Nineteenth Century
Glass

Silveria vase; Stevens & Williams, circa 1900; height 6½ inches. Signed "Onyx" compote; Dalzell, Gilmore & Leighton, circa 1889; diameter of top 6 inches. Silvered Glass perfume bottle, cut purple over crystal glass; signed "E. Varnish & Co./ London," circa 1851; height 6½ inches. *Author's Collection*

Novelty-Type Cameo Glass. Vase imitating carved ivory, with applied glass windows on both sides; designed by Kretschman and decorated with gold and enamels by Jules Barbe; Thomas Webb & Sons, circa 1887; height 9 inches. Vase in the "Chien Lung" style, engraved by Daniel and Lionel Pearce; Thomas Webb & Sons, circa 1885; height 5 inches. Covered rose jar with pierced ormolu top and collar; etched cameo design of flowers and leaves in Chinese-red on yellow Pearl Satin body; height 8¾ inches. Vase of opaque ivory-colored glass with gold and enamel decoration by Jules Barbe; Thomas Webb & Sons, circa 1885; height 8 inches. *Author's Collection*

NINETEENTH CENTURY GLASS

ITS GENESIS AND DEVELOPMENT

Revised Edition

by

Albert Christian Revi

Schiffer Publishing Ltd

Box E, Exton, Pennsylvania 19341

Acknowledgments

My wholehearted thanks to Fred Carder of Corning, New York; John Northwood II and H. W. Woodward of Brierley Hill, England; and Professor Aldo Polato of Venice, Italy, for their technical counsel and for information and documents placed at my disposal.

To the editors of *The Crockery & Glass Journal*, *The Glass Industry*, *Hobbies* and *The Spinning Wheel*, my sincere gratitude for allowing the use of material written by me expressly for their publications.

I am indebted to the following institutions for photographic illustrations: Alfred University Museum, Alfred, New York; The Corning Museum of Glass, Corning, New York; Musée des Arts et Metiers, Paris, France; The Smithsonian Institution, Washington, D.C.; and The Toledo Museum of Art, Toledo, Ohio.

To photographers Wade H. Knight, Dallas, Texas; H. Hall of Stourbridge, England; and Osvaldo Bohm of Venice, Italy, my deep appreciation for their splendid work.

ALBERT CHRISTIAN REVI

Dallas, Texas

REVISED AND ENLARGED EDITION, JULY 1967

Copyright, 1959, 1967, by Albert Christian Revi

ISBN 0-916838-43-9

Library of Congress Catalog Card No.: 59-15032

MANUFACTURED IN THE UNITED STATES OF AMERICA

To my wife

Contents

Introduction

Glass has been man's servant since before the dawn of history. Primitive peoples in widely scattered localities throughout the world are known to have used a natural glass called obsidian for arrowheads, spearheads, knives and tools. In more advanced cultures, obsidian was used for ceremonial masks, small sculptures, jewelry and mirrors. The glass found in nature represents molten volcanic rock masses which were extruded and cooled too rapidly to permit crystallization.

Just when glass was first made artificially is unknown to us but it must have occurred very early in the cultural history of mankind. Some authorities believe it was coincident with the development of the potter's art, but they hasten to add that there is a great difference between a glaze and glass. It is quite probable that each was an independent discovery.

In 1876, the scientist Velain suggested that the discovery of glass was accidental. He gave as an illustration the lightning stones, called *pierres de foudre* by the French peasants, who believed them to be the cause of lightning fires. Actually such lightning stones are glass formed by the burning of grain and the fusion of the ash resulting from the fire caused by the lightning.

The ancient natural historian Pliny gave the following account of the origin of glass:

"In Syria there is a region known as Phoenice, adjoining to Judaea, and enclosing, between the lower ridges of Mount Carmalus, a marshy district known by the name of Cendebia. In this district, it is supposed, rises the river Belus, which after a course of five miles, empties itself into the sea near the colony of Ptolemais. The tide of this river is sluggish, and the water unwholesome to drink, but held sacred for the observance of certain religious ceremonials. Full of slimy deposits, and very deep, it is only at the reflux of the tide that the river discloses its sands; which, agitated by the waves, separate themselves from their impurities and so become cleansed. It is generally thought that it is the acridity of the sea water that has this purgative effect upon the sand, and that without this action no use could be made of it. The shore upon which this sand is gathered is not more than a half mile in extent; and yet, for many ages, this was the only spot that afforded the material for making glass.

"The story is that a ship, laden with niter, being moored upon this spot, the merchants, while preparing their repast upon the seashore, finding no stones at hand for supporting their cauldrons, employed for the purpose some lumps of niter which they had taken from the vessel. Upon its being subjected to the action of the fire, in combination with the sand of the seashore, they beheld transparent streams flowing forth of a liquid hitherto unknown: this, it is said, was the origin of glass."

Pliny's story is a plausible one for it has been found by actual experiments that sufficient heat can be generated by an open fire to melt a soda-silica glass. But while the discovery of glass *could* have been made in the manner Pliny described, the facts, supported by archaeological finds and analysis, indicate that glass was discovered several hundred years before the Phoenicians plied their trade routes.

The question of just where and when glass had its beginning will probably remain a mystery for some time to come. A small ball-bead in the Ashmolean Museum in Oxford has the distinction of being the oldest piece of dated glass ever to have been found. It bears the cartouche of Amenhotep (1551–1527 B.C.). There are many examples of Egyptian glass from this period and the style of workmanship certainly indicates an advanced period in glass technology. Earlier examples of glass have been found in Egypt, the dating of which is questionable, but on one thing most authorities do agree—they are anterior to the Eighteenth Dynasty. (1546–1350 B.C.).

Speaking of ancient glass to the Newcomen Society in 1924, Sir W. M. Flinders Petrie said: "The oldest pure glass is a moulded amulet of deep lapis lazuli color, of about 7000 B.C. Fragments of green opaque glass inlay appear in the First Dynasty, about 5000 B.C. Striped black and white glass amulets came in the Eleventh Dynasty, about 3800 B.C. An elaborate fused-glass mosaic of a calf is in the jewelry of 3300 B.C. from Dahshur. Blue translucent beads appear about 1570 B.C. All of these occurrences of *datable* glass in Egypt were probably due to importation from Asia."

In 1926 Petrie stated that ". . . not a single piece of glass was made in Egypt prior to about 1500 B.C. . . . There was certainly no evidence until one came down to the period 1500 B.C., about which time one also came across sculptural records bearing representations of Syrian workmen being brought into Egypt, carrying with them the vases of metal or glass which they had produced. There was no question that the Syrians were far ahead of the Egyptians up to this period in the matter of art and industry, and when one remembers that examples of glass had been found in Syria—in the Euphrates region—which could be definitely dated back to 2500 B.C., one had little difficulty in attributing to the Syrians the glasswares which were imported into Egypt prior to 1500 B.C."

A. Lucas, formerly a Director of the Chemical Department, and an Honorary Consulting Chemist in the Department of Antiquities of Egypt, takes exception to Petrie's statements in his book, *Ancient Egyptian Materials and Industries* (third edition, revised, London, 1948).

"At what period glass was first produced is uncertain," says Lucas, "and there is little doubt that it was made exceptionally and in small amount before it came into general use, and when occasionally early specimens are found in Egypt there is no need to assume that they are of foreign origin and have been imported."

The pros-and-cons concerning the genesis of glass have been bandied back and forth for many years, and they will very likely continue to be a subject for discussion among authorities, but the rich blue glass beads from Deir el Bahri, found in the coffin of Maït, a "child queen" of King Mentuhotep (2196–2172 B.C.), are of an undisputed date even though their provenience is questionable.

There are strong indications that glass had its origin in Asia Minor, probably in Mesopotamia. The excavations in a cemetery of the Third Dynasty of Ur (2450 B.C.) unearthed a large quantity of glass beads. This evidence led Petrie to believe that there may have been glass producing centers in this region far anterior to its production in Egypt. H. Frankfort found a cylinder of light-blue glass at Tell Asmar, northwest of Baghdad, which he dated to the dynasty of Gutram, or more probably to the dynasty of Akkad, about 2600–2700 B.C. It appeared to be quite free of striae or inclusions, indicating an advanced means of glass production. Whether the manufacture of glass was continued in this region is uncertain.

The famous Sargon Vase in the British Museum, inscribed with the name of the Assyrian King Sargon II (722–705 B.C.) is considered to be of Egyptian origin although it was found in the ruins of Nineveh. The translucent greenish glass was built up on a sand core, a technique prevalent in those times since blown glass was as yet unknown. Thompson's excavations at Nineveh brought forth several cuneiform tablets, obviously glass factory records, which indicate that the art was well known in this area. The translations reveal the Assyrian names for various kinds of glass and the directions and formulas for their manufacture. In the writings was a detailed account of how to build a glass furnace, which included the rather macabre practice of making sacrifice to unborn human embryos, thereby propitiating the spirits of incomplete beings whilst the glass was in the process of being made.

In Roman times the glass industry was firmly established in Palestine, Syria, Sidon and Mesopotamia and might well have been the result of a long, slow decline of the industry in Egypt following the magnificent cultural era of the Eighteenth Dynasty. From the end of the Eighteenth Dynasty up to the Christian Era, the quality of the glass degenerated. Under the stimulus of the Ptolemaic revival it was spread aboard to Greece, Italy, Palestine and Syria.

Our first mention of glass in India occurs in the time of the Singalese kings, probably as a result of the conquests in that part of the world by Alexander the Great. For some time it had been thought that the Chinese imported glass, but more recent evidence reveals that they were manufacturing their own glass about 550 B.C.

Glass appears to have been first used as a gem, with a value equal to the natural stones deemed precious at that time. Even as late as the Ptolemaic period, glass gems were still held in high esteem. In Frederic Neuburg's *Glass in Antiquity* the author states: "Emerald-green glass appears to have exercised a fascination over the peoples of antiquity. The emerald vessels mentioned by the Rabbis were certainly glass. Pliny gives an account of the great emerald pillar in the Temple of Melkart (the city-god) in Tyre, which was reputed to shed a glimmering radiance in the night time. Here probably was a similar phenomenon to the Egyptian emerald obelisks and the emerald tiles of Isaiah."

There are several mentions of glass throughout the Old and the New Testaments. Most of the references have been interpreted to mean "mirrors" made of metal and glass, but some are unmistakably references to glass vessels and gems. In Proverbs (XXIII: 31) the word "kos" denotes a drinking-vessel. In Revelation (XV: 2 and XXI: 18) the term "hyalos" is taken in the sense of "pure glass."

Until the advent of blown glass (100 B.C. to A.D. 100) glass vessels were made on a sandy, clay core covered with cloth and tied on with a string, to which a rod of metal or wood was attached as a handle. The sand core was dipped in a small crucible of molten glass and rotated quickly a few times to distribute the metal fairly evenly. Where decorative patterns were desired, thin rods of glass, usually of a contrasting color or colors, were wound about the article while the glass was still soft. The wavy effects found on these early specimens of core-molded glass were produced by dragging the applied rods up and down with a small tool. The article was then rolled on a stone slab to produce a uniform and smooth surface; the foot and handles, if required, were made separately and added thereto. Finally the rod was withdrawn and the sandy core scraped out. The inner surfaces of core-molded vessels have a rough texture not found in blown wares.

"Small figures and certain other objects," writes Lucas, "such as larger and more elaborate pieces of inlay, can have been made only by moulding." Glass inlays, often erroneously referred to as enamel, paste or Pate de Verre, were always cut and molded, and then cemented into position; they were not formed from powdered glass as suggested by the latter appelations.

The pressing of glass objects, hailed as a unique advancement in the early nineteenth century, was an actuality in ancient Egypt during the Eighteenth Dynasty—as evidenced in small press-molded cups and amulets. The revival of mold pressing in the nineteenth century is credited to Enoch Robinson, a carpenter in the employ of the New England Glass Company of Cambridge, Massachusetts. The end result of this carpenter's intrusion into the glass trade changed the whole course of not only the New England Glass Company but the entire industry as well.

Most people think of Deming Jarves as the father of the pressed glass industry in America, and perhaps rightly so. It was during Mr. Jarves' association with the Boston & Sandwich Glass Company at Cape Cod, Massachusetts, that he played his major role in this particular phase of the glass trade. While he was connected with the Sandwich works, Jarves registered several patents for "improvements" in pressing glass articles.

Even more or less contemporary writers like the Reverend Dionysius Lardner (A *Treatise on the Origins, Progressive Improvements, and Present State of the Manufacture of Porcelain and Glass*, Philadelphia, 1832), Apsley Pellatt (*Curiosities of Glass Making*, London, 1849), and George Dodd (*The Curiosities of Industry and the Applied Sciences*, London, 1857), agree that the invention of pressed glassware was an American contribution to the glass arts. But in *Reminiscence of Glass Making* (New York, 1865) Mr. Jarves modestly admits that as far back as 1814 he had been importing "Holland salts made by being pressed in metallic moulds, and from England glass candlesticks and table centre-bowls, plain, with pressed square feet, rudely made, somewhat after the present mode of moulding glass."

The art of press-molding glass objects spread quickly over the Continent and England. The firm of Baccarat in France supplied most of Europe and other parts of the world with elaborately designed pressed-glass articles for the table and decorative use. By 1833 the making of pressed glassware was introduced at Newcastle, England.

At first the invention of press-molded glassware caused unrest among the glass workers who were fearful this new technique would mechanize them out of their jobs. Instead, it proved to be a boon to the industry. In the last quarter of the nineteenth century more than just a few American and European glass factories sustained themselves and their workers very well by producing huge quantities of press-molded wares which they marketed on a world-wide scale.

In making Millefiori Glass the ancients combined glass threads of many colors which they fused into a rod so that cross-section disks showed a very colorful and intricate pattern. In forming these rods as many as 150 pieces of colored glass were drawn out into threads measuring no more than a thousandth of an inch in thickness. The cut disks were laid side by side and rolled in a matrix of colorless glass, or placed in position side by side in a mold and put in a furnace where they fused together at their edges. An ancient Millefiori bowl made by the mosaic glass process has bees represented between blossoms as if hovering over a bed of flowers.

In *Glass in Antiquity* Neuburg reveals that: "In filigree glass, colored (or more frequently white) opaque threads were twisted with threads of colorless glass and drawn out while in a plastic state, then twined and coiled to produce charming effects. Only limited use was made of filigree glass, but it is occasionally found employed for the rims of bowls or mosaic glass."

Transparent glass was a rarity in ancient times, perhaps because this quality was not necessary for the uses for which it was intended. In Egypt, during the Eighteenth Dynasty, opaque white glass was made by the use of tin oxide; turquoise blue glass derived its color from the use of copper; copper was also the coloring agent in the reddish glass which resembled the jasper stone of ancient times, not the copper ruby of more recent date. Green glass was also produced with copper or iron as a colorant. Antimony and lead produced a fine yellow glass of an opaque quality. Basically the coloring agents used by the ancient glassmakers remained the same throughout many centuries.

In the seventeenth century Neri published his formulas for an almost endless variety of colored glasses which included several formulas for the manufacture of glass gems. By the late eighteenth century and early nineteenth century a spectrum of colors were produced in Bohemian, German and French glass factories.

With the discovery of the ductility of glass, about the first century B.C., the product changed from a luxury item for a few into a necessity for many. Forming glass articles with the aid of a blowpipe and a contact mold made possible the production of large quantities of cheaper and better glass articles. In 1934, D. B. Harden wrote: "It was a short road thereafter that led first to blowing glass in moulds that bore elaborate patterns, and then to blowing vessels at the end of the blowpipe—in other words, free-blown glass.

"These developments must have occurred about the beginning of the Christian Era, and are probably due to workers on the Syrian coast. There is a group of mould-blown vases belonging to Syrian workshops of about that time, many examples of which bear signatures of artists in Greek characters as part of the moulded design. The two best names are Ennion and Artas, and their vases have been found on both eastern and western Mediterranean sites. These Syrian craftsmen were undoubtedly among the first makers of mould-blown glasses, and it is highly probable that one of their members invented the process."

The era of mold-blown glass was accompanied by a marked improvement in the quality of the metal. Whereas the qualities of transparency and freedom from color and impurities were unimportant to earlier glassmakers who were primarily interested in imitating the precious stones of their times, the invention of glass blowing and the manifold uses made possible by its invention made these qualities at once desirable. Some indication of the high value placed on colorless, transparent glass can be realized from these words founds in the Bostock-Riley translation of *The Natural History of Pliny*: "Still, however, the highest value is set on glass that is nearly colorless or transparent, as nearly as possible resembling the crystal, in fact. For drinking vessels glass has quite superseded the use of silver and gold."

It was reported that the Emperor Nero paid 6000 sesterces (about $2,500.00) for two small crystal-glass cups. At a time when glass had become a more or less common household material—manifested in tablewares, bottles for wine and other liquids, unguent vases and toilet articles, seals and signets—this sum seems quite out of line. But those wares made for the common use were of a greenish or purplish tint common to glass made from impure materials, and were not possessed of the crystalline qualities held in such high regard at that time.

Cut and engraved glasses predate the Christian Era by some fifteen centuries. Beginning with the simple wheel-cut designs found on specimens of Egyptian glass attributed to the New Kingdom and the metal drilled products of about 1500–500 B.C., the art advances slowly to those fabulously engraved glass cameos of the Roman period—about the first century B.C. The most noteworthy specimen of ancient Cameo Glass is the Portland-Barberini vase now housed in the Gold Room in the British Museum. On a par with this magnificent cinerary urn is the Naples amphora, a two-handled vase with Bacchanalian rites superbly depicted in white relief designs on a deep blue ground. The ancients' technical advancement in this period of Cameo Glass production is evidenced by a fragment in the British Museum collection, composed of not less than five layers of colored glass—each layer of glass cut away in a relief design of the most exquisite and intricate workmanship. The perplexing abrasion technique known as "Diatreta" is discussed at length in this book.

Cut and engraved glasses again appear in the early seventeenth century. It took on many forms from the ethereal stippled designs produced with a diamond point to rococo motifs cut deeply in the surface of the glass. The art was widespread in Europe and continued to be a popular means of glass embellishment right on through the eighteenth century, with the designs reflecting the taste of the times. The invention of flint glass in England, about 1675, provided English craftsmen with a hard glass capable of taking on a brilliant finish when cut and polished.

Window glass is first mentioned by Lactantius at the close of the third century. It made its most important appearance again in medieval times when it was used in the colored glass windows of cathedrals. In France, Gregory von Tours (ca. A.D. 593) and Bishop von Protus (ca. A.D. 609) used colored glass for windows. A century later glass was exported to England. When rebuilding the cathedral at Rheims, A.D. 969–988, Bishop Adalberon used colored glass windows depicting Biblical scenes. While this is recorded as one of the earliest uses of stained glass for windows, it is not to be construed as having been the first. The scarcity of historical records from the third to the ninth centuries prevents a more accurate chronicle of the development of glass made and used in western Europe during this period.

During the dark ages in Europe, the Islamic world was going through a vigorous intellectual development. In *Properties of Glass*, George Morey states: "It was during this period that the use of glass weights was developed to the highest accuracy by the Arabs. These apparently were not made until about 300 A.D., reached their highest accuracy about 780, and by 1300 had been abandoned. The manufacture of glass was mentioned by Jabir ibn Haiyan (the 'Latin Geber') about 776."

Decorating glass with enamels and lustrous stains attained a new perfection in the hands of Islamic craftsmen. Prior to this period there were other evidences of enameled glassware, some dating back to Egypt during the reign of Thutmose III, about 1500 B.C. Several fragments of fire-painted (enameled) glass and a vessel decorated with a design of human figures can be found in the Cairo Museum dating from about the same period as the enameled jug bearing the cartouche of Thutmose III in the British Museum's collection. Between this early period and the first century A.D., very little evidence is available to indicate that the art was in more or less continuous use. The Paris plate—attributed to Antioch or Syria, about 200 A.D.—is a prime example of ancient unfired painting on glass. The mythological story of the Judgment of Paris is expertly depicted in shades of gray, violet, yellow, brown and black on a reddish ground in what was known as the "reverse picture technique" in the eighteenth century.

In the first quarter of the sixteenth century, enameled glassware reached a new high in the very capable hands of the Venetians. The enameling techniques manifested themselves in similarly decorated wares from the Netherlands, Germany and Spain in the late-sixteenth and early-seventeenth centuries.

Morey's monograph gives us a splendid account of the rise of Venice as a glass center. The author writes: "Probably as an indirect result of the Crusades and the fall of the Eastern Empire, glass manufacture in Venice entered a period of development about the beginning of the eleventh century which soon made that city the center of the glass industry, which dominant position it maintained for at least four centuries. . . . Glass manufacture in Venice became a large-scale industry, which was jealously protected as a monopoly. An elaborate guild system was set up in 1279, which provided a system of apprenticeship requiring eight years for its completion. In 1291 the glass works were moved to the island of Murano, a separate borough of the city, and drastic measures were taken to prohibit the exportation of scrap glass, called cullets, and the immigration of workmen. Syrian craftsmen were imported, who brought with them technical recipes and procedures from Byzantium and the Egyptian orient. The technical excellence of the Venetian glassware gives evidence of the highest degree of craftsmanship and the beauty of its design has never been surpassed."

From Venice came the first attempts to revive the ancient achievements. They developed the art of filigree glass to its utmost during the sixteenth century. Intricately-wrought patterns were developed from threads of white and colored glass. The delicate pattern of air traps and filigree threads found in their Vetro di Trina glass are superb technical examples of the glassmakers art. Marcantonio Sabellico (*De Situ Venetae Urbis*, written in 1495) has this to say about the wares made on the island of Murano: "A famous invention first proved that glass might feign the whiteness of crystal, and they began to turn the material into various colors and numberless forms—but consider to whom did it first occur to include in a little ball all the sorts of flowers which clothe the meadows in spring." That Sabellico was referring to Millefiori rods encased in a solid glass ball is rather obvious and this establishes the development of the first Millefiori paperweight (though it may not have been so used) at that time. Other examples of early Venetian Millefiori wares are in scant evidence and those found compare unfavorably with the wares produced in the mid-nineteenth century by French and Bohemian glass factories. The chalcedony, or Schmelzglas, made in Venice was undoubtedly inspired by the ancient productions of stone glasses. Their marblelike texture, sometimes splashed with Aventurine, imitated to perfection the gem stones. Crackled glass was entirely a Venetian invention; and silvering mirrors, though not of their invention, reached a very high standard of excellence not found in any other part of the world at that time. The development of the Venetian techniques in the nineteenth century leaves nothing to be desired; they are in every respect as fine as those wares made three centuries earlier.

The manufacture of fine glass spread rapidly over the Continent and England during the fifteenth century. Partly responsible for this further development of the industry was the publication of Neri's book *L'Arte Vetraria* (Florence, 1612). In it Neri described in detail the manufacture of lead and borax glasses, and colored glass in a profusion of tints and shades, including the splendid gold-ruby glass so often credited to Kunckel. Latin, French, English and German translations of Neri's book were published during the seventeenth and eighteenth centuries. Prior to 1612 the art was clouded in mystery and superstition. Neri's work represents the first scientific approach to the production of glass.

The preponderance of colorless glass over colored wares in collections of eighteenth century glass would lead one to believe that the public's taste was more inclined toward the former. Actually, though, the favor of the masses has been fluctuating between colored and uncolored glassware since they first had a choice. During the eighteenth century, high grade wares were predominantly manufactured from transparent white glass (crystal). Those factories producing the more common wares were only able, at best, to offer their trade a transparent glass with greenish or purplish tinges which were due primarily to the impure ingredients in the glass batch. Consequently the preponderance of common wares manufactured in this period were tinted with brilliant shades of amber, purple, green and blue.

One of the principal means of embellishing glass in the eighteenth century was pattern molding. Hereby a gather of glass was blown into a mold whose inner surface carried a design in intaglio. Blowing the plastic glass inside this mold produced the configuration in relief on the surface of the blow. This was then removed from the mold and further expanded by blowing. The pattern, though somewhat enlarged and diffused over the surface of the expanded blow, retained its original design. Diamonds, ogivals, ribs and flowers represent the most common motifs employed by glass manufacturers for eighteenth-century pattern-molded wares.

Engraving colored glassware was an uncommon practice in the eighteenth century. This expensive means of embellishment was more usually a technique reserved for top-grade crystal glass. English, Irish and a few American factories supplied the needs of the American colonies. The superbly engraved glasses produced by Bohemian factories during this period were just a prelude to the magnificant portrait-picture intaglios made in the first half of the nineteenth century by Bimann.

Enameled wares appeared in the eighteenth century in all of the glass-producing countries in Europe and also in America. The simple little enameled glass bottles produced in Germany and France during the eighteenth century are often mistaken for similar wares made by Baron Steigel at his Mannheim, Pennsylvania, glassworks. Enameled beakers and *humpen* continued to be made in Bohemia throughout the seventeenth and eighteenth centuries. Prominent in this field of glass decorating in England were Michael Edkins and the Beilby family; the latter best known for their armorial designs on stemmed goblets; the former for his exquisite decorations in the Chinese manner on milk-white glass.

The nineteenth century can be considered the Golden Age in glass history—for at no other time, since its discovery more than 5000 years ago, were more accumulated glass skills and decorative techniques manifested in the comparatively short space of one century. While some of the methods of glass production were changed or improved upon in the nineteenth century, the end results were nearly the same in appearance. For the most part the tools of the trade have remained unchanged for centuries.

The industrial revolution, the relaxation of government controls on the industry (specifically in England), plus a pride of craftsmanship born of freedom, were a few of the contributing factors to this Golden Age of Glass. It is our earnest endeavor to graphically illustrate the visible evidences of this period in glass history and in every case where possible to acquaint the reader with their earlier prototypes.

"—— and there is no new thing under the sun.
Is there any thing whereof it may be said, See, this is new?
It hath been already of old time, which was before us."

Ecclesiastes 1:9–10

Nineteenth Century Glass

Pearl Satinglass

For many years Pearl Satin Ware, sometimes called Pearl Ware, or Mother-of-Pearl Satinglass, has proved to be one of the most popular collectibles offered to a glass-conscious public. The various patterns in which this ware can be found, plus the many shades and combinations of color which may be encountered, make it to many collectors the most interesting of all the glasses fabricated in the nineteenth century

The earliest use of a symmetrical or controlled pattern of air traps in a glass body as a decorative feature—the basic principle of Pearl Satinglass, was made manifest in the Venetian's intricate Vetro di Trina. The air traps were formed by the crisscrossing of opaque white glass threads imprisoned between two walls of glass.

Benjamin Richardson, who was considered the father of the English flint glass industry in his day, took out what we believe to be the earliest patented process descriptive of Pearl Satin Ware in the nineteenth century. His invention for "An Improvement In The Manufacture Of Articles In Glass, So As To Produce Peculiar Ornamental Effects", was filed July 27, 1857, and sealed January 26, 1858. The process for manufacturing this peculiar ornamental effect in a glass body was quite simple. A gather of glass was blown into a mold which carried the pattern in projected form. The result was a piece with surface indentations. The parison (the piece still in its molten state) thus indented was dipped in fluid metal to coat the exterior surface. The air traps preserved between the indented molding and the glass skin provided the ornamentation.

2

Purple Pearl Satin ewer-vase with gold decoration. Height 13 inches.

Another method for achieving this result was to place the molded piece in a cup of glass blown to receive it, the worker then blowing and shaping the mass further into the article desired. The several layers in each case could be the same color or of different colors, according to the desired effect the worker wished to obtain. Nowhere in Mr. Richardson's patent enumerations did he allude to giving the article a lusterless finish either with acids or sandblasting, as is usually found in the later productions of Pearl Ware.

Another method used in England and America late in the nineteenth century to produce this type of ornamentation was to line a heated mold with glass tubes, either crystal or colored, and blow into this mold an inflated gather of glass. The hollow tubes adhered to the surface of the blow and the parison was rolled on the marver to firmly embed the tubes of glass into the surface of the mass. By deftly twisting the blow while it was still in a plastic state, the worker produced articles of glass with pearly swirled stripes on the outer surface.

There is one type of Pearl Satinglass produced in the late nineteenth century that did not depend on air traps within the body for its pearly effect. The outer skin of the triple-cased article was a thick layer of crystal glass that had been pattern-molded forming heavy bosses thereon. When acidized these bosses presented a lovely pearly effect.

On February 8, 1881, a patent was issued jointly to William B. Dean and Alphonse Peltier, both residents of Brooklyn, New York, for the manufacture of glass articles utilizing a controlled pattern of air traps within the walls of a glass body as a means of ornamentation. Messrs. Dean & Peltier's method for producing such a ware followed almost verbatim the principles set forth by Benjamin Richardson some twenty-three years earlier in England. No mention was made in the Dean-Peltier patent specifications to suggest a lusterless finish on the surface of the glass.

Soon after the Dean-Peltier patent was registered it was assigned to the Mt. Washington Glass Company of New Bedford, Massachusetts. It played a major role in the legal dispute between the New Bedford works and the Phoenix Glass Company over the rights to produce such a ware in America. In 1886 Thos. Webb & Sons of Stourbridge, England were licensed by the Mt. Washington Glass Company to produce this and other types of patented wares under their license.

Mt. Washington Glass Works' Pearl Satin vase in deep rose. Height 7 inches.

Recorded in the English Patent Offices in London are the specifications for somewhat similar ornamentation filed by Alfred Landier and Charles Houdaille, both of Paris, France. Their factory was located near Sèvres. Messieurs Landier and Houdaille's papers are dated September 21, 1885. The specifications state that the decorative effect of the pattern-molded body, covered with a skin of glass to close in the air traps, would be analogous to that produced by cutting or engraving. Again no mention was made of finishing the article with a lusterless surface.

Letters patent were issued to Frederick Stacey Shirley of the Mt. Washington Glass Company, June 29, 1886, in which he related his method for producing shaded and bicolored articles of glass in cased glass, Plush (Satinglass), and "Pearl Satin Ware." The process Shirley outlined in his specifications followed closely those so clearly outlined by Benjamin Richardson in 1858, and which were later registered in this country by Dean and Peltier. There were two additional processes mentioned in the Shirley papers. First, Shirley suggested that the pattern-molded body be covered with a sensitive metal, one that could be developed into different colors and shades of color by reheating certain portions of the article in a furnace. Second, he suggested a lusterless surface for the article, produced with the aid of an acid-roughing dip or by sandblasting, and all calculated to give the finished product a "velvet-like finish or an appearance resembling the skin of a peach," and "a pearl-like appearance."

Joseph Webb, manager of the Phoenix Glass Company's Works at Water Cure, Beaver County, Pennsylvania, also patented a process for fabricating Pearl Satin Glass as of July 6, 1886. Mr. Webb's method followed the cupping process explained by Benjamin Richardson almost thirty years earlier. In a subsequent patent issued to Joseph Webb on May 17, 1887, the manufacturing process did not differ perceptively from his first patent. Still a third patent was issued to Mr. Webb on March 6, 1888, in which he prescribed the use of two molds: one to pattern the inner wall or shell of the article, the other to be used after the outer shell of glass had been applied. The finished product displayed a crisscrossed network of pearly indented lines in the surface of the article.

In 1889, Thos. Webb & Sons of England patented a process for manufacturing cameo relief designs on articles of Pearl Satin Ware. After the body of the article had been prepared in the usual way an additional plating of opaque white or colored glass was applied to it. A design was painted on the surface of this additional plating with acid-resisting inks and the article subjected to an acid bath. The acid bath dissolved away all the opaque white or colored casing not protected with the resist, leaving a design in shallow relief on the surface of the article. A great deal of care was exercised at this stage of the work, for if the article were allowed to remain too long in the acid bath the action of the acid would have laid open some of the air traps. The same technique was employed to produce cameo relief designs on plain Satinglass articles.

Author's Collection
Blue Pearl Satin rosebowl with cameo relief in white. Thos. Webb & Sons, 1889.
Height 4 inches.

August 7, 1885, a patent covering a method of producing Pearl Satin-glass was issued in London to William Webb Boulton, head of the firm of Boulton & Mills which had the Audnam Bank glasshouse for over seventy years until the early part of this century. According to verified reports Boulton was merely a business man and in no way a craftsman. He had a very good manager named Thompson, and it was most likely this man or some other member of his staff who was responsible for an invention worthy of a patent.

Other English glasshouses manufactured Pearl Satin Ware. Stevens & Williams of Brierley Hill, Staffordshire, sold it under the name "Verre de Soie" as early as 1886 according to H. S. Williams-Thomas, director of the firm. A vase produced by a method described earlier, the one in which tubes of glass were utilized, is in the private collection of Fred Carder of Corning, New York. At the time of its manufacture Mr. Carder was art director for Stevens & Williams; he described it as "Verre de Soie with air traps."

Soon after Fred Carder came to America and founded the Steuben Glass Works at Corning, he again manufactured his "Verre de Soie with air traps." Several fine examples are on permanent view in the Public Library at Corning. According to Mr. Carder these later productions date from about 1905. There is little to distinguish Mr. Carder's later Verre de Soie from those articles made earlier; the only difference seems to be in the inner casing, which in the later ware was made from a milky, translucent glass which Mr. Carder termed "Alabaster" glass. The Corona, Long Island, works of Louis C. Tiffany also manufactured a Pearl Satin Glassware contemporary with Mr. Carder's and very similar in appearance.

It will not surprise many collectors to learn that much of the Plush, Satinglass, and Pearl Satinglass produced in the late nineteenth century emanated from Bohemian and French factories; some pieces have been found bearing the Sèvres mark usually identified with porcelains of the period. Wholesale distributors of Bohemian glassware advertised "Plush" and "Pearl Satin" wares in American trade journals between 1886 and 1888. C. F. A. Hinrichs & Company offered "Bohemian Satin," and "Satin Moire Glassware with applied Thorny and Floral Decorations." A. Klingenberg, a representative for foreign glasshouses, announced that they had new shipments of "Moire Antique Satinglass"

Blue Pearl Satin Vase with applied crystal threading.
Original glossy finish. Height 13 inches.

to show their customers. Neuman and Lunick advertised "Bohemian Satin Moire Glassware in Patterns of Damask, Vertical, Diagonal, Snow Glass (Coin Dot), etc."

Lazarus & Rosenfeld, New York City, wholesale distributors of "Bohemian Art Glassware," advertised elaborate table lamps, fairy lamps and vases in "Rose-De-Boheme," "Green-De-Boheme," "Yellow-De-Boheme," "Couleurs-De-Boheme" and "Pearl Satin." All the items shown in their 1888 full-page, full-color advertisements in the *Crockery & Glass Journal* were elegantly decorated with enamels and gold in floral, fruit and bird designs. These cheaper Satinglass products, supplied by factories at Steinschonau and Altrohlau, Bohemia, had a disastrous effect on the sale of American and English wares of finer but similar character. Glass manufacturers used many different means to color articles of Pearlware and Satinglass. Mr. Shirley suggested that heat-sensitive metals be used for the outer skin of the article. By simply reheating a portion of the article, different colors and combinations of color were

Public Library, Corning, N. Y.
Verre de Soie vase with air traps. Made by Fred Carder, Steuben Glass Works. Circa 1905. Height 5 inches.

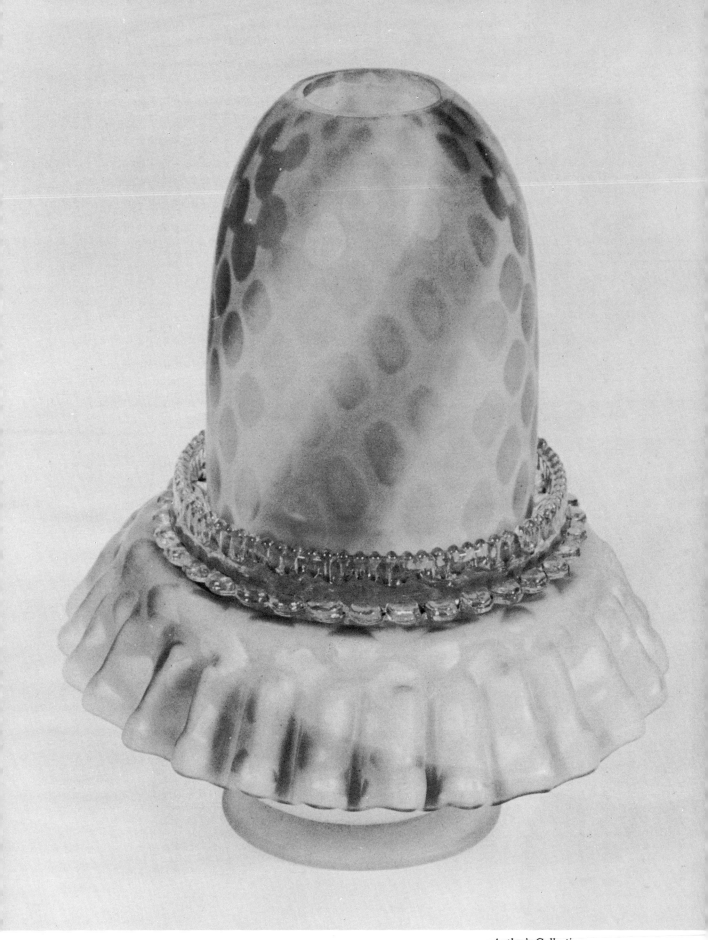

Author's Collection
Rainbow-striped (blue, rose, yellow and apricot) Pearl Satin fairy lamp.
Circa 1885. Height 6 inches.

brought about. An interesting process called "die-away" by the glass trade was also used to produce shaded glassware. The rainbow-striped specimens so dear to many collectors were produced by laying what are termed "bull-colored" rods of glass on the body of the article before it was fully formed. On some pieces mica flecks and bits of variegated colored glass were picked up on the gather and made an integral part of the decoration. The decorating possibilities for this particular type of glassware were vast and in an era of overembellishment every known technique was employed.

Some ornamental features used to decorate Pearl Satinglass were: silver deposit, colorful enamels, silver and gold leaf, coralene, applied glasshouse decorations of leaves, flowers, fruits, etc. Gold, silver, ormolu and pewter mountings have also graced specimens of nineteenth century Pearl Satin Ware.

In 1925 the United States Glass Company manufactured pressed and molded black Satinglass—centerpiece bowls with wide, flaring edges, candlesticks, vases, compotes with baluster or twisted stems, small trays and dishes for candy, and ashtrays. Most of the black Satinglass was designed with smooth, flowing lines and could still be considered stylish today. It has come on the antiques market in recent years, and many collectors and dealers have greatly overrated its age, rarity and value.

Coralene

$\mathcal{A}$ patent for the Coralene decorating process was issued to Arthur Schierholz of Plauen, Thuringia, in the German Empire, on July 7, 1883. Schierholz explained in his patent that "ornamental and other articles of glass, whether blown, cast, or pressed, such as statuettes, vases, and the like, were decorated by first applying designs with enamel of a sirupy consistency, either colored or transparent, and strewing thereon small glass beads, either colored or not, so that when the glass was subjected to heat sufficient to melt the enamel, the beads would become cemented to the glass, and thus provide it with a peculiar refracting vitreous coating that imparted great brilliancy to the colors." Schierholz elaborated on his patent by including a means for decorating sheet glass and cathedral glass (stained glass) in the same manner.

Many patents registered abroad at that time were short lived, and this was true of Schierholz's patent for Coralene decorations. As early as 1886 several wholesalers of Bohemian glass were offering "Coral Beaded," "Coralene Beaded," "Beaded Glassware," and "Lustra," decorated fancy wares in the trade journals. The Coralene decorated Burmese vase shown in our illustration was made at the Mt. Washington Glass Company, New Bedford, Massachusetts, around 1886.

It is quite possible that Coralene decorated articles marked "Patent" refer to the Schierholz process; but it does not necessarily mean that they were manufactured in Germany.

Lately a great many pieces of genuine art glass, mostly Pearl Satin, plain Satinglass and Burmese, have appeared on the market with newly applied coralene decoration. The perpetrators of this particular fake have

Opalescent crystal vase with Coralene decoration of a peacock in many different colors.
Shell feet and rim of vase decorated with gold. Height 8 inches.

copied the old designs faithfully using a flat finish yellow paint over which they have applied a transparent adhesive or glue. Tiny glass beads, of the kind experimentally used for highway safety devices, were applied to the article and adhered to the adhesive agent. The fakes can be readily detected—the beads fall off at a touch.

Author's Collection
Pale green glass tumbler with rigaree decoration around base. Slightly opalescent rim developed by reheating. Coralene decoration of yellow rose with green shaded leaves.

Amberina

$\mathcal{I}$t is highly probable that the production of parti-colored glass from a homogeneous metal was known to the ancients for the phenomenon must certainly have occurred in the more than five thousand years of glass production which preceded the invention of Amberina art glass. However, in Apsley Pellatt's *Curiosities of Glass Making* (London, 1849) we find our first brief mention accorded to a parti-colored red and green glass composed of homogeneous stock. "Flint glass manufacturers," he wrote, "produce beautiful red from a mixture of copper and iron, and sometimes accidentally; for instance, when the ordinary metal mixed specially for light green medical bottles is nearly worked out, it will assume the complementary color—namely, a ruby red; so that the same bottle will be parti-colored red and green."

Such "accidents" occurred (and the metal would strike red in reheating) most often during the "fire polishing" process when mold marks were being removed from the mold-blown bottles by reheating. The pieces to which this happened were considered undesirable and ended up on the cullet heap.

Many glasshouse workers in England and America must have witnessed this phenomenon at some time or other, but the commercial aspects of this occupational nuisance were not recognized until Joseph Locke applied it to the development of Amberina. The patent for Amberina was dated July 24, 1883, and was granted to Joseph Locke "assignor to W. L. Libbey, of Newton, and Edward D. Libbey, of Bos-

16

ton, Massachusetts." It was the first patented method for producing shaded and parti-colored glassware from a sensitive, homogeneous metal. A very small amount of gold in solution was colloidally dispersed in a transparent amber-glass batch. Articles formed from this melt were allowed to cool below a glowing red heat and specified parts were reheated at the glory hole. This rapid cooling and reheating struck a red color in the reheated portions, causing in the finished product a shading of amber to ruby red. The patent also provided for the development of a violet shade, and greenish, bluish and other tints through the controlled use of the caloric available to the glassworker by reheating articles through the small aperture of the glory hole, or the larger aperture of the castor hole.

Collection: Toledo Museum of Art
Amberina mug cut in the Russian pattern. New England Glass Works. Circa 1884.

This first patent for Amberina was followed by a series of similar patents issued either to Locke or to Edward D. Libbey. The next to appear was dated November 13, 1883, and covered Mr. Locke's method for producing a lamp globe of two different colors from the same homogeneous stock. It called for the globe to be formed from a sensitive amber glass, and for cooling and heating the globe unequally to develop darker colors where desired.

In an era of extravagant cut glass it is not surprising to find the New England Glass Company also manufacturing cut Amberina. An interesting method of producing blanks composed of sensitive Amberina glass was patented by Edward Libbey on July 29, 1884. The line drawings which accompanied his specifications illustrated a shallow dish which, after being suitably shaped in a mold, was reheated to produce a rather deep ruby color on its outer surface only. When the design was cut through the ruby color to the undeveloped amber color on the inner surface of the article it presented a rich and interesting object of art. A superb example of this technique exists in the collection of the Toledo Museum of Art.

In 1884, W. L. Libbey & Sons announced "Amberina at greatly reduced prices." This may have been prompted by C. F. A. Hinrich's advertisement in the Crockery & Glass Journal dated February 21, 1884, in which they offered the trade "Ruby Amber Glassware" at prices far below the cost of Libbey's Amberina. On November 12, 1885, Libbey reported that the strike at their factory was over and they were ready to fill orders for Pomona and Amberina; later announcements of Amberina price reductions by Libbey indicates that they were hard hit by the cheap copies of their beautiful shaded ware.

A patent issued to Edward D. Libbey, on June 15, 1886, for a plated glassware clearly explains the method used by the New England Glass Works to produce their "Plated Amberina." Hereby a piece of opal or opalescent glass, plated with a gold-ruby mixture, was reheated to develop a deeper color at portions which would blend into the lighter part of the glass, not sufficiently reheated to develop any color. When sensitive amber and gold-ruby metal (Amberina) was used, the result would appear in the Amberina shading; a sensitive cobalt and ruby glass mixture would produce a plated ware shading from blue to ruby. The patent papers further stated that colored casings of canary, blue or green could be substituted effectively for the opalescent casing. While there is no mention of pattern molding to produce the ribbed effect on the surface of the glass—a characteristic of plated Amberina—this had no particular bearing on the specifications necessary for this patent.

The name "Amberina" was, according to the application for trade-mark papers dated April 4, 1884, in continuous use by W. L. Libbey & Son since December, 1882. Labels bearing the Amberina trade mark have been found on several pieces of Amberina, and plated Amberina too. A few years ago we saw a piece of plated Amberina with an original paper label attached thereto reading "N. E. Glass Co./1886/Aurora." It is quite possible that "Aurora" may have been the name originally used for this ware.

Amberina art glass was made at the Libbey Glass Company of Toledo, Ohio, around 1900, and discontinued after a few years. It was again revived—or at least an attempt was made to revive interest in it—around 1920. This was a very short-lived venture, and it seems only a small quantity was manufactured. This later Amberina, usually marked "Libbey" in script letters in the pontil of each article, is rich in color and most of the forms are in excellent taste.

Collection: Mr. & Mrs. William E. Hammond
Signed "Libbey" Amberina cream and sugar set. Height 4½ inches.
First quarter twentieth century.

Rose Amber

*T*he Mt. Washington Glass Company also produced a shaded glassware in every way similar to Locke's Amberina. Their ware with colors shading into each other was manufactured under the trade name "Rose Amber." While trade-mark papers were granted to Frederick S. Shirley on May 25, 1886, for Rose Amber, and Mr. Shirley stated that the name had been in continuous use by the New Bedford works since August 1, 1884, no patent papers covering the manufacturing process used to produce this parti-colored glassware are on file in the patent offices in Washington, D.C. either in the name of the Mt. Washington Glass Company or any of the men connected with this firm at that time.

The February, 1886, issues of the trade journals ran full-page notices of the injunction granted to the New England Glass Company in their suit against the Mt. Washington Glass Company for the infringement of their patent on "Amberina Glass." The Circuit Court of the United States, District of Massachusetts, handed down an opinion on February 17, 1886, enjoining the New Bedford firm from producing their Rose Amber wares. At no time thereafter was there any release from this injunction noted in any of the trade journals or newspapers. In the opinion of several patent attorneys, Locke could never have patented the method today.

The injunction of 1886 seems not to have prevented the Mt. Washington Glass Company from producing Rose Amber. The following account taken from the pages of the *New Bedford Board of Trade Report* of

20

Rose Amber parfait glass with handle, molded in the "Optic" pattern.
Mt. Washington Glass Works, 1886. Height 5 inches.

1889 bears us out on this point. "Amberina, or rose amber, which is a transparent and effective combination of glass, shading from ruby to the most delicate amber tint, in which the popular optical and hammered effects are produced, is made here, and the circumstances of its introduction on the market is interesting. When ruby glass, which, by the way, receives its coloring from an oxide of gold, comes from the pot, it is amber in color. In making red glass the articles were reheated, when the red color developed. It was the practice to reheat first one end of the vessel and then the other. When one end of the article was reheated the result was the ware now known as amberina, but in this state it was considered as unfinished. At length two companies, of which the Mt. Washington was one, conceived the idea of trying the public with this variegated ware. It caught the popular fancy and was all the rage for about two years. The amount of gold used in the glass is indicated by the fact that the residuum in the bottom of the old pots in which this glass is made is carefully chipped off, and globules of gold are found precipitated, sometimes to the value of thirty or forty dollars.

"The success of amberina suggested to F. S. Shirley, the agent of the works, that an opaque shaded ware would be a novelty. The introduction of Burmese ware opened a new era in glass making and created a sensation at once."

Pearl Satinglass. Brown vase with gold "Federzeichnung" decoration; height 5 inches. Rose-colored vase with applied glass threading and thorny handles; height 7½ inches. Rainbow footed bowl, applied thorny decoration, signed "Patent"; height 5 inches. Rose-colored vase in the hobnail pattern; height 6 inches. *Author's Collection*

Smith Brothers opal glass vase decorated with gold and silver iris and leaves; height 9 inches. Crown Milano covered rose jar; height 11 inches. Opal glass vase with polychrome and gilt decoration; signed "Webb" (Thomas Webb & Sons), circa 1885; height 11 inches. *Author's Collection*

French *art nouveau* Cameo Glass, circa 1900. Vase in silver stand; dark green cameo relief design on a crackled light green ground; signed "E. Michel"; height 9 inches. Bowl-vase of mottled yellow glass with etched cameo decoration of maidenhair fern enameled with orange, yellow, and green; signed "Daum-Nancy"; height 5 inches. Vase of beige-colored glass with etched cameo relief design of seaweed and shells in reddish-brown; signed "Le Gras"; height 8½ inches. *Author's Collection*

"Wild Rose" Peach Blow vase decorated with gold tracery; New England Glass Company, 1886; height 9 inches. Hobbs, Brockunier & Company's facsimile of the Morgan Peach Blow Vase and stand in acid finish; height 11 inches. Mt. Washington Peach Blow vase decorated with enamels and gold in the "Queen's" design; height 9 inches. *Author's Collection*

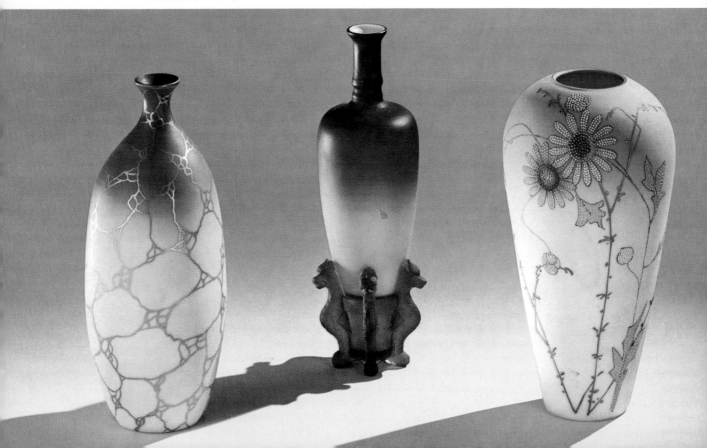

"Moss Agate" vase with cut decoration all over; Stevens & Williams, circa 1888; height 5 inches. Lithyalin decanter, possibly by Egermann, circa 1830; height 7 inches. Lava Glass vase, Mt. Washington Glass Company, circa 1878; height 6 inches. *Author's Collection*

Burmese Glass. Cup and saucer decorated with the "Queen's" design; diameter of saucer 4½ inches. Rare lyre-stem candlestick; height 11 inches. Hobnail ("Pattern 131") sugar bowl; height 5½ inches. Decorated molasses pitcher; height to top of metal mount 7 inches. All made at the Mt. Washington Glass Company, circa 1886. *Author's Collection*

Plated Amberina pitcher; New England Glass Company, circa 1886; height 10 inches. Montieth Amberina bowl designed by Joseph Locke; New England Glass Company, circa 1884; diameter 8 inches. Alexandrite custard cup and saucer; Thomas Webb & Sons, circa 1900; diameter of saucer 4 inches. Daisy and Button pressed Amberina canoe; Hobbs, Brockunier & Company, circa 1886; length 8½ inches. *Author's Collection*

Agata Glass. Bowl-vase decorated with mottled blue mineral stain on a mat ground; height 5 inches. Facsimile of the Morgan Peach Blow vase; height 8½ inches. Pitcher with applied "shell" handle; height 9 inches. The small toothpick holder in the foreground is the New England Glass Company's opaque green ware; original paper label on base; height 1⅝ inches. *Author's Collection*

Pressed Amberina

One piece of pressed Amberina that can be definitely attributed to the New England Glass Company is the small stork vase shown in the illustrations. It was one of the many designs sketched by Joseph Locke in 1884 in his capacity as head designer for the Cambridge works.

In February, 1886, W. L. Libbey & Son, as proprietors of the New England Glass Company, licensed Hobbs, Brockunier & Company of Wheeling, West Virginia, to manufacture "pressed Amberina." Hobbs, Brockunier & Company produced Amberina in the "Hobnail Diamond Pattern, under the Libbey Patent, in a great variety of shapes and articles" according to their advertisements in the *Crockery & Glass Journal* dated March, 1886. The "Hobnail Diamond Pattern," listed in the Wheeling firm's trade catalogues as "No. 101 Pattern," is better known to present-day collectors as "Daisy and Button." Shards of several pressed-glass patterns, including "Daisy and Button Amberina," have reportedly been dug up at the site of the Boston & Sandwich Glass Works on Cape Cod. Many of these patterns are known to have been produced in glass factories a considerable distance away from Sandwich. In view of this, serious researchers and collectors continue to have reservations about the validity of Sandwich's claim to pressed "Daisy and Button Amberina."

Scotney & Earnshaw of London, England, registered design No. 64088, the "Daisy and Diamond Pattern," on December 22, 1886. This firm was listed in the *Pottery Gazette Diary* under "Agencies for Foreign

Pressed Amberina vase. Designed by Joseph Locke, 1884.

Manufacturers" from 1884 to 1901, and specialized in the wholesale distribution of "American tumblers." Many pieces of "Daisy and Diamond" pressed glass—crystal, colored, and Amberina—have been found bearing Scotney & Earnshaw's registry number, and since Scotney & Earnshaw were not glass manufacturers we attempted to discover who actually made these wares. Unfortunately the records in the London Patent Office did not contain this information; but we did find a link between Scotney & Earnshaw and Hobbs, Brockunier & Company which leads us to believe that the South Wheeling glassworks made articles in the "Daisy and Diamond Pattern" for export.

A transparent, homogeneous glassware shading from pale amber to a delicate rose tint in the reheated portions of the article was press-molded by the firm of Cristalleries de Baccarat of France. Known to collectors as "Baccarat's Amberina" it was introduced by that firm in 1916 and catalogues illustrating such wares were distributed to the trade and the public at large that same year. Baccarat's "Rose Teinte' " made another appearance in 1940 when the firm again produced their beautiful shaded glassware.

The greater portion of Baccarat's Rose Teinte' was pressed in their three major designs—helical twist, pinwheel and laurel—in a vast amount of boudoir accessories, vases, bowls, tablewares, stemware, tumblers, decanters, candlesticks, chandeliers and a host of useful household and decorative articles. Large, low-footed compotes were made especially for the Turkish market.

The marks "Baccarat" and "Depose" found on this ware refer to the designs which the firm of Baccarat patented, rather than to the formula or method of production used to manufacture this sensitive shaded ware. The glass is very similar to the Amberina and Rose Amber wares made by the New England Glass Company and the Mt. Washington Glass Works. The amount of gold salts dispersed throughout the amber glass melt was much smaller than that used by the American factories, hence the rather pale rose tints in the reheated portions of the article.

Baccarat also produced a sensitive, homogeneous glassware shading from opaque white to opaque rose in the developed portions of the article. It resembles in every particular the coloring of the New England Glass Works' "Wild Rose" Peach Blow glassware. Baccarat's shaded white to

Pressed Amberina "Toy Tumbler" toothpick holder. "Pattern 101,"
Hobbs, Brockunier & Co., 1886.

rose opal wares were pressed in the same molds used for their "Rose Teinte'," and they were contemporary with this glassware. The shaded rose to white opal glassware was also marked "Baccarat" and "Depose" in small block letters somewhere on each article or a part thereof.

Painted Amberina

On April 9, 1895, a patent was issued to Andrew Stock and Emil Mueller of Pittsburgh, Pennsylvania, covering a process for manufacturing shaded and parti-colored glassware by painting the glass partially with a paint composed of copper oxide and yellow ochre. This first partial painting was fixed by placing the article in a muffle and bringing it to a high temperature. After the article had cooled it was painted all over with this same compound and again reheated in a muffle. The reheating brought out the ruby color in the first coat of paint and changed the second to a yellow, amber or green color. Such wares can be encountered by collectors today. They are easily detected, especially when portions of the painted coloring have been worn away with use. It also has an iridescence which is peculiar to wares painted with metallic stains.

Alexandrite

At the beginning of the twentieth century, not later than 1902, Thos. Webb & Sons manufactured a parti-colored transparent ware of great beauty. The glass shaded from a pale citron-yellow color to rose and then to blue in the reheated portions of the article. It was produced from a homogeneous melt and unevenly turned to develop the rose and bluish tinges. Webb's sold their product under the name "Alexandrite." The small violet vase shown in our illustrations is a fine example of this beautiful glassware.

Stevens & Williams also produced an Alexandrite glassware by plating a body glass of transparent yellow with rose and blue glass. The outer casings of blue and rose were cut through to the yellow glass, producing an exceptionally beautiful effect.

By courtesy of the Stourbridge Corporation
Alexandrite violet vase. Thos. Webb & Sons.
Circa 1900. Height 3 inches.

Shaded Opalescent Glassware

Glasses with raised opalescent white designs on their surface were a popular item in the late nineteenth century. Inexpensive tablewares and decorative articles were produced by Hobbs, Brockunier & Company of Wheeling, West Virginia; Alexander J. Beatty & Sons of Steubenville, Ohio; Phillip Arbogast of Pittsburgh, Pennsylvania; John Bryce & Company of Pittsburgh; King & Company of Pittsburgh; and Doyle & Company of the same city. There were still other manufacturers of this type of glassware, both foreign and domestic. The wares produced by these various companies differ in form and in coloring, but the basic manufacturing technique in each case is the same.

Shaded opalescent glassware was manufactured in this way. A colored bulb of glass was heavily coated with a sensitive crystal glass containing bone ash and arsenic. It was blown into a pattern mold to produce a raised decoration on its outer surface, after which it was cooled slightly and then reheated at the glory hole. The raised designs, having cooled below a glowing red heat, upon reheating, struck an opalescent white color. The finished product was an article of glassware with a colored background on which a raised opalescent white design appeared.

This ware can be found in a multitude of patterns, with background colors ranging from transparent crystal right on through the entire spectrum. Hobnail, Dew Drop, Bullseye, Optic, Spot Resist, Opalescent Bar, Opalescent Rib, Checkered Bars, Zig Zag, Seaweed, Floral, and a host of other well-known patterns were manufactured. Some of the designs, such

30

Ruby-colored pitcher with developed opalescent design. Height 11 inches.

as Opalescent Rib, Checkered Bar and Zig Zag, were patented designs. The last named were registered by William Henry Barr, assignor to Alexander J. Beatty & Sons, on April 3, 1888.

In 1886, C. F. A. Hinrichs sold imported opalescent hobnail glass—called "Lustred Pea-spotted"—in a variety of colors.

On June 1, 1886, William Leighton, Jr. and William F. Russell, both assignors to the Hobbs, Brockunier Company, patented a means for producing opalescent glassware. The article to be made was first pressed in a full-size mold to form nodules or bosses on its exterior surface. Being composed of a sensitive opalescent glass, upon reheating at the glory hole, the bosses struck an opalescent white. Pressing the articles in full-size molds insured a more precise spacing of the nodules.

On November 20, 1888, John F. Miller of the Buckeye Glass Company, Martin's Ferry, Ohio, patented a means for producing a rather attractive opalescent glassware. Their "New 528 Venetian Ware" was advertised in full-page illustrated advertisements in color in the various trade journals. It was produced in "crystal, canary, blue and rose opalescent" in a variety of table wares. Being blown in full-size molds it was cheaply manufactured and priced accordingly. Nevertheless, it was an attractive glassware and sold exceptionally well.

On February 14, 1889, Thomas Davidson, the enterprising son of the founder of George Davidson & Company, Ltd., the Teams Glass Works, Gateshead-on-Tyne, England, patented a process for producing pressed, shaded, opalescent glassware. Articles such as ornamental dishes, vases, jugs, tumblers, and so on, were made of clear glass at the base, gradually becoming more opaque towards the top. To a batch of, say, 560 pounds of sand, 210 pounds of alkali, and 84 pounds of sodium nitrate, was added 70 pounds of calcium phosphate, 84 pounds of calcspar, and 35 pounds of arsenic. The proportions of these last three ingredients were variable. The articles were pressed and molded in the ordinary way, then allowed to cool slightly, and then reheated. The reheated portions of the articles struck an opalescent color of the shade of the body metal or opalescent white.

Flashed Glassware

*T*he popularity of Joseph Locke's Amberina prompted the production of what is known as "flashed wares" to the trade. An article of glass was formed and the inner surface of the object was partially coated with a thin plating of glass of another, more dominant, color—usually a ruby red. The result was a parti-colored, shaded glassware.

Most of the wares known to collectors as "Rubena Verde," "Rubena Crystal" and "Blue Amberina" were manufactured in this way. Not only was it a cheaper means of producing a shaded glassware, but it also circumvented Mr. Locke's patented method for producing his Amberina glass. Occasionally such shaded glasses were plated over with a sensitive opalescent metal, pattern molded and reheated to form a raised opalescent design on the finished product.

Flashed Wares can be easily detected by examining the rim of the article for the several casings.

On May 5, 1891, Francis Lannoy of Tiffin, Ohio, patented a unique method for producing flashed glassware. The method consisted of joining and causing to adhere the edges of two pieces of glass of different shades, then coating the combined pieces thus made with molten glass, and blowing the mass into its ultimate shape. The line of demarcation between the two or more colors was even more apparent in this ware.

Archibald L. Brown of Chicago, Illinois, patented a means for producing "Colored Flashed Ornamental Glass" on June 8, 1897. Brown prepared the glass by grinding away a portion of the surface and then applying a mixture of gutta-percha, gum and coloring matter. The article was baked in a kiln at a low temperature for several hours to fix the color to the surface of the glass. Brown's patent also contained a new method for grinding away portions of the coloring to produce ornamental design on the glass.

On September 29, 1891, William Buttler of Washington, Pennsylvania, patented a means for flashing color on pressed and blown glass. The articles to be colored were dipped into a pot of colored glass with a very low melting point. Since the uncolored wares were made from a glass of a higher melting point they retained their shape throughout the flashing process.

Several patents for producing flashed colored glassware were registered abroad. On May 5, 1814, Joseph Price of Gateshead-on-Tyne, England, patented a means for flashing crystal glass with opal (opaque white) glass. On July 4, 1882, Rice Williams Harris patented a technique for producing flashed glass by blowing crystal glass into a cup of colored glass in which a hole had been opened to allow heat and gases to escape, thereby obviating strains and air bubbles between the layers of the glass. Two patents for flashing color on crystal glass were registered by Fontaine & Cie. of Aachen, Germany, on February 10, 1902, and July 1, 1902. Both patents provided for the preparation of pressed disks, rings, stars, letters, figures, rosettes, crowns, leaves, and so forth, which were later picked up on a gather of crystal glass and incorporated into the body glass. The Fontaine process assured a uniform color in the finished decoration.

Around 1887 C. F. A. Hinrichs offered the trade imported Bohemian bi-colored (flashed) glassware pattern-molded with "Polka Dot or Bull's Eye patterns" in "Rubena" (shaded crystal to ruby glass), "Rosina" (shaded light to dark ruby glass), and "Blurina" (shaded light blue to ruby glass).

Burmese

By adding small amounts of fluor-spar, feldspar and oxide of uranium to essentially the same ingredients used by Joseph Locke to produce Amberina, Frederick S. Shirley manufactured his popular translucent, homogeneous, shaded ware known as "Burmese." Mr. Shirley patented his formula for Burmese December 15, 1885, thus reserving the rights to produce it for the Mt. Washington Glass Company.

In order to better understand the manufacturing process involved in the making of Burmese let us go over Shirley's formula as found in his patent enumerations:

> 100 pounds of white sand
> 36 pounds of refined lead oxide
> 25 pounds of pearl ash (purified potash)
> 7 pounds of niter
> 5 pounds of bicarbonate of soda

——made translucent by the addition of:

> 6 pounds of fluor-spar
> 5 pounds of feldspar

This charge weighing 184 pounds produced a well-known mixture for translucent white or opal glass. To this mix Mr. Shirley added:

> 2 pounds of oxide of uranium
> 1 & ½ pennyweights of prepared gold

The addition of two pounds of uranium oxide made the ordinarily translucent white opal glass melt a pale yellow in color. Adding the small amount of gold, made soluble in a solution of aqua regia and colloidally dispersed throughout the entire batch, made the glass sensitive to thermal changes. After the article was formed from this glass it was allowed to cool below a glowing red heat and reheated at the glory hole. The reheated portions of the article struck a salmon-pink color which shaded down into the original body color of pale yellow.

Author's Collection

Footed Burmese bowl with applied Burmese decoration.

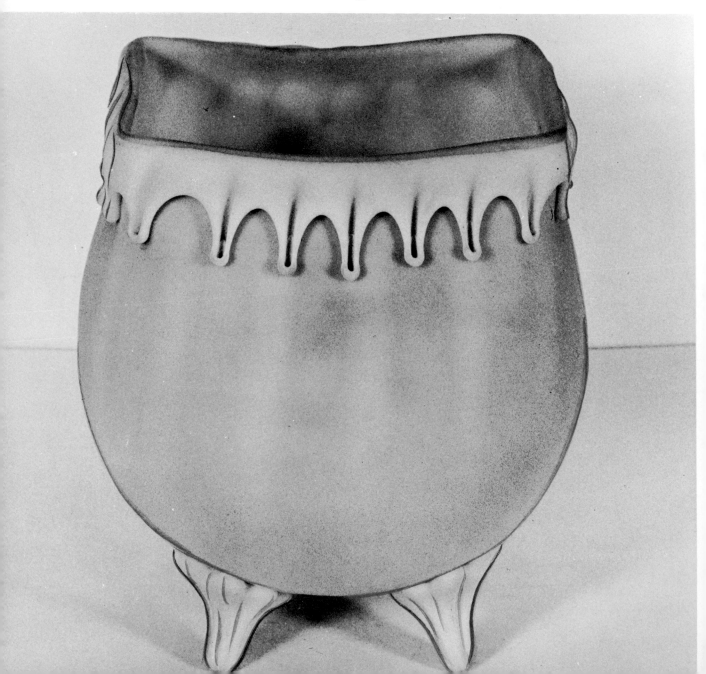

Long before Shirley employed oxide of uranium as a colorant for Burmese this ingredient was being used by European and American glasshouses. Uranium imparts a very handsome wine-yellow color to glass, the metal stained by this oxide exhibiting a fine canary-green fluorescence when viewed by reflected light. In Bohemia it was known as "Annagelb" and "Chrysopras" glasses; the former a transparent uranium-yellow glass, the latter an opaque uranium-yellow with opalescent qualities. Annagelb was known at the Boston & Sandwich Works as "Canary yellow."

Author's Collection
Large Burmese bowl with applied Burmese decoration in its original glossy finish.

Gold too is a powerful colorant when introduced into a glass batch. At one time gold-ruby glass was very high in price, on the pretext of its content of the expensive metal, gold. This, however, is unjustifiable, one part of gold being sufficient to transform fifty thousand parts of glass into a deep ruby metal. The tinctorial power of gold toward glass is so great that even one part in a hundred thousand will produce a light red glass. Moreover the solvent capacity of glass for gold is very small, and if an excess of gold be introduced into the batch, the glass will only dissolve sufficiently to give a deep ruby glass, the surplus being left behind as a fused button in the bottom of the pot.

The gold must always be in a liquid form and used as a very dilute solution. This solution is sprinkled over the sand used in the batch, the sand being well stirred to ensure that all particles are wetted with the solution. In view of this, the report of a gold ring accidentally falling onto a gather of glass and producing Amberina coloring must be erroneous.

So little gold and uranium was used in the manufacture of Burmese glassware that an overemphasis of these facts can be quite misleading. From a batch weighing about two hundred pounds, containing less than $1.00 worth of uranium oxide and less than $3.00 worth of gold, hundreds of articles could be made. The amount of gold and uranium contained in each piece of Burmese is infinitesimal.

On June 16, 1886, Frederick Shirley's formula for Burmese was patented in England. Not long afterward Thos. Webb & Sons purchased a license to produce Burmese at their works in Stourbridge. The glass was named "Queen's Burmese Ware" and most of the articles produced by Webb were so marked, either with a paper label or incised in the glass itself. On September 5, 1887, Thos. Webb & Sons registered a design for a flower-shaped top for vases and bowls which they produced in fancy colored wares—including Burmese. The registry number, 80167, can be found etched or engraved on some of these wares.

For some time Stevens & Williams experimented to produce a similar ware without infringing on Mr. Shirley's patent. John Northwood II, whose father conducted these experiments, told us that they did produce a similar ware. It was, however, never marketed; in fact, it never got beyond the experimental stages at Stevens & Williams. A small *bobêche* on a shelf in Mr. Northwood's studio workshop is all that remains in England of this attempt to produce a competitor to Burmese.

Decorated Burmese fairy lamp. Signed "Thos. Webb & Sons,
Queen's Burmese Ware, Patented." Circa 1886.

In the early fall of 1886 suits were entered by the Mt. Washington Glass Works against the Phoenix Glass Company for infringing on its patents dated December 15, 1885, June 29, 1886, and February 8, 1881. The last two are referred to in the chapter on Pearl Satin Glass.

In rebuttal, the Phoenix Glass Company had the law firm of Connally Bros. draw up a list of particulars giving their legal opinion of Mr. Shirley's claims against them. In essence the Connally Bros. firm stated that in their opinion the patent dated December 15, 1885 (covering Burmese and Peach Blow) was too broad in its coverage and neglected to give credit to the production of shaded wares patented by Joseph Locke (Amberina). They also stated that shaded glasswares were well known prior to Burmese and that giving the article a plush or velvety finish with acids or sandblasting was also a well-known art far anterior to Shirley's patented method.

On October 14, 1886, a memorandum in one of the trade journals stated that a letter from Mr. Shirley to the editor promised an answer to this opinion by Connally Bros. It finally came out in the December 16, 1886, issue. Mr. J. E. Maynadier, Attorney and Counselor at Law, submitted his opinion for the Mt. Washington Glass Company. Mr. Maynadier stated, in effect, that the patent covering Mr. Shirley's Burmese glass was original in the strict sense as understood by patent attorneys and judges. That while Mr. Locke's patent for Amberina glassware did in some instances resemble the Shirley claims, it was not broad enough

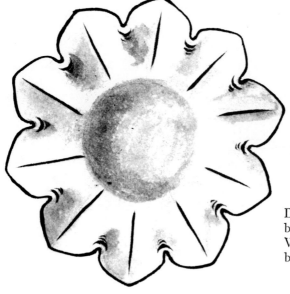

Design No. 80167, a decorative top for vases, bowls, etc., was registered in London by Thomas Webb & Sons Ltd. on September 5, 1887. It has been found on Queen's Burmese Ware and on other art glass produced by this firm.

Collection: Mr. & Mrs. William E. Hammond
Burmese table lamp. Mt. Washington Glass Works. Circa 1886. Height 19 inches.

to include them. Shirley's attorney dwelt on the fact that Locke's specifications particularly stated that his was a transparent ware; Mr. Shirley's Burmese being almost opaque, certainly translucent, circumvented the Locke coverage. The outcome of all the differences between the Mt. Washington Glass Works and the Phoenix Glass Company was never divulged in any of the subsequent issues of any of the trade journals; we can only assume that they were either reconciled or the matter was simply dropped by both sides as too costly a fight to continue pressing.

Though an elliptically-shaped paper label reading "Mt.W.G.Co., Burmese, Dec.15th,1885" can sometimes be found on the New Bedford ware no trade mark or trade-name papers for Burmese exist in the files at the Patent Offices in Washington, D.C.

In the *New Bedford Evening Standard* the following account appeared, datelined December, 1886. "Some months ago the Standard contained an account of Manager Shirley presenting to Queen Victoria several articles of Burmese ware manufactured at the Mt. Washington Glass Works in this city. The Queen liked the beautiful dishes so much that she has ordered a tea set of the same ware. The set has been finished, and is ready for packing. It is beautifully ornamented, many of the pieces with flowers in enamel work, the leaves being composed of minute beads of solid gold and glass of various tints. Some of the pieces are decorated with vine and leaf painting in modest colors which harmonize well with the delicate canary and salmon of the ware, and others have neat traceries of gold. Everything in the ornamentation is of original design by Mr. Albert Steffin, foreman of the decorating works. The set includes a dozen small cups and saucers, a dozen small plates, sugar, cream and slop bowl, six bread plates, a large flower bowl, and four vases, two of Egyptian and two of Etruscan pattern. All the handles are of solid gold or plain pattern and Etruscan finish. It is probably the finest set of ornamental glassware ever made."

In 1889, a report printed by The Board of Trade, New Bedford, Massachusetts, had this to say about the Burmese wares made at Mt. Washington: "The decorating is done in a three-story building on the premises, which is entirely given up to this department. Albert Steffin is the superintendent in this department and designed the elegant decorated Burmese sent to the queen. This pattern has now become famous and is known as the 'Queen's design.' It conventionalizes a number of flowers and is in raised enamel. Much of the decorating is done with pure gold, reduced with acids, and the effect of the rich gold with the mellow shades of the Burmese is very lovely. The maidenhair fern design on lamps and shades of lusterless white glass is one of the most tasteful pieces of glassware ever put on the market. Some others of the latest designs are the 'tapestry,' the 'Persian,' the latter giving the effect of inlaid enamel, the new lace pattern, and the 'Egyptian' design, in which the pyramids and palms are conspicuous. There is also a design of fish swimming in a net of gold which is very attractive. The colors are of mineral composition and are fused into the material by baking in the kilns. At the same time they undergo a chemical change which develops the brilliancy and transparency. The salt, pepper, and sugar sifters, in the form of decorated eggs of glass, originated here and have proved a very successful Easter specialty. The decorated ware turned out here is of the highest grade, prepared for the finest trade." We regret to say that since this book was initially printed (1959) undecorated pieces of Burmese glass have been embellished with many of the designs mentioned above, the "Egyptian" and "Queen's" designs in particular.

A small vase which in every way resembles Mr. Shirley's Burmese glass is in the author's collection. It was produced by Fred. Carder at the old Steuben Glass Works about 1908. Mr. Carder's "Peach Blow" differs but a little from Shirley's Burmese in color; if anything, it is perhaps a more vivid hue.

We would like to bring out one interesting fact revealed in the Burmese patent enumerations. Shirley claimed that "should it be desired, the workman by reheating the edges to a melting-point, can restore the original yellow color on the part so reheated, thus producing varied effects of color-shadings not previously obtainable." This should answer the question raised by many collectors concerning the yellow color found on the rim of some articles of Burmese glassware.

Peach Blow Glassware

*T*he publicity attendant on the sale of a Peach Blow porcelain vase for eighteen thousand dollars on March 8, 1886, precipitated the manufacture of glass and pottery reproductions of this ware. The vase, one of the thousands of art objects sold by the American Art Institute for the estate of Mrs. Mary Morgan, was reported to have once been in the collection of a Chinese mandarin named Wang Ye. The exquisite glaze was described in the *Crockery & Glass Journal* for March, 1886, as being the color of "crushed strawberries," a desirable hue for this kind of porcelain, but difficult to attain. The several accounts of the sale were amusing and at times confused, for while one reporter would state that the vase was sold to Mr. Walters of Baltimore, Maryland, another, supposedly quoting Mr. Walters, would deny this statement. Mr. Walters did buy Mrs. Morgan's Peach Blow vase, but because of the adverse publicity surrounding its purchase it was hidden away in a vault for more than fifty years before it was placed on exhibition in the Walters Art Gallery in Baltimore, Maryland.

Newspapers and magazines were quite critical of the bottle-shaped vase; their references to "the crazy Widow Morgan" and her "plug-ugly of ceramic art" were numerous. Nevertheless the word Peach Blow fell from the lips of thousands. B. D. Baldwin & Company of Chicago, Illinois, introduced a line of beauty aids under the trade name "Peach Blow" and belles of the day were not in fashion unless their cheeks and lips were so tinted.

HOBBS, BROCKUNIER'S "CORAL"

Three American manufacturers produced a glassware simulating the coloring of the Morgan Peach Blow vase. Hobbs, Brockunier & Company made what we consider to be the best facsimile of the vase by plating an opal glass body with a transparent amber glass made sensitive to caloric changes by colloidally dispersing gold salts throughout the melt. After plating the article with this sensitive skin of glass, the upper portion of the article was reheated at the glory hole and struck a ruby color at those parts. The finished product shaded from yellow in the base to a deep cherry red in the upper regions.

The Wheeling facsimiles of the Morgan Peach Blow vase sold exceptionally well according to sales reports for the year 1886. Other articles, decorative and utilitarian, were made of this same glass and these, too, were favorably received. Hobbs, Brockunier's advertisements of their "Coral, sometimes called Peach Blow," report that it was sold in the "Coral and Lustreless" finish. In 1887 it was reported that "other firms in the Wheeling area are working on this same ware" (Peach Blow glassware).

The manufacturing process employed in making Wheeling Peach Blow glass was a patented means belonging to the New England Glass Company (see Plated Amberina). We cannot trace any recording of an agreement between these two companies over the use of this process by Hobbs, Brockunier & Company. Such an understanding might possibly have been included in the agreement reached between these two firms at the time the Wheeling works were licensed to produce pressed Amberina under the Libbey patent.

From the pages of the *Crockery & Glass Journal*, November 25, 1886, we have this informative account of the wares made by the Wheeling works in their Coral glass: "At Hobbs, Brockunier & Co.'s trade is excellent. The demand for their lusterless coral, known to the trade as peachblow, is beyond expectations, and keeps up remarkably well. This firm is now making tasty holiday goods. Pears, peaches, and other fruits in coral, richly tinted, look natural enough to eat." The fruit pieces are rare in this ware. Other factories, both in America and abroad, also made glass fruits in shaded colors but these were shaded by the die-away process. Wheeling fruits, such as the pear we illustrate here, have been colored by reheating.

Between 1908 and 1930 Fred Carder of Corning produced a Peach Blow glassware very similar in color to the Hobbs, Brockunier's Coral. Mr. Carder plated a translucent alabaster glass with gold-ruby metal and reheated the whole object to produce a beautiful cherry-red coloring over the entire outer casing. The articles made by Carder are sometimes marked "Steuben" in the pontil.

MT. WASHINGTON "PEACH BLOW"

The term "Peach Blow" was positive magic. Applied to the right merchandise it could have sold anything. Frederick S. Shirley of the Mt. Washington Glass Company filed trade-name papers on the terms "Peach Blow" and "Peach Skin" securing exclusive use of the appelations, as applied to glassware, for the New Bedford Works on July 20, 1886.

Substituting a small amount of cobalt or copper oxide as a colorant, instead of the oxide of uranium used in making Burmese, Shirley produced a homogeneous glassware shaded pale gray-blue to a delicate rose tint in the reheated portions. Mr. Shirley suggested this substitution of cobalt and oxide of copper in his patent papers for Burmese glassware.

The Mt. Washington Peach Blow wares were manufactured in forms and shapes that were also used for their Burmese glassware. Pattern-molding, applied glass decoration, and gold and enamels created interesting and beautiful designs on articles for table and decorative use. The subtle coloring of this glassware was not appreciated in its day which accounts for its being in scant evidence now.

"Peach Blow" labels from trade-mark papers issued to F. S. Shirley.

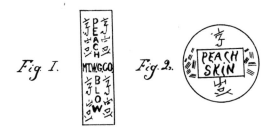

Fig. I.   Fig. 2.

"Coral" (Peach Blow) pear. Hobbs, Brockunier & Co., 1886. Height 5 inches.

Pair of Wheeling Peach Blow vases with spangles throughout the glass and twisted
amber glass handles. Height 10¼ inches.
Collection Mansion Museum, Oglebay Park, Wheeling, W. Va.

Wheeling Peach Blow bowl with
lavender lining. Height 4 inches.
*Collection Mansion Museum,
Oglebay Park, Wheeling, W. Va.*

WILD ROSE

The public's enthusiastic response to such late nineteenth century shaded wares as Amberina and Burmese was responsible for the further experimentation with heat-sensitive glasses made by the New England Glass Works. One of the products resulting from this research was patented by Edward D. Libbey on March 2, 1886. It was advertised and sold under the name "Wild Rose."

In a few words, Mr. Libbey's Wild Rose was produced by combining an opal glass and a gold-ruby glass in one pot. The sensitive glass mixture thus formed was reheated to produce color in the reheated portions of the article. The result was a translucent shaded rose to white homogeneous glassware of great beauty. The factory name for this ware was "Peach Blow."

Mr. Libbey's specifications circumvent previous patents for shaded wares like Burmese and Amberina, which methods provide that all the ingredients be mixed simultaneously in one batch, by simply combining two different kinds of glass. The dissimilarity in production methods

Collection: Mr. & Mrs. William E. Hammond
Decorated Mt. Washington Peach Blow pitcher.
Height 9 inches.

Gundersen-Pairpoint Glass Works, New Bedford, Massachusetts
"Peach Blow," wholesale prices

Top Row, left to right:

#469 Cornucopia 7"	$4.00
#471 Nut Dish	4.50
#469 Cornucopia 7"	4.50
#466 Tappan Tulip Vase 8½"	3.75
#3146 Compote	5.00
#466 Tappan Tulip Vase 8½"	3.75

Middle Row, left to right:

#466 Tappan 3-Foil Vase 8½"	4.00
#373 Creamer	3.50
#474 Cup	3.25
#474 Saucer	2.50
#372 Sugar	3.50
#466 Tappan 3-Foil Vase 8½"	4.00

Bottom Row, left to right:

#470 Rolled Top Candlestick 8½"	4.00

#468 Bon-Bon Dish	5.00
#470 Rolled Top Candlestick 8½"	4.00
#475 Hat Cigarette Holder ...	2.50
#470 Candlestick, Crimped 8½"	4.00
#468 Bon-Bon Dish	5.00
#470 Candlestick, Crimped 8½"	4.00

Photograph indicates maximum possible color range from delicate pink to deep crimson. Majority of pieces, however, were made in the delicate pink.

(First four items in the bottom row are glossy finish. Balance of items in photo are dull velvet finish.)

seems trifling; however it was sufficiently different to thwart any claims of patent infringement.

Articles of Wild Rose glassware were pattern molded, decorated with gilt and enamel designs and also acidized to a lovely satin finish. Sometimes pieces were left in their original glossy state. The vase shown in our illustrations was decorated by Joseph Locke for his daughter Nora. The intricately etched relief designs covering the entire surface of the vase have been outlined and highlighted with gold traceries and a dark brown mineral stain.

The closing sentence of the last paragraph in Mr. Libbey's patent papers, although broad in its meaning, gives us our clue to the New England Glass Company's opaque green ware which we mention in the chapter on Agata glassware. By simply adding the proper amount of copper oxide to an opal glass batch Libbey produced a homogeneous opaque green glassware. The Cambridge product is distinguished from a similar ware produced by the Mt. Washington Glass Works by its mottled blue metallic stain decoration.

Author's Collection
"Wild Rose" (Peach Blow) vase, etched and decorated by Joseph Locke. Height 7 inches.

Joseph Locke patented a process on July 13, 1886, for producing a glass-ware whose inner and outer surfaces shaded white to rose. This was accomplished by plating a sensitive opal glass (Wild Rose) with a sensitive transparent white metal and reheating in certain portions to develop the red tones in both the inner and outer casings.

At about the same time that shaded glassware was being produced in America the firms of Thos. Webb & Sons and Stevens & Williams of England were manufacturing shaded wares which they termed "Peach Glass" or "Peach Bloom." Webb's Peach Glass was described on page 299 of the *Pottery & Glass Gazette* for 1885 as "a new art glass—a delicate blend of color shaded so as to resemble a peach." Webb's Peach Glass was similar in appearance to Hobbs, Brockunier's "Coral" in that it was a cased ware shading from yellow to cherry-red in the upper portion. Stevens & Williams' "Peach Bloom" was very much the same in appearance. Both English factories sometimes used their peach glasses in conjunction with cameo relief designs producing articles of considerable beauty.

Bohemian glass manufacturers were selling "Peach Blow" glass at prices far below the cost of American and English wares soon after it became popular. I. Vogelsang Sons, 90 Warren Street, New York City, importers of Bohemian glass, advertised "Peach Blow imitations at one-fourth of the price of real Peach Blow." Although these Bohemian wares in no way compared with the fine wares made in America and England, their cheapness forced our better products off the market.

About 1952, the Gundersen-Pairpoint Glass Works of New Bedford, Massachusetts (successors to the Mt. Washington Glass Company and its successor, the Pairpoint Corporation) reissued the popular wares produced by the Mt. Washington Glass Company in the late 1880s—"Peach Blow," "Burmese" and "Rose Amber." It was not their intent to make reproductions of the original wares. Unfortunately, a few unscrupulous people took this as a grand opportunity to pass off these wares as old glass and a great many collectors and dealers were taken in. Now these Gundersen-Pairpoint wares are highly prized by collectors for what they actually represent—a serious attempt to recreate fine glass of an earlier period.

An original photo illustration of the forms in which the Gundersen-Pairpoint "Peach Blow" wares were made is shown, accompanied by the wholesale prices asked for these wares. Since not all the forms for "Peach Blow," "Burmese," and "Rose Amber" are shown, we are also including a wholesale price list enumerating more of the articles offered in "Peach Blow" and "Rose Amber" by the Gundersen-Pairpoint Glass Works:

	Peach Blowl	Rose Amber
#57 Old Fashion Contour Glass		$5.00
#58 Flip Vase 4¾" diam.; 6½" high ..		3.50
#58 Large Water Tumbler		2.25
#120 Wine Glass	3.00	
#457 Jug		7.50
#457 Fruit Glass		2.00
#466 Tappan Tulip Vase 8½"	3.75	4.25
#466 Tappan 3-Foil Vase 9½"	4.00	4.25
#2077 Dividend Glass 4½"............	1.50	1.00
#2077 Large Dividend Decanter .. with Stopper		7.00
#4068 Swan 4"	4.00	
#4068 Swan 6"	4.75	

Author's Collection
Peach Blow vase with applied crystal decoration. Thos. Webb & Sons. Circa 1886.

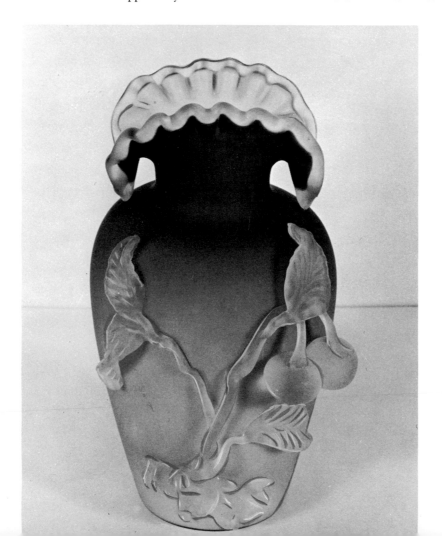

Agata

Early in the year of 1887, full-page advertisements announcing W. L. Libbey's "latest novelty, Agata Art Glass," appeared in the *Crockery & Glass Journal* and other trade papers. The method of producing this novel type of glassware was patented January 18, 1887, by Joseph Locke. According to Mr. Locke's patent specifications the article to be ornamented was first partially or wholly coated with a metallic stain or mineral color of the color desired, and thereafter the part of the glassware so stained was either spattered or had applied to it a volatile liquid, such as benzene, alcohol or naptha. The volatile liquid would evaporate leaving a mottled surface on the glassware which was fixed by placing the article in a muffle.

This technique for decorating glassware was mostly confined to the New England Glass Work's Wild Rose Peach Blow. It is usually encountered in a glossy finish, the mat-surfaced pieces being rare. The mineral stains used on Agata were the same as those Locke employed to decorate his Pomona glassware.

Pattern-molded Agata, Agata facsimiles of the Morgan Peach Blow vase, and Agata lined with opal glass are rare examples of this ware.

The Cambridge works also produced an opaque green ware which they decorated with a narrow band of mottled blue metallic stain around the top or midsection of each article.

Agata had been in production less than a year when the New England Glass Works was closed down and the factory removed to the Midwest. It was not made again.

Opaque green table lamp with mottled blue mineral stain decoration. Height 20½ inches.

Pomona

*P*omona, the Roman goddess of the fruit of trees, lent her name to one of the more subtle products of the New England Glass Works, and the delicate gelid appearance of Pomona glass has long been a source of eye pleasure to collectors of this ware.

Joseph Locke's first patented method for producing Pomona was issued April 28, 1885. The article to be produced was made and shaped from homogeneous crystal glass in the usual way, after which it was covered entirely with a wax or acid-resisting material. On the portion of the article which was to have the iced or frosted ground a series of curved lines were cut through the resist with a wheel or some other cutting agent. This necessitated a great many lines crisscrossing each other. The outline for the ornamentation found on almost all pieces of this ware was also cut through the resist before the article was subjected to the action of the etching acid which ate into the glass wherever the resist was removed. The relatively simple task of scratching through the resist with an etching needle was assigned to several young women who daily turned out hundreds of such articles.

The object having been etched, the wax or acid-resisting pellicle referred to in the patent was removed. The outlined ornamentation was filled in with colored mineral stains and the piece was fired in a muffle to fix the colors.

It soon became apparent that Locke's original method for manufacturing Pomona was far too expensive for the company to continue using

56

Pomona cream and sugar set, decorated with blue berries, red stems and gold leaves.
New England Glass Works, 1886. Height 3 inches.

and so he experimented further, searching for a cheaper means of producing somewhat the same effect. On June 15, 1886, a patent was issued to Joseph Locke covering this less expensive way to make Pomona glassware.

In his later patent, which Locke explained would hasten and simplify the operation of etching to produce a stippled or frosted ground, the article to be treated was first protected at points where it was to be left smooth and plain for decoration by means of a pellicle or layer of wax. The portion of the article to be etched had applied to it a thin layer of some finely pulverized acid-resisting powder—such as asphaltum or resin. The fine coating of acid-resisting powder was made to adhere to the surface of the object by means of a thin layer of oil or varnish. The particles adhering to and touching the body of the article protected the article at such points from the acid in the usual acid bath. All parts of the surface not protected by the powdered resist were acted upon by the acid, leaving a fine stippling all over the body of the article. The texture of the stippling was governed by the fineness or coarseness of the powdered resist.

andgrand

Collection: Smithsonian Institution
Specimens of Pomona made by the New England Glass Company, Cambridge, Mass.,
and presented to the U.S. National Museum in 1886.

In neither of Locke's patent specifications do we find any reference to pattern molding the body glass, although one seldom will find a specimen that has not been so treated; nor did Mr. Locke limit the glass body to a transparent crystal metal.

In an interview with Joseph Locke which appeared in the *Crockery & Glass Journal* for 1901, he stated that Pomona glassware was colored with amber, blue and rose-colored mineral stains. The amber stain, more often encountered than any other color in Pomona, is a dilute nitrate of silver. The pale blue stain has a manganese base. According to Locke, Pomona was ahead of its time and was not a popular item.

Locke illustrated his first patent papers with a tumbler on which the initials of his patent attorneys, Crosby & Gregory, appeared. The top of the tumbler was decorated with a band of acanthus leaves. His second specifications were illustrated with a small footed vase, girdled about its tapered midsection with a band of flowers resembling wild roses. Other motifs found on this ware are designs of blue berries with red stems and gold leaves, butterflies and sheaves of wheat, grass, butterflies and pansies, a tracery of blue lines, and a vintage design which we found on a pitcher belonging to his daughter.

Collection: Alfred University Museum
Pomona pitcher etched and decorated by Joseph Locke. firstgrind

A delicately etched Pomona finger bowl engraved with the initials "I.H.B." and surmounted with a royal crown was acquired in Spain where it was reportedly received from a member of the Spanish royal family. The letters were said to represent the initials for "Imperator Hapsburg-Battenburg." It very likely represents one of the pieces from a very large service made after 1893 by the Libbey Glass Company of Toledo, Ohio. On July 15, 1893, H.R.H. Infante Don Antonio de Orleans appointed Messrs. Libbey & Company glass makers to his royal house, with the use of his royal coat of arms for signs, bills and labels. The grant was signed by Pedro Jover Fovar, Superintendent of His Royal Highness's Household. This distinction followed close behind the Infanta Eulalia's visit to the Libbey exhibit at the Columbian Exposition of 1893, and Libbey's presentation to the princess of a glass dress. (See chapter on Spun Glass.)

Joseph Locke commented on his Pomona glassware in an interview granted in 1900 to the editor of the *Crockery & Glass Journal*. "Pomona," he said, "was twenty years ahead of the times. Connoisseurs bought it and were willing to pay a big price for it. Owing to the changes made in the New England Glass Company, and for various reasons, it was dropped. It could be sold now more readily than then, as the people are educated to an appreciation of such wares. 'Pomona' ware was needle-etched and colored with iridescent tints of delicate pinks, lavenders and amber. The shapes were bowls, vases and fancy pieces in artistic designs."

Frosted Glassware
(Craquelle and Overshot Glassware)

Frosted or iced glassware was a sixteenth-century invention of the Venetians that spread rapidly throughout the Continent after it was successfully copied by Bohemian craftsmen. It was produced by plunging the red-hot glass into cold water and then reheating and reblowing it. This process produced the effect of ice or frosting on the outer surface of the glass, the interior surface remaining smooth to the touch. Although these wares appear to be covered with fractures, they are perfectly sonorous.

Apsley Pellatt produced what he termed "Venetian Frosted Glass" at his Falcon Glass Works about 1845–1850. Pellatt claimed that the art of making this glass was known and practiced only by the Venetians until

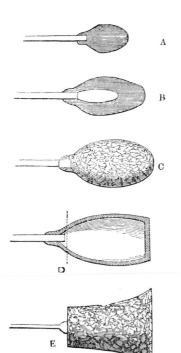

Illustrated explanation of the manufacture of "Venetian Frosted Glass" from Apsley Pellatt's *Curiosities of Glass Making*. "A, is the first gathering; B, the second, expanded by blowing; while at nearly a white heat, it is suddenly plunged into cold water; if immediately rewarmed and blown the effect will be as C; flatten the bottom, and whet off at D; attach a ponty, as E, and finish the article as usual; but in the latter process, the less heat the better, or it will melt out the frosting."

61

revived by him in the mid-nineteenth century, but several examples of this type of glassware, attributed to Spanish and other Continental factories in the seventeenth century, contradict this statement. We illustrate a drawing from Mr. Pellatt's book *Curiosities of Glass Making* explaining this technique as practiced at the Falcon Glass Works.

Another means for producing an iced effect on a glass body was to roll the inflated gather over a marver that had been previously covered with fragments of pounded glass. The fragments adhered to the plastic metal and the gather was heated again, slightly, and formed into the desired article.

At first, frosted glassware of this type was made only in transparent white or crystal glass simulating ice; but by the mid-nineteenth century fashion decreed it should be colored, and so it was. Transparent ruby, rose, yellow, blue, green and combinations of various colors were either picked up by the plastic gather from the marver or the crumbs of glass were sprinkled on the glass body. More often, though, the body glass itself was colored, the pounded fragments with which the article was covered being of transparent white or crystal glass. Many kinds of craquelle glass were exhibited at the Paris Exposition of 1878 by several European manufacturers. Some showed two colors up to a certain point, and three colors above; some showed deep cracks, while others had a smooth, uniform surface.

On October 4, 1883, Hobbs, Brockunier & Company ran a full-page color advertisement illustrating their "Craquelle" glassware in "Rose, Sapphire, Old Gold and Marine Green." Melon-ribbed finger bowls and plates, nappies and cruets, and some leaf-shaped dishes were shown along with many articles of tableware of plainer design. Large bowls with "shell" feet were also illustrated.

Iced glassware, better known to collectors as "Craquelle" and "Overshot" was produced at the Boston & Sandwich Glass Works on Cape Cod, and at the Reading Artistic Glass Works established by Lewis Kremp in Reading, Pennsylvania, in 1884. Undoubtedly other American glass factories produced craquelle glass for this ware enjoyed great popularity in the last quarter of the nineteenth century.

Several methods for manufacturing iced or crackled glassware were registered in England in the last half of the nineteenth century. These were modified versions of the early Venetian and Bohemian methods of

Ruby Craquelle wine bottle and glasses. Clichy, France. Circa 1850.

manufacture. A most novel and beautiful iced effect on glassware was patented in England on September 17, 1883 by Carl Pieper for Dunkel & Compagnie, of Herzogenrath near Aachen, Germany. The article to be decorated was first given a frosted finish with acids or sandblasting. It was thereafter covered with a type of glue commonly used by cobblers and then placed in a muffle at a low temperature. The glue, on drying, would fly off in flakes together with pieces of the glass, bringing about the desired effect of ice or the frost flowers on a windowpane.

Eugene A. Savary of West Hoboken, New Jersey, patented a process very much like Carl Pieper's on April 11, 1893. Savary's patent was followed by still another, just like it, registered by Philip J. Handel of Meriden, Connecticut, November 22, 1904. On March 6, 1883, Augustus N. Lindsley of New York City patented a means for producing "opalescent mottled and crackled glass" for light shades and globes. Hugo Thuemler of Pittsburgh, Pennsylvania, registered his patent for crackled glass and porcelain wares on May 21, 1901.

Collection: Robert Lehman
Ice Glass jug, with blue rim and plain glass handle. Italian. Seventeenth century. Height 8 inches. (Photo: The Corning Museum of Glass)

Crown Milano and Albertine

$\mathcal{P}$ainting and enameling was by no means a novel means of decorating opal glassware in the nineteenth century, but by giving it an exotic name like "Crown Milano" the Mt. Washington Glass Company was able to arouse enough interest in enameled opal glassware to warrant its production on a large and profitable scale.

The most famous piece of ancient painted opal glass is the Daphne Vase which dates from about the third century A.D. The sixteenth-century Venetians produced an opaque milk-white glass which they also decorated with colorful enamel designs. In the eighteenth century, English, Continental, and Chinese glass manufacturers were producing opaque white enameled glasswares imitating in form the "Blanc de Chine" porcelains of the period. By the mid-nineteenth century, painting white opal glass with a mat ground or finish was quite a common practice in some Bohemian, English and French factories. American enterprise, more specifically that of Albert Steffin and Frederick Shirley, brought decorated opal glass to the pinnacle of elegance in our country.

On July 6, 1886, Frederick S. Shirley and Albert Steffin were issued a joint patent for a means for decorating white opal glassware, particularly lamp shades and lamp bases. The articles, having a convex ribbed surface, were decorated by placing against this ribbed surface a perforated corrugated stencil. Dusting the perforated stencil with a small bag of pulverized carbon produced an outline design for the decorator to follow in applying the floral or other connected ornamental patterns which did

65

Crown Milano pitcher.

Crown Milano vase with handles; beige ground with russet and gold decoration. Original paper label. Height 6½ inches.

not appear distorted in the finished product. Lamps of this description were exhibited at the New Bedford Industrial Exposition of 1887.

Most Crown Milano was produced in this way. A blank of white opal glass, either free-blown, pattern-molded, or pressed, was first given a bisque finish with the aid of an acid-roughing dip. To this mat-finished surface enamels were applied, fairly thin in consistency except on those parts where a raised design was desired. The colors most often used were soft shades of beige, brown and pink, but vividly colored items like the covered rose jar and the rare creamer shown in our illustrations are also to be found. Applied glass decoration in the form of ornate handles, finials and prunts of different descriptions are not unusual in this ware.

Trade mark papers were issued to the Mt. Washington Glass Company on January 31, 1893, for Crown Milano. The mark consisted of the block letters "C"and "M" arranged as a monogram and in connection with the representation of a crown—the crown being placed above the monogram. It was carefully pointed out that the design may differ slightly. In some cases the crown could be omitted entirely, while the essential feature, the monogram "C M," would always be in evidence. The covered rose jar in our illustrations is such an exception, having the initials "C M" within a diamond-shaped figure usually associated with the Royal Flemish trade mark. The papers further state that the monogram "C M" was not limited to articles of opal glassware and it would appear that it wasn't, for the author has seen a few pieces where the body glass was a soft uranium-yellow color, perhaps undeveloped Burmese glassware.

The jug-vase we illustrate bears an original paper label identifying it as the Mt. Washington Glass Company's "Albertine." In every physical attribute it emulates Crown Milano: body glass of white opal, and enamel decoration in soft muted shades of beige, pink and green with accents of gold and white enamel. Another specimen so labeled which we have examined at close hand was painted to resemble Burmese, the white body glass showing in the base and inside the article. It is interesting to note that in 1887 A. H. Mews & Company of Cambridge, Massachusetts, produced pottery blanks in plain biscuitware for decorators which they named "Albert" or "Albertine Ware."

Soon after the Pairpoint Manufacturing Company of New Bedford, Massachusetts, took over the Mt. Washington Glass Company, in 1894, they issued an illustrated catalog of their combined wares—silverplated

Collection: John Maxfield
Opal glass covered jar decorated yellow, orange, and gold; signed "Pairpoint." Height 7½ inches.

Collection: Richard Cole
Decorated opal glass box; biscuit-colored ground with gold and silver decoration of iris flowers and leaves. Signed "Pairpoint Manufacturing Company / #4624–57." Made circa 1895. Overall length 6 inches.

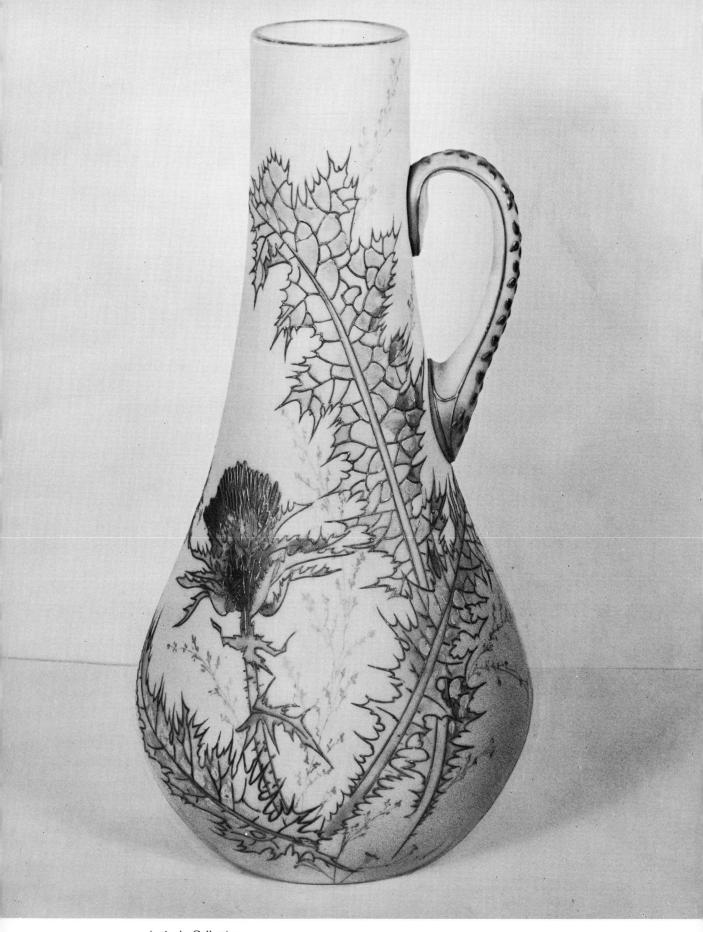

Albertine jug-vase. Height 13 inches.

objects and art glass. Crown Milano, Albertine and Royal Flemish pieces with silverplated mounts and fixtures were shown alongside other decorated opal glass articles that were almost exactly the same in appearance. These similar wares were identified in the catalog as "Decorated Porcelain," "Dresden Decorated," "Royal Worcester," and "Colonial Decorated." This would explain why so many pieces of Mt. Washington's decorated opal wares that appear to be Crown Milano or Albertine do not bear these identifying marks.

About 1896 the Pairpoint Manufacturing Company produced decorated china using blanks purchased from a pottery in Limoges, France. These wares were marked with a crown and laurel wreath and sold under the name "Crown Pairpoint Ware." The same mark can be found on shiny and mat-finished opal glasswares with decorations almost identical to those found on Crown Milano wares. The 1909 edition of *Trade Marks of the Jewelry and Kindred Trades* listed the "Crown Pairpoint Ware" mark as "discontinued"—apparently it was no longer in production in 1909.

The gilded and enameled opal glass vase shown in our illustrations represents a ware in every way similar to Crown Milano. Made by Thos. Webb & Sons, sometime between 1880–1890, it bears their incised mark in the base of the vase.

Some novel salt, pepper and condiment containers were introduced late in the nineteenth century by a few factories. They were manufactured by blowing a gather of milk-white glass in full-size molds of various forms, then acidized to a bisque finish and decorated with colored enamels to resemble Easter eggs, tomatos, etc. On May 28, 1889, Albert Steffin registered a design for an egg-shaped "salt box or condiment holder" with a perforated metal top. This was followed by another design for a condiment or salt cellar in the shape of a tomato dated December 31, 1889. Both types appeared in the Mt. Washington Glass Company's illustrated advertisements in the *Crockery & Glass Journal*. On September 12, 1893, Mr. Steffin registered another design for a condiment holder in the shape of a fig and having a cone-shaped, perforated metal top. An open dish formed to represent a full-blown flower supported on a base of leaves was also registered by Mr. Steffin on April 25, 1893.

Similar designs for condiment dispensers were registered by Alfred E. and Harry A. Smith. The Smith brothers' design patent, dated April

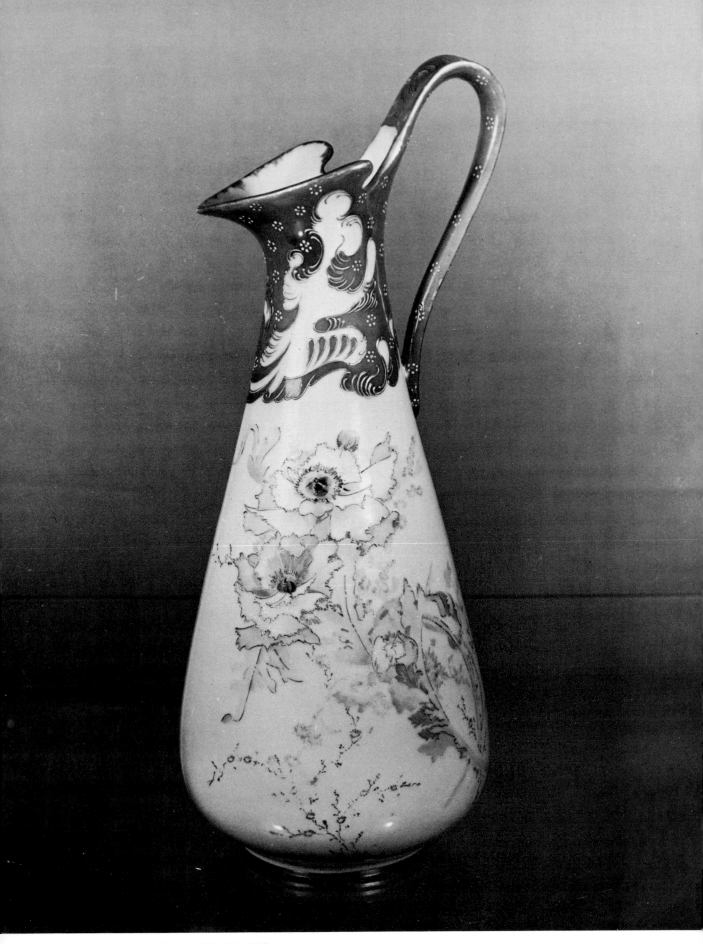

Collection: John Maxfield
Porcelain ewer-vase decorated russet, yellow, and gold; marked with green crown and
"Pairpoint Limoge"; impressed mark "2015" (same mark in red underglaze). Height
12½ inches.

11, 1893, represented an egg-shaped dispenser in a tilted position instead of standing upright, thereby circumventing Mr. Steffin's patented design of a few years earlier.

Joseph Locke, assignor to W. L. Libbey & Son of Toledo, Ohio, registered two designs for condiment dispensers on December 3, 1889. The first design is a representation of a cube or dice with dots thereon, so arranged that the dots of the two opposing sides should aggregate seven. The other design represented a thimble, the lower portion to be the receptacle for the salt or other spice while the top was made of metal, perforated to allow the contents to pour out.

Royal Flemish,
Napoli, and Verona Glass

A patent was issued to Albert Steffin on February 27, 1894, for decorating glassware which we recognize as the Mt. Washington Glass Company's "Royal Flemish." Raised lines of heavy enamel were painted on a glass surface in such a way as to form segments, which were later colored to appear like sections in a stained glass window. The different panels, or segments, were painted with contrasting colors to heighten the illusion. It would appear that Mr. Steffin was a bit tardy in registering this patent, for Royal Flemish wares were advertised by the New Bedford firm in the *Crockery & Glass Journal* as early as 1889.

Articles of glassware decorated, according to Mr. Steffin's specifications, with vitrifiable mineral colors (transparent enamels) resembled closely the Islamic glasses of the fourteenth century. The patent papers do not specify what kind of glass was employed, but manifestly it appears from those examples found that a crystal glass was used, its surface being first prepared to a mat finish with an acid-roughing dip. Most of the wares were colored in shades of brown, beige and gold, but there are as many exceptions to this rule as there are with Crown Milano wares.

On January 31, 1893, trade-mark papers were issued to the Mt. Washington Glass Company for their Royal Flemish cipher. The trade mark was to consist of the letters "R" and "F" arranged as a monogram, the "R" being reversed thereon so that the stem of the "R" formed the stem of the "F," the whole being inclosed in a diamond-shaped figure.

On May 22, 1894, Albert Steffin patented a novel means for decorating

Royal Flemish covered jar. Mt. Washington Glass Works.
Circa 1889. Height 8 inches.

Royal Flemish vase. Circa 1889. Height 14 inches.

glassware which the Mt. Washington Glass Company called "Napoli." Steffin's specifications revealed that his new decorating technique produced an illusion of depth and solidity by tracing the outline of a design on the outer surface of a transparent crystal or colored glass vessel with gold or silver, and painting the rest of the decoration on the inside with colored enamels.

This kind of decoration was difficult to do, therefore Steffin suggested that the external outlines of the design be used as a guide for the internal decoration. He also pointed out that this new method of decorating glass could save time and money, since both could be permanently affixed to the surface of the glass with one firing.

Collection: John Maxfield

Royal Flemish jug decorated red, russet, green, yellow, blue, and black, with outline and decorations in gold. Height 8½ inches.

Collection: Chrysler Art Museum of Provincetown
Signed Royal Flemish vase decorated with peacock in various shades of purple. Glass jewels set into tail feathers and cock's comb. The segments of the decoration have been done in various shades of blue and heavily encrusted with gold. Height 12¾ inches.

Collection: Chrysler Art Museum of Provincetown
Signed "Napoli" vase; crystal glass externally decorated with raised web-like decoration in gold. Internally decorated with yellow chrysanthemums, green leaves, and brown stems. Height 15½ inches.

Collection: Mrs. J. M. Miller
Signed "Napoli" covered jar decorated with Palmer Cox's Brownies.

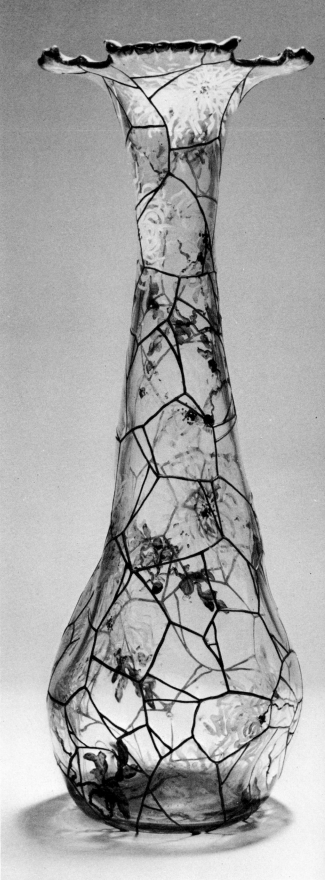

Napoli glass was usually decorated with designs similar to those found on Royal Flemish and Crown Milano wares, but there were exceptions to this rule. The covered cookie jar shown in our illustrations has been decorated with Palmer Cox's Brownies engaged in one of their amusing escapades.

In 1894, the Mt. Washington Glass Company introduced a ware very similar to Napoli and Royal Flemish which they called "Verona." For this they used transparent colored or crystal glass blanks handsomely decorated with colored enamels and gold.

Collection: George D. Rust
Cream and sugar set decorated in the Napoli glass fashion, but bearing Royal Flemish markings. Such mistakes happened occasionally at the Mt. Washington Glass Company's decorating department. Height 3 inches.

Smith Brothers

*T*he father of Messrs. Alfred E. and Harry A. Smith, who constituted the firm of Smith Brothers, was a pioneer in the glass decorating business in this country. He came here from England about the year 1851, at which time the art was in its infancy, under contract with the Boston & Sandwich Glass Company, and he encountered many discouraging obstacles. In the first place, the taste of the people had not been educated to an appreciation of the work. When Mr. Smith left England, the excavations at Nineveh and Pompeii had created a demand for productions similar to ancient pottery on which Grecian and Roman borders and figures were painted in black, and the demand for such goods had reached the proportions of a "rage." The first difficulty in reproducing these articles here was encountered in the effort to obtain suitable ware to decorate. The workmen couldn't make the glass vases. There were hardly two blanks alike and it was a good deal of trouble to match the vases into pairs. When the goods were put on the market, the dealers sent word that they were not satisfied with these wares.

Alfred Smith was in the employ of his father at this time and was the first artist in this country to put enamel colors on a cone shade. The experiment was not a success. The colors which the decorator had at his disposal were manufactured in a crude way, being simply glass ground to an impalpable powder. But the glass of which the shades were made was so easily fusible that they would not stand the ordeal of fire in the kiln.

Collection: Mrs. R. A. McMurry
"Santa Maria" vase. Design copyrighted in 1893 by A. E. Smith, New Bedford, Mass.

Nearly discouraged, Mr. Smith looked about to see in what direction his art could be utilized and rendered profitable. At that time fluid lamps were in common use, and the experiment of gilding designs on the lamps and pedestals was tried. It was found that the glass would stand fairly well a "gold fire," or the temperature required to make gold unite with the glass, and the new idea was an instantaneous and brilliant success. Everybody wanted decorated lamps and hundreds of thousands were made. Occasionally enamel colors were tried, but the glass was unsuitable. The problem was solved years later by Messrs. Smith. The blank shades were imported and Smith Brothers was the first decorating firm to order shades prepared for their purpose from abroad. Subsequently all the decorators followed their example.

In addition to gilding lamps, Mr. Smith introduced a new style of apothecary's ware, which was afterwards driven from the market by the invention of the recessed labels.

After a few years the elder Smith severed his connection with the Boston & Sandwich Company and established the Boston China Decorating Works, managed by Levi Cooley, who was formely employed by Mr. Smith at Sandwich to fire kilns.

In the Spring of 1871, Alfred E. and Harry A. Smith came to New Bedford under contract with William L. Libbey and established a decorating department at the Mt. Washington Glass Works, then operated by Libbey. The decorating department was a success from the start. After three years, Smith Brothers hired the department, bought stock, and conducted the business. The reputation of the firm of Smith Brothers became world wide, the brothers ranking first in their particular line. They graduated some of the best workmen in the country, and employed some of the best artists from abroad.

Four years later Smith Brothers moved to their own location at 28 and 30 William Street in New Bedford. At first ordinary work was required, but later the demand for better things turned their attentions to decorative articles. Beautifully decorated vases were sent to the silver plating works for mounting, a great many being decorated by Reed & Barton and the Meriden Brittiana Company. What came to be known everywhere as the "Smith Vase" was first made here, and no vase ever had so great a run of popularity. Finally the pattern was copied. Horace Partridge placed it in the dollar stores and the country was soon flooded with reproductions.

Old photograph showing a view of Smith Brothers show rooms, circa 1895.

The lamps, vases and shades painted by the Messrs. Smith were exquisitely beautiful and artistic. Some of the best effects were obtained on shades of white with a bisque finish. Oriental scenes were painted in the most delicate colors and were of dreamy beauty. When lighted, the effects were lovely. Conventional designs in enamel and gold, with Etruscan or burnished finish were very popular. The firm also decorated shades on special order and local landscapes were frequently utilized. Baccarat, of Paris, once sent the finest decorated shades to this country, but such work as that done by the Smith Brothers drove the foreign manufactures from the market.

Smith Brothers also engaged in glass cutting. A number of beautifully cut and engraved glasses were turned out at their factory. Their display at the 1889 exhibition was a revelation to this country and they received many awards for their wares.

Most of the articles bearing the Smith Brothers trade mark of a rampant lion within a shield and the words "Trade Mark" were mold-blown and show the marks perceptively. The painted designs were lovely and graceful and this was their saving grace. The Santa Maria vase shown in our illustrations was made to commemorate the Columbian Exposition of 1893. Its design was registered at the Copyright Offices in Washington, D.C. by A. E. Smith in 1893.

Cracker jars, syrup jugs, mustard pots, ribbed salt-and-pepper shakers, jardinieres, cuspidors and "Tete-a-Tete" sugar and creamer sets were also among the many articles sold by the Smith Brothers.

L. A. Littlefield, a manufacturer of trimmings for glassware and an electroplater, supplied the silver plated tops for the many articles of table-

Author's Collection
Green opal glass vase with black transfer and gilt decoration. Signed "Richardson's Vitrified Enamel Colours." W. H. B. & J. Richardson, Wordsley, England, manufacturer. Circa 1847. Height 8 inches.

ware manufactured and decorated by the Smith Brothers. His advertisements appear in the trade journals late in the year 1886.

The Mt. Washington Glass Company supplied the Smith Brothers with some of the opal glass blanks which they decorated with enamels and gold. This accounts for the striking similarity between their wares and those of the New Bedford glass works.

At least two firms in England produced glassware with vitrified enamel decorations. In 1847 Richardson's registered two designs for such wares dated July 6 and August 16. Examples of their wares are usually marked "Richardson's Vitrified Enamel Colours." Most of the articles are painted with simple but elegant designs in black, but later on more sophisticated styles appeared, painted with several different colors. Messrs. George Bacchus & Son produced similarly decorated opal glassware with transfer-printed motifs in black, sepia and other colors, and also decorated with polychrome enamels. Their wares are sometimes signed "Geo. Bacchus & Son's Vitrified Enamel Colours."

The C. F. Monroe Company

$\mathcal{T}$he C. F. Monroe Company of Meriden, Connecticut, produced painted opal glassware which bore their trade names "Wave Crest Ware," "Kelva," and "Nakara." Having bought their blanks from abroad and also from the Pairpoint Corporation of New Bedford, Massachusetts, they, too, bear a striking resemblance to the wares we have discussed in previous chapters. All of the articles were formed from an opaque white glass blown into shape in full-size molds. The decorations are reminiscent of Crown Milano glassware.

For the most part boudoir accessories such as powder boxes, jewel boxes, hair receivers, and collar and cuff containers were produced. Other decorative articles like vases, jardinieres, ash containers and cigar humidors were also manufactured, along with a host of household articles and tablewares.

On October 4, 1892, Carl V. Helmschmied, a designer and decorator working for the C. F. Monroe Company, patented a "Design for a Table-vessel" which he described as consisting of "an alternating series of concave and convex surfaces spirally disposed in the direction of the height of the vessel, and a spiral rib between such surfaces." This design can be found on many pieces of signed Wave Crest, from salt shakers to jewel boxes. A former decorator for the C. F. Monroe Company told us that the names given their decorated opal wares—Wave Crest, Nakara, and Kelva—were determined by the background color and the designs used to decorate these wares. While this may have been their intention in the beginning, it is obvious from the many pieces we have examined that there were many exceptions to this rule.

Author's Collection
"Opal-Ware" jewel box and clock. Signed "Wavecrest." Circa 1890.

Trade-mark papers were issued to C. F. Monroe Company for "Wave Crest Ware," May 31, 1898. On August 2, 1904, they registered their "Kelva" mark. "Nakara" seems not to have been registered in the patent offices in Washington, D.C. The firm went out of business during World War I and there were no successors according to the Meriden, Connecticut, Chamber of Commerce records.

Similar wares were produced by the H. M. Rio Company of Philadelphia, Pennsylvania. These are marked "Keystone Ware." The name was not registered at the trade-mark office.

Charles F. Monroe wished to expand his business and articles of association were drawn up March 19, 1892, listing the following stockholders: C. F. Monroe, William James Goulding, Edward Miller & Company (per E. Miller, Jr., Treasurer), E. W. Smith, H. Wales Lines, Rufus M. Wilson, The Charles Parker Company (per W. H. Lyon, Secretary), Mrs. George Ball, Frank M. Ball, Albert Babb, A. Pritchard, E. J. Doolittle, David Smith, D. H. Schneider, George A. Church, I. L. Holt, George H. Wilcox, M. Seips, C. Berry Peets, George R. Curtis, Carl V. Helmschmied, and M. B. Everitt.

Author's Collection

Illustration from design patent (*left*) issued to C. V. Helmschmied, October 4, 1892. Wave Crest Ware cream pitcher (*right*) with Carl V. Helmschmied's patented body form. Rose-beige ground with blue and mauve violets, green leaves and stems. Original paper label; silver-plated top. Height 3¼ inches.

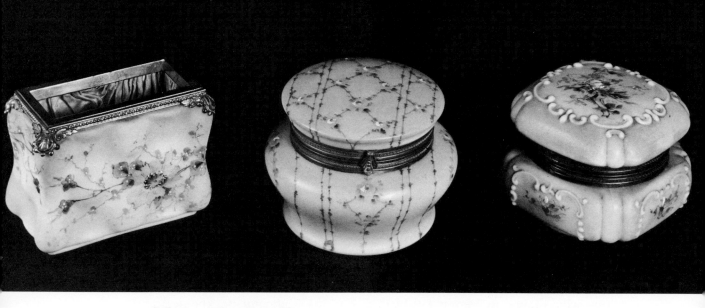

Collection: Arthur. W. Cunette
Letter holder and two jewel boxes in decorated opal glass made by the C. F. Monroe
Company, Meridan, Connecticut, circa 1895.

Mr. Monroe held 201 shares of stock, the remaining 199 shares were divided between the rest of the stockholders. On April 23, 1907, the corporation's stock was increased from $40,000 to $100,000.

Richardson & Atterbury
Patents for Enameled Glassware

Henry Gething Richardson, a member of the firm of Hodgetts, Richardson & Son, patented a method for "Improvements In Producing Ornaments, Designs, And Inscriptions On Or In Glass," on December 16, 1879. A thin vessel of flint glass was formed in the usual way, having a wide-open mouth. The design was painted or otherwise produced in enamel colors on the inside of the vessel after it had cooled. After the colored enamel design had set or hardened, the thin-walled vessel was heated to a low redness and a smaller vessel of opal or other colored glass lowered into the vessel on the end of a blowpipe. By blowing, the worker expanded the smaller opal glass vessel, causing it to fill and attach itself to the thin vessel on which the design had been executed. The two vessels, thus combined into one unit and having the enamel design imprisoned between them, were blown and tooled into the desired article.

Mr. Richardson's patent specifications provided another means for producing this effect by painting a design in colored enamels on an opal glass or other colored ground and then immersing this in a pot of fluid crystal metal to lock in the enamel design between two walls of glass.

The designs were so painted that when the parison was expanded it would not distort the pattern too much. The designs were also painted on the wall of the vessel only after it had been brought to almost full size by the gaffer. The footed tazza we illustrate is a prime example of this interesting technique.

About ten years later, on March 5, 1889, to be more precise, a similar

Turquoise blue tazza with enameled violets and fine cut mitre edge.
Manufactured by Hodgetts, Richardson & Son. Circa 1879.

patent for enameling glassware was issued to Thomas B. Atterbury of Atterbury & Company, Pittsburgh, Pennsylvania. Mr. Atterbury's specifications suggested that a gather of hot glass be rolled over a marver, the marver or plate having had a design cut into its surface and the indentations filled with pulverized glass or enamel. The plastic glass picked up the colored enamel in the design incised on the marver and was reheated at the glory hole to flux.

The patent illustrations shown by Mr. Atterbury in his specifications suggest the use of floral designs, but he also mentions the possibility of utilizing this process to form names, letters and figures on bottles or window glass; bands, stripes and all manner of decorations could be readily and cheaply applied to glassware of any kind. Atterbury's patented method was used by the Whitall, Tatum Company of Millville, New Jersey, to produce their "Sail Boat," "Faithful Dog," "Eagle" and "Remember Me" paperweights.

Venetian Techniques

MILLEFIORI

$\mathcal{T}$he Venetian influence in the manufacture of nineteenth-century glass actually goes back to ancient Egypt during the time of the Roman occupation and earlier, when the Egyptians were producing glass articles composed of what we now term Millefiori rods. Deming Jarves, in his book *Reminiscence of Glass-making* (New York, 1865) tells of ancient Egyptian glassware that contained "mosaic similar to the modern paperweight." The ancient geographer Strabo relates that an Egyptian priest presented the Emperor Hadrian with several glass cups in mosaic—sparkling with every color, and deemed of such rare value that they were used only on great festivals.

The first explanation of these works of art is to be found in the *Collection of Antiquities* by Count Caylus, who described them as "composed of delicate different-colored fibres of glass joined together with the greatest nicety, and conglutinated into a compact homogeneous mass by fusion." Winkelmann, in his *Annotations on the History of the Arts among the Ancients*, describes these same specimens as "pictures made of glass tubes," and further on describes in great detail two small pieces which were brought to Rome in 1765. The first piece was a representation of a bird, possibly a duck, with brilliant, colorful plumage. The other piece, about one inch in diameter, exhibited ornamental drawings of green, white and yellow on a deep blue ground.

94

Footed crystal glass decorated with engraved leaves and stems, and millefiori sections,
to simulate flowering vines. Baccarat; circa 1850. Height 4¼ inches.

The method of producing Millefiori, or "mosaic rods" as Mr. Jarves termed them, was brought to the Italian peninsula by Alexandrian craftsmen about 30 B.C. By this method a bundle of variously colored glass rods were so arranged that its end resembled a rosette or mosaic picture. Bound tightly together and subjected to intense heat, this bundle of multicolored rods was fused into one rod which could, while in a plastic state, be pulled to any length and still retain its original pattern in miniature.

The earliest Millefiori articles were produced by slicing the rods either obliquely or straight across and placing the little cross-section disks side by side in a terra-cotta mold. The mold, with its contents, was subjected

Author's Collection
Small Venetian scent bottle inlaid with portrait rods of Pope Pius IV (1846–78); Ferdinand I, Emperor of Austria (1835–48); Francis Joseph, Emperor of Austria (1848–1916); Giuseppe Garibaldi; and the famous Ponte Vecchio of Florence, Italy.
Length 3 inches.

Millefiori ewer. Venetian; sixteenth or seventeenth century.

to heat in a furnace where the disks fused together at the edges. This crude method of production limited the utility and size of the articles that could be made from Millefiori rods.

With the discovery of the ductility of glass, sometime during the first century A.D., Millefiori articles were manufactured differently. Into a heated mold, lined with cross-section disks, a bulb of transparent, plastic glass was inserted and expanded by further blowing. The little cross-section disks became embedded in the plastic metal and could then be handled like any other blown glass. Irregularities in the surface of the finished product were ground down to a smooth finish.

Some of the more intricate rods were produced in the following way: molten glass was poured into a pattern mold (often in the shape of animals, dancing figures, butterflies, stars, etc.) to form the core or central motif of the finished rod. The patterned core, taken up on a punty, was dipped several times into a pot of fluid glass of contrasting color until it was well coated. Rolling the rod on a marver, the glass worker made it into a well-shaped cylinder which could be pulled to a great length, and still retain its original pattern in miniature. Successive coatings of different colored metals, plus additional pattern molding, made for more elaborate designs in the finished product.

About 1845, Pietro Baggliagli, a Venetian glass manufacturer, produced at his works in Murano Millefiori articles in which he used portrait rods. These early nineteenth-century portrait rods were not much better than those produced by ancient glassmakers in Palestine about the second and first centuries B.C., but twenty years after Baggliagli, Jacopo Franchini and Vincenzo Moretti produced portrait rods of which the physical details were remarkable indeed. In producing portrait "murrini" the various features of the physiognomy and costume were made up separately, the separate parts being composed of tiny glass rods of various shades and colors no thicker than the lead from an ordinary pencil. These tiny colored rods of glass were arranged and bound together before being subjected to heat which fused the rods into a single unit. These separate units were drawn out while still in a plastic state, diminishing in size but retaining their original design.

The facial features, eyes, nose, mouth, beard or mustache, were placed in position in a mold and the rest of the countenance filled in with tiny flesh-colored rods of glass. As many as four different skin tones were used

Millefiori paperweight. Made by Charles Kaziun about 1950.

giving the finished portrait a realism never attained before or since in a glass rod. The costumes were also previously made up in parts and arranged and added in the same way.

An early prototype of the mid-nineteenth-century paperweight was made by the Venetians in the late fifteenth century. A solid ancient Venetian ball, consisting of fragments of Millefiori and filigree cane, was illustrated in Apsley Pellatt's *Curiosities of Glass Making*. The paperweights made by the French with such a high degree of craftsmanship were produced by arranging small sections or "set-ups" of Millefiori rods in an upright position on a bed of plastic glass. A punty was attached to what was to be the underside of the weight and the whole was dipped into a pot of fluid crystal glass where it acquired a heavy coating of metal. Shaping and polishing followed and the article emerged to dazzle the layman with its intricacies.

About 1910 Fred Carder produced what he termed "Tessera." Actually, it was Millefiori glassware produced according to the earliest technique by lining a mold with small cross-section disks and allowing them to fuse at the edges in a muffle.

The very recent productions of paperweights by Charles Kaziun in America and Paul Ysart in Scotland rival even the finest Millefiori weights produced in the mid-nineteenth century.

FILIGREE GLASS, LATTICINIO AND VETRO DI TRINA

The production of what is correctly termed "Filigree Glass" began about the first or second century B.C. The ancients produced simple filigree rods by twisting two or more opaque colored rods of glass rope-fashion while they were in a plastic state and subjected them to extreme heat to fuse the rods together. These early rods were limited in use to decorating the rims of bowls and vases.

In the sixteenth century the factories at Murano and Altare developed this art and produced filigree rods in many different ways. Georges Bontemps, director of the crystal manufactory of Choisy-le-Roy in 1823, was the first to publish an important work on the processes employed by the glassmakers of Murano in the fabrication of Filigree Glass. We believe Mr. Bontemps' own words will best explain the various manufacturing techniques.

"To obtain canes with spiral threads, which, on being flattened, produce a network of equal meshes, the interior of a cylindrical mold either metal or of crucible earth is surrounded with canes of colored glass alternating with rods of transparent glass. Then the workman takes at the end of his pipe some transparent glass, with which he forms a massive cylinder able to pass into the mold surrounded by the little rods, and which is heated to a little below red heat. After heating the cylinder also, he puts it into the mold, pushing it down in such a manner as to press against the rods; he then lifts up his tube while retaining the mold in its place, and thus lifts the rods with the cylinder. He heats them again, and marvers in order to render the adhesion more complete. Finally, heating the extremity of the cylinder, he first cuts off that extremity with the shears, heats it again, seizes it with pincers and draws it out with his right hand, while with his left he turns his pipe rapidly over the arm of his chair. Whilst the rod is thus becoming longer, the threads of colored glass wind spirally around it. When the workman has completed a rod of the wished-for dimensions, about a quarter of an inch in diameter, and the lines are sufficiently closely wound, he cuts it off with his pincers, heats anew the extremity of the trunk, and seizing and drawing it out whilst he rolls his pipe rapidly round, he thus proceeds to the production of a new rod, and so on, until the whole column is finished."

The canes shown were executed by the following processes as related in Bontemps' treatise.

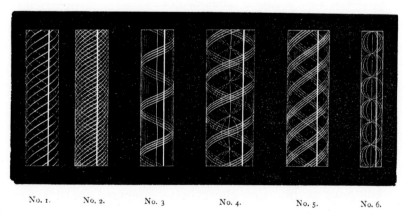

No. 1.   No. 2.   No. 3   No. 4.   No. 5.   No. 6.

Specimens of filigree canes (see text). Illustration from *Marvels of Glass-Making in All Ages* by Alexander Sauzay (London, 1870).

"To manufacture canes which, on being flattened, produce network in squares, three or four rods of colored glass of a simple thread, alternated with rods of transparent glass, are placed in a cylindrical mold having both extremities of the same diameter; afterwards the interstices in the interior of the mold are filled up with transparent rods, in order to retain the colored ones in their position, and then the operation goes on as before."

The canes represented in figures 1 and 2 on page 101 were obtained by this process.

"To obtain canes producing, when flattened, chaplet beads, a globe of glass is blown, the extremity of which opposite the tube is opened so as to produce a little open cylinder. It is flattened so as only to admit canes, and into this sheath there are introduced five or six canes of single colored threads, alternated with transparent ones; the end opposite the tube is heated and closed. The workman presses on the flattened cylinder whilst an assistant draws up the air through the tube so as to take it from the interior and produce a flat solid mass in which the colored canes are inserted. The workman places successively a small mass of hot transparent glass on each side of the flattened cylinder, and marvers it in order to make the mass again cylindrical. He thus obtains a small column, in the interior of which are arranged the colored threads on the same diameter. He afterwards proceeds as for the preceding canes, by heating and drawing out the extremity whilst he rolls the tube rapidly over the arms of his chair.

"By this twisting, the line of colored threads is presented alternately in front and sideways, and produces chaplet grains.

"It may be understood that the canes of colored glass placed in the center of the column, being, from the twisting, crossed one over the other, seem to present chaplet grains formed of threads having an uncolored space between them, which arises from the canes of uncolored glass alternating with the colored ones."

The cane represented in figure 6 on page 101 was obtained by this method.

"It often happens that the chaplet grains are combined with the squares in the preceding canes, by using the cylinder prepared for the chaplet grains to insert in the mold prepared for the canes in squares."

Cane No. 4 on page 101 was made by this process.

By courtesy of the Stourbridge Corporation
"Venetian Filigree" compotier made by
John Northwood for Stevens & Williams.
Circa 1887. Height 8 inches.

Tumble-up. Red filigree canes on a milk-white ground. Height 8 inches.

Reticulated Class

"Sometimes a zigzag line is placed in the center of a cane. For that a solid cylinder is first prepared of transparent glass, of half the diameter of that to be drawn out, and a small colored cane is fastened to the side of this cylinder; the whole is covered with a fresh layer of transparent glass, in order to produce a cylinder of the necessary dimension to go into the mold of the canes with threads. The small colored column, not being in the center of the cylinder, will twist spirally round that center from the movement of drawing and twisting, and will produce a zigzag on being flattened."

Figure 3 on page 101 represents this technique.

To produce articles of Filigree Glass, the worker first lined a heated mold with sections of filigree rods. Often several different kinds of glass rods were used alternately around the sides of the mold. A bulb of hot, plastic glass was blown into the mold and emerged with the filigree rods adhering to its surface. The mass was rolled on the marver to weld the rods to the crystal body and it was then blown and hand-tooled into the desired article.

"Vetro di Trina" and "Latticinio" are names given to specific types of Filigree Glassware. Articles of Vetro di Trina glass exhibit either milk-white loopings similar to "Nailsea" or "Verre Moire" on a crystal ground, or vertical or crisscrossed, milk-white stripes on a crystal ground.

"Latticinio," sometimes called "Vetro di Trina with air traps," is the name given to articles of glass in which a network of milk-white lines appear on a crystal ground, with an air-bleb imprisoned in each of the diamonds formed by the crisscrossing of these white threads between two walls of glass. Apsley Pellatt explained the means of production in *Curiosities of Glass Making*. Two cuplike formations, one with milk-white canes spirally applied inside the cup, the other with milk-white canes spirally applied outside, were combined, the former over the latter, to produce the reticulated effect described above. Dr. Pazaurek refers to this ware as "Netzglaser" in his interesting monograph on nineteenth-century Bohemian and German glassware.

A Venetian glass technologist with whom we discussed the Vetro di Trina glassware insists that the air-blebs were the result of pattern molding, the process now in use by Muranese glass manufacturers.

Collection: The Corning Museum of Glass
Vetro di Trina with air traps goblet.
Possibly English or Continental. Late
eighteenth or early nineteenth century.

STRIPED GLASS

A type of glassware known to present-day collectors as "striped glass" was produced in Assyria about 100 B.C. and revived in the sixteenth century by the Venetians. Here, a bulb of plastic glass was blown into a heated mold lined with colored or white rods alternating with crystal rods. When withdrawn the colored and crystal rods adhered to its outer surface. Just as a drop of water added to a cupful will not be discernible from the whole, so the crystal rods when placed on the body of the crystal glass lose their individuality and only the colored rods are seen by the eye. By deftly twisting the inflated parison while it was still in a plastic state, the worker obtained the effect of colored and opaque threads spiralling around the body of the finished article.

An interesting variation was produced by "combing" perpendicular or horizontally applied glass threads into a wavy pattern.

On July 15, 1885, William Webb Boulton patented an invention for "Improvements In Decorating Glass With Stripes." Boulton first prepared a rod of glass with two or more stripes and then cut this rod into smaller rods, each section then being worked on the blowpipe with an additional gather of glass, and formed into articles of glassware with stripes thereon. Glass in the Venetian style being popular at this time, Boulton & Mills' wares must have sold very well.

The Venetian techniques of glass manufacture were imitated by the Bohemian, French and English glass factories in the mid-nineteenth century. The Bohemian factories of Neuwelt and Josephinenhutte produced some very fine Millefiori and Filigree wares. Gustave Pazaurek illustrated several superb examples in *Gläser der Empire und Beidermeirzeit*.

The glasshouses of St. Louis, Clichy and Baccarat in France manufactured some of the finest examples of Millefiori in a multitude of intricate paperweights and decorative articles. The production of Filigree and Striped Glass articles also reached a high degree of craftsmanship in the capable hands of the French glassworkers.

In England, the Venetian techniques did not become widely used until the last quarter of the nineteenth century. Prior to this, a few paperweights and some decorative articles made of Millefiori and Filigree rods had comprised the smallest segment of their output. Some excellent specimens of these wares were in evidence at the 1951 Exhibition of Glass at Stourbridge, England. The pieces shown were credited to the mid-nineteenth

Striped glass ewer. Height 12 inches.

century, about 1840–1845. (Several drinking glasses, the stems of which were formed from Filigree rods, were attributed to the eighteenth century.) In 1887, Stevens & Williams of Brierley Hills successfully produced and marketed glass articles which they termed "Venetian Filigree." Mr. Williams-Thomas, director of this firm, told us that the output was not great as the cost of production was of necessity very high.

The production of glass articles utilizing Millefiori and Filigree rods did not come to America until shortly after 1850. In 1860, Christian Dorflinger of White Mills, Pennsylvania, invited a large group of glassworkers from the St. Louis district of France to come to work for him in America. Among them was Nicholas Lutz.

It is, to all intents and purposes, impossible to distinguish articles of glass made by Nicholas Lutz from those produced by other capable glassmen. Though it has been claimed that certain types of applied crystal prunts on Filigree, Striped and Threaded Glassware positively identify the maker as Lutz, the fact is that similar decorative prunts were in use hundreds of years before the Christian Era. Applied prunts were one of the earliest means of glass embellishment.

In the nineteenth century, labor was an expensive factor in the economy of the American glass factories; consequently the cost of producing Millefiori and Filigree rods was high. Some enterprising German importers, located on West Broadway in New York City, imported Millefiori and Filigree rods from Italy at a price which allowed for their resale to glass factories in the United States at much less than production costs here. Advertisements appeared in the trade catalogues at that time advising manufacturers of the availability of Millefiori and Filigree rods, as well as rods of colored glass and clods of Aventurine, at a "right" price. A controversy will always arise whenever a correct attribution of the wares manufactured from these imported rods is attempted.

Aventurine Glass

*A*ccording to Professor E. Peligot of France, "Aventurine is a yellowish glass in which there are an infinite number of small crystals of copper, protoxide of copper, or silicate of that oxide. When it is polished, this glass presents, especially in the light, a glittering appearance for which reason it is used in jewelry.

"Many attempts have been made to discover the secret of its manufacture. The skillful chemist, Hautefeuille, has succeeded by persevering efforts in making this glass in considerable quantities: he has just published in the last report of the Societe d'Encouragement [October, 1860] a memoir in which he freely indicates the processes he has followed.

"When the glass is very liquid, iron or fine brass turnings enclosed in paper are added; these are incorporated into it by stirring the glass with a red-hot iron rod. The glass becomes blood red, opaque, and at the same time milky and full of bubbles; the draught of the furnace is then stopped, the ash-pan closed, the pot with its lid on is covered with ashes, and it is allowed to cool very slowly. The next day on breaking the pot the Aventurine is seen formed."

In 1865 the chemist Pelouze invented an Aventurine as fine as the finest produced in Venice. The formula he gave was as follows: 250 parts sand, 100 of carbonate of soda, 50 of carbonate of lime, and 40 of bichromate of potash.

The Venetians, who are credited with the discovery of Aventurine, combined rods of Aventurine with their intricately devised filigree glassware and also sprinkled fine kernels on the body of glass objects. Imitators have never been able to produce Aventurine with that true golden color

110

Chrome (green) Aventurine jug. Late nineteenth century.

typical of the Venetian product. The Dalla Venezia family of Venice has been a source of supply to glasshouses all over the world for more than two hundred years.

"The Glass of the Golden Star," as the Chinese poetically call Aventurine, was sold to foreign factories in large clumps or rods by Muranese manufacturers, and these were broken into pieces of suitable size and applied where needed. Particles of green (chrome), pink (chrome in the presence of tin), and bronze Aventurine can be found in nineteenth-century wares of English, Continental and American manufacture. An item in a current newspaper advises us that blue Aventurine is now available in costume jewelry.

The May, 1877, issue of the *Crockery & Glass Journal* contained a short note to the effect that H. Henkins had patented "gold glassware (granulated gold vases) after the Venetian technique." Unfortunately the writer did not elaborate on this statement, and we do not know where Mr. Henkins was working at this time. Many Continental glass manufacturers exhibited Aventurine glass articles at the Paris Exhibition of 1878; it seems that at this late date Aventurine glass had come into more or less universal use, and glass factories all over the world were no longer dependent on Venetian sources for their supply.

In 1899 a patent was issued jointly to Edward and Sidney Walsh of Janvier, New Jersey, covering a method for making large articles from pieces of Aventurine. The clods of "Goldstone" were crushed into small bits and spread out in a mold. The mold was placed in a kiln until the pieces melted and fused together. To prevent the copper crystals suspended in the glass from oxidizing, outside air was excluded from the kiln. Irregularities in the surface of the finished article were smoothed down on a wheel.

In recent years the Fostoria Glass Company of Moundsville, West Virginia, produced green Aventurine glassware. The chrome (green) Aventurine glass was made by supersaturating a high lead glass with chrome oxide. During the melting of the glass batch all the chrome oxide is dissolved in the glass, but as the glass is cooled down to the temperature at which it will be worked or pressed, it is not able to hold in solution all the chrome oxide at the lower temperature. This results in chrome oxide crystals being formed in the glass and these crystals are large enough to reflect light giving the typical appearance of the Aventurine glass.

Articles of glass that appear to have been lightly dusted with gold were manufactured in this way. Powdered gold was either sprinkled on the parison prior to its being fully blown and shaped, or the parison was rolled on a marver that had been covered with powdered gold. When the parison was expanded the gold dust was diffused over the surface of

Collection: Smithsonian Institution
Black and gold vase with crystal and gold shell handles and applied foot.
Union Glass Co., 1905.

the article, producing the desired effect described above. This technique
was widely used in the mid-nineteenth century by the Venetians. Julian
de Cordova, president of the Union Glass Company of Somerville, Massachusetts, presented the Smithsonian Institution with a large selection
of glassware in the Venetian style, several of the pieces having been decorated with gold dusting. The presentation was made by Mr. de Cordova
in February, 1905.

Peloton Glass

Wilhelm Kralik of Neuwelt, Bohemia, patented a novel type of glassware which he named "Peloton Glass." At the time the patent was registered, on October 25, 1880, Kralik was in the employ of Count Harrach, owner of one of the largest glass factories in Bohemia.

To produce articles of this novel type of art glass, the hot glass was withdrawn from the furnace and was dipped or immersed, either before or after it was worked into shape, in a reservoir containing suitably prepared filaments or threads of glass until the desired quantity of these filaments had adhered to the hot glass. Kralik stated further that these filaments could also be projected or thrown onto the hot parison, or the parison could be rolled over the marver which had been previously covered with the filaments in various colors. The article was reheated several times at the glory hole and then either pressed or hand-tooled into the desired form.

The filaments were prepared by a process known as drawing or spinning glass; they were then submitted to a breaking apparatus, and were thus prepared in pieces of the desired dimensions.

The vermiculated decoration produced by the application of these filaments could be of one tint or of various shades or tints by using filaments of different colors. They were applied to either a transparent colored or clear background, or, as was most common, against an opaque white or colored ground. In most cases the filaments themselves were opaque white or colored glass. Sometimes the finished article was given a satin finish in an acid bath.

According to Mr. Kralik's enumerations, glass beads or fragments of glass could have been combined with the filaments so as to obtain a decoration in different forms and colors. Some pieces were further embellished with colorful enamel designs.

About 1885 J. B. Graesser of Zwickau, Germany, issued a catalog of his fancy glass productions in which several pieces of Peloton glass were illustrated in color. Apparently Count Harrach's glassworks were not the sole source for these wares. On February 6, 1880, John George

Collection: Mr. & Mrs. A. R. Morris
Peloton Glass covered cracker jar.

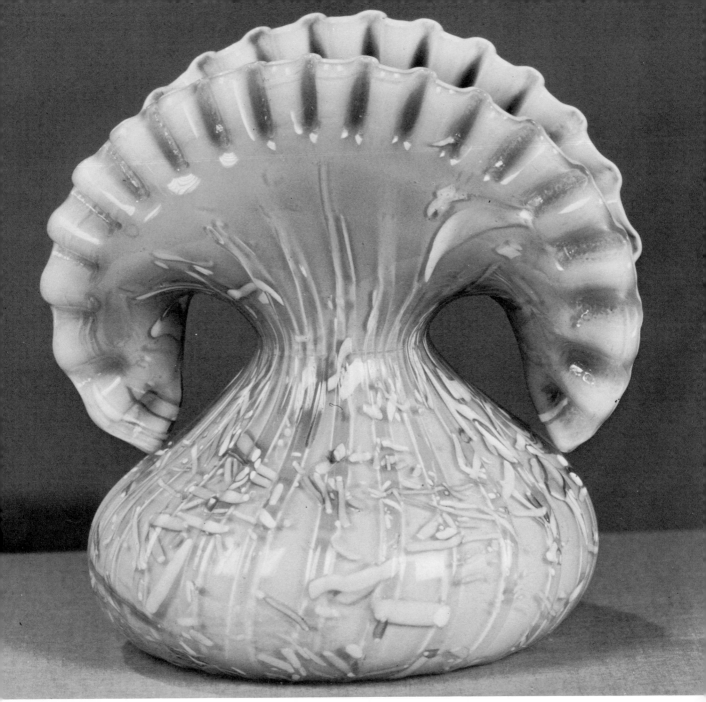

Peloton Glass vase, shaded white to rose; decoration consists of applied filaments of blue, rose, yellow, and white glass. Height 4¾ inches.

Sowerby of Gateshead-on-Tyne, England, registered a patent for producing sheets of glass with threads of colored glass scattered over its surface. The decorating technique is somewhat like Kralik's Peloton glass, but Sowerby suggested that his glass was to be used in the production of stained-glass windows.

Threaded Glassware

The art of decorating glassware with applied glass threads, so widely practiced in the nineteenth century both in America and abroad, derived from an ancient Egyptian technique.

Early glassworkers of the Nile Valley decorated their glass objects by winding them about with varicolored threads of glass which they "combed" into featherlike patterns with a tool similar in appearance to a buttonhook. The designs made by the threads of glass were warmed into the surface of the article and smoothed out by rolling the object on a marver.

After the advent of blown glass in the first century A.D., when glass articles came into wider use, threads of glass were wound about objects for a practical purpose—to enable greasy hands to gain a better grip. Decorative aspects were not overlooked, however, for often these applied threads were of a contrasting color to the body glass.

Until the mid-nineteenth century, glass threads were applied by hand. The worker simply took up on a punty a gather of glass of any desired color. A slight touch of the gather to the body of the article was enough to start the process. The plastic metal adhered to the body of the article at the point of contact and the worker then began to rotate the article away from the punty, thus drawing the gather into a thread of glass which he applied to the neck or body of the article.

Then in 1876 William J. Hodgetts of the firm of Hodgetts, Richardson & Sons of Wordsley, England, patented a mechanical apparatus for applying glass threads to glass articles. It was first registered in England on May 6, 1876, and on November 26, 1878, letters patent were issued to Mr. Hodgetts in America.

118

This glass threading machine consisted of a mechanism for sustaining and revolving a glass bulb or cylinder in proximity to a gather of heated glass from which threads were to be drawn, at the same time causing the bulb and the thread-yielding gather to move past each other in the direction of the length of the bulb or cylinder. Through an ingenious use of two kinds of half-screw boxes, the motion of the bulb could be directed either forward or backward past the thread-yielding gather, thus applying a second coil of thread about the bulb or cylinder. In this way the threads could either be made to wind in parallel with the first coil of threads or to overlap each other.

Mr. Hodgetts suggested that windowpanes and door panels could be made from glass cylinders so decorated with varicolored glass threads. Cylinders, after threading, could be split and flattened into sheets.

Another means for producing decorative effects with threaded glass was to pattern-mold the body glass in Venetian Diamond or another design prior to threading it. Often the body glass and the threads were of contrasting colors. The shimmering effects produced were striking. Applied raspberry prunts and rigaree decoration were often added to such pieces, especially those produced in England and on the Continent. The sophistication of the European designs is a telling factor in determining their origin.

Mr. Hodgetts' machine was patented in several countries, but with little alteration in the design this apparatus could be duplicated and still not infringe upon his patent rights. Such a machine was patented on

Collection: Mr. & Mrs. Ned Stinnett
Large Threaded Glass footed bowl.

December 8, 1877, by William Henry Stevens of Wordsley, near Stourbridge. The main function of Hodgetts' threading machine was duplicated in Mr. Stevens' patented design, although the apparatus itself was
a little different. Later, on September 10, 1880, William Henry Stuart
of Stafford, England, patented still another means for applying decorative glass threads to glass articles. Mr. Stuart's idea included rolling the
plastic parison in pulverized glass or enamel prior to threading the bulb.
Reheating would cause the finely pulverized glass or enamel to melt and
run, while the glass threads remained intact and in place on the bulb.

In the *Pottery Gazette* for February, 1877, one writer mentions the
"Allasantes" or "Sidonian" glass patented by a member of the Webb
firm. In such wares, colored threads of glass were attached to glass articles and expansion caused by heat developed these threads into very curious but pleasing designs. The writer was no doubt referring to a patented
method for ornamenting glassware taken out by Thos. Wilkes Webb on
June 9, 1876. One portion of Mr. Webb's patent dealt with the application of glass threads in a haphazard fashion to produce a motif consisting
of random designs of colored trailings of glass, giving the impression of
an ancient type of glassware. A somewhat similar write-up was found in
an American trade paper of the same year. The rest of the patent we shall
discuss in the chapter on applied glasshouse decorations.

On February 20, 1885, John Northwood, the engraver of the first
Cameo Glass reproduction of the Portland vase, patented a machine for
producing Threaded Glassware which did away with even more of the
handwork still entailed and tended to make the threading more uniform.
The plastic parison, wound about with threads of glass of various colors,
was introduced into a machine lined with projecting blades of different
lengths. By a pulling and pushing operation the threads were combed into
featherlike patterns reminiscent of some ancient Egyptian glassware.

Marvering and the warming in process caused the threads to sink into
the body metal giving the article a smooth surface; even so, a careful
study of wares made under Northwood's patent will reveal a slightly
raised touch on the threaded portions. All such pieces examined by the
author have been marked "Patent" in the base with glossy letters; the
rest of the article being acidized to a satin finish. The shell-shaped dish
shown in our illustrations is an example of Mr. Northwood's patented
method for producing this decorative effect.

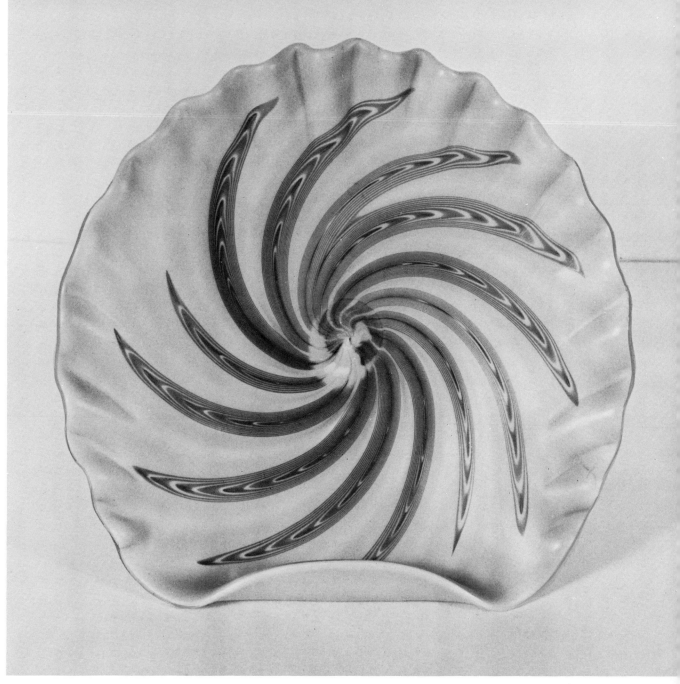

Threaded Glass shell-shaped dish by John Northwood's patented process.

Several pieces of this ware were exhibited in the Brierley Hills Council House from the collection of the inventor's son, John Northwood II. This ware has been considered an American product and attributed to the Mt. Washington Glass Works. It is important, in the light of the foregoing, that such erroneous attributions be corrected.

Stevens & Williams of Brierley Hills carried Threaded Glassware another step forward by painting the threaded body with enamels. Oscar Pierre Erard was the artist most prominently associated with this "Tapestry" ware which was made at Stevens & Williams about 1892. Soon afterwards it was copied by the Bohemian factories.

In 1902 the Albert Glass Works of Stourbridge, England, manufactured threaded glassware and fancy epergnes with threaded decorations.

Collection: Stevens & Williams Ltd.
"Tapestry" vase decorated by Erard. Circa 1892.

These were advertised in the *Pottery Gazette Diary* by L. & L. Hingley & Son (formerly Mills, Walker & Company, Ltd.), wholesalers of fancy glassware to the trade.

Occasionally Filigree Glassware and Pearl Satin Ware were further embellished by adding threads of glass to the body of the article. The pitcher and ewer-vase shown in our illustrations are wonderful (and difficult to acquire) examples of this technique.

European and American factories were quick to adopt machine threading for their wares. Its obvious advantages of uniformity and facility could not be overlooked. In an interview with Leslie Nash, son of Arthur Nash, the motivating genius in the Tiffany Glass factory, I learned that his father brought with him from England a machine for applying glass threads to glass articles. The use of such machinery had become so wide

Author's Collection

"Verre Moire" fairy lamp—threads of white glass in a "pulled" pattern on a colored ground. Manufactured simultaneously by English, Continental and American glass factories. Circa 1880.

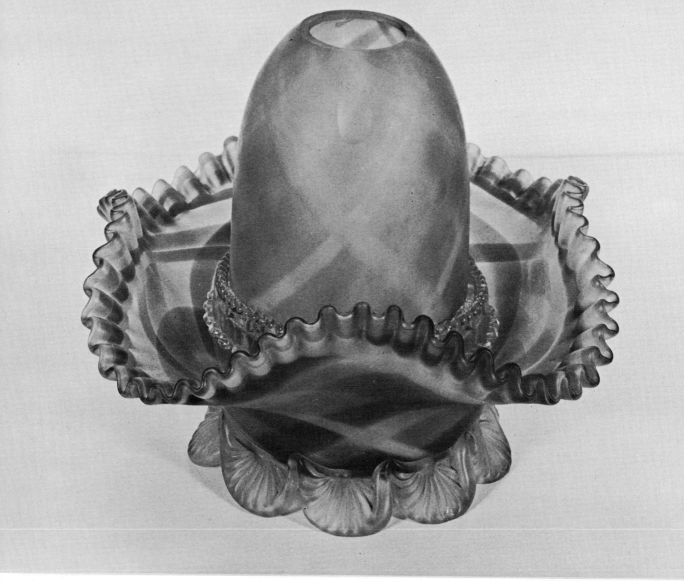

Collection: Mrs. Claranell Lewis
"Tartan" fairy lamp. A design consisting of a combination of threads of glass of different shades of color arranged to form a plaid closely resembling a Scotch Tartan. Registered by Henry Gething Richardson of the Wordsley Flint Glass Works, near Stourbridge, February 24, 1886.

a practice that almost every glass factory of any real size had one in its shop. Each factory would add some modification to suit its special needs.

At the Sandwich Historical Society's museum on Cape Cod there are exhibited several pieces of Threaded Glass. Tall-handled lemonade glasses, cologne bottles, punch cups, and pitchers predominate, but there are a few other articles, all rather loosely attributed to this venerable factory and thought by many to be the singular work of Nicholas Lutz. It is true that fragments of machine Threaded Glass were unearthed at the old factory site and this does establish the production of such wares at Sandwich, but there is not enough evidence to warrant the positive attribution of all the pieces shown.

It is well to remember that fine examples of Threaded Glassware were made in considerable quantity by almost every important glass factory in England as well as in the United States, and that definite attribution is often extremely difficult if not impossible.

In January, 1886, The Phoenix Glass Company of Water Cure (Beaver), Pennsylvania, offered "Verre Moire" wares under the name "Venetian Threaded." Their illustrated advertisements showed tankard pitchers and matching tumblers, vases, and other decorative wares. They also announced that they were distributors of Clarke's Fairy Lamps in America.

Stevens & Williams of Brierley Hill, England, registered their patent for "Jewell" glassware on September 6, 1886. The method of its manufacture involved the following procedures: First, a bulb of glass, crystal or colored, was threaded all around on a machine very similar to the one patented by William J. Hodgetts in 1876. Next, the threaded parison was blown into a cup of glass and subsequently blown into a ribbed mold. This last step forced the air-traps formed between the threads of glass and the outer casing of the article into vertical rows of air-blebs.

Author's Collection
Tangerine-colored "Jewell" glass finger bowl and plate made by Stevens & Williams, Brierley Hill, England. Diameter of plate 5 inches.

Different versions of Jewell glass were produced by using John Northwood's pull-up machine to comb the applied glass threads into a variety of patterns. Stevens & Williams engraved the registry number, 55693, on all of their Jewell glass productions.

Count Schaffgotsch produced the same kind of glassware at his factory in Josephinenhutte, Germany, soon after Stevens & Williams Jewell glass was introduced.

On July 20, 1905, Harry Wilkinson, "a glass house manager living in Dennis Park, near Stourbridge," received a patent for an "Improved Method of Ornamenting Glass Articles." Wilkinson produced bead-like decorations on glassware by winding glass threads about a ribbed parison and reheating the bulb at the furnace to melt the threads at points where they did not adhere to the glass body. The patent papers do not say who Mr. Wilkinson was working for at the time of his patent, but in 1921 he established the Stourbridge Glass Company, Ltd., with W. A. Price as one of his partners.

Author's Collection
Blue finger bowl and plate with air-trap pattern. Made at the Josephine Glass Works, Josephinenhutte, Germany. Diameter of plate 5 inches.

Spun Glass

By a lengthy process of retrogression we could trace the development of today's fiber glass back to the ancient Egyptian method of decorating glass objects with applied threads of varicolored glass, but for all practical purposes glass fibers as we know them today were not within the realm of reality until the late eighteenth century or early part of the nineteenth century.

We find in the *Memoires de L'Académie des Sciences* for the year 1713 this report by the well known physician and naturalist Rene-Antoine de Reaumur (1683–1757): "If they succeed in making glass threads as fine as those of spiders' webs, they will have glass threads of which woven stuffs may be made." Later reports proved Reaumur to be correct.

In a treatise on glass written by the Rev. Dionysus Lardner and dated 1832, the following explanation of the manufacture of glass fibers is found: "It has already been mentioned that glass may be spun into very long and minute threads, with great velocity, when the mass from which it is drawn has been previously heated. For this operation the use of a blowpipe is required, and the manner of its performance is very simple.

"The lump of glass being sufficiently softened by the flame, another piece of glass is applied to it, when the two, cohering together, and being then drawn apart, are seen to be connected by minute filaments. A fine thread being thus obtained, its end is applied to a wheel or reel, and the heat of the glass being maintained, while the wheel is turned with considerable velocity, a thread may be drawn continuously out as long as the workman pleases, or until the store of glass is completely expended.

127

"The thread thus made is extremely flexible and delicately fine. Its firmness depends in a great measure upon the heat whereat the glass is maintained, and upon the velocity where-with the wheel is turned; the greater these are, the firmer will be the thread.

"Many hundred feet of these filaments may be drawn out from a heated mass in the space of one minute. Its pliancy and elasticity are proved by the facility with which, when in the state just mentioned, it may be bent and retained in various forms, and by the energy where-with its original shape is resumed at the moment of release from its constrained position."

In those early years glass was treated in this manner in order to afford a pleasing exemplification of some of its properties, or for purposes of ornament. When it was desired to produce colored threads, the glass employed was imbued with a very deep tint, for, when drawn out in such minute filaments, it would otherwise appear nearly colorless.

From *L'Echo du Monde Savant, &c.* No. 58, dated February 15, 1837, and translated from the French, we have this interesting report: "We do not find in these researches, that the ancients were acquainted with the art of spinning and weaving glass, or of giving it any required shade of color. This invention, therefore, must be considered as belonging to the nineteenth century, and the honor of the discovery is due to M. Dubus Bonnel, an ingenious Frenchman, a native of Lille, and for which he obtained patents in Great Britain and various countries of the European Continent in 1837.

"When we figure to ourselves an apartment decorated with cloth of glass, and resplendent with lights, we must be convinced that it will equal in brilliancy all that the imagination can conceive; and realize, in a word, the wonders of the enchanted palaces mentioned in the Arabian tales. The light splashing from the polished surface of the glass, to which any color or shade may be given, will make the room have the appearance of an apartment composed of pearls, mother-of-pearl, diamonds, garnets, sapphires, topazes, rubies, emeralds, or amethysts, etc. Or, in short, of all those precious stones united and combined in a thousand ways, and formed into stars, rosettes, bouquets, garlands, festoons, and graceful undulations varied almost *ad infinitum*."

Not mentioned in this account, but nevertheless manufactured by Mr. Bonnel, were some magnificent robes for the clergy, sparkling with jewel-like colors and mingled with gold threads.

From *The History of Silk, Cotton, Linen, Wool, and other Fibrous Substances, Including Observations of Spinning, Dying and Weaving,* published in 1845, we have the following pertinent data: "The warp is composed of silk, forming the body and groundwork on which the pattern in glass appears, as effected by the weft. The requisite flexibility of glass thread for manufacturing purposes is to be ascribed to its extreme fineness; as not less than from fifty to sixty of the original threads (spun by steam engine power) are required to form one thread weft. The process is slow; for no more than a yard of cloth can be produced in twelve hours. The work, however, is extremely beautiful and comparatively cheap, in as much as no similar stuff, where bullion is really introduced, can be purchased for anything like the price for which this is sold; added to this, it is, as far as the glass is concerned, imperishable. Glass is more durable than either gold or silver, and besides, possesses the advantage of never tarnishing."

Experiments with glass fibers were carried out with hollow tubes of glass early in the nineteenth century. Deacher found in his experiments that no matter how fine the hollow tube of glass was drawn it still retained the hole throughout its length.

At the Universal Exposition of 1855 there was exhibited the animal group shown in our illustrations. It is a life-size representation of a lion, with splendid hair and bristling mane, stifling a serpent. The skin and hair of both serpent and lion are made of glass fibers. This group was the result of thirty years labor by its maker, Monsieur Lambourg. It was

Collection: Conservatoire National des Arts et Metiers, Paris
Lion and Serpent by Lambourg. Circa 1855.

placed on permanent exhibition in the glass room at the Conservatoire des Arts et Metiers at Paris, France, in 1862. The *Dictionaire des Arts et Manufacturers* speaks thus of this group and its maker. "A very clever enameler (lamp worker) of Saumur has made an extremely interesting application of threads of spun glass, using it to imitate the hair of animals. He assimilates the colors to those of natural skins, and after having cut the threads of a suitable length, he attaches them by one end on a solid surface, copying the arrangement of the skin he wishes to imitate. I have seen at his house tigers, striped hyenas, and other animals of natural size, admirably modeled and covered with the glass hair of which we speak.

"The imitation is so perfect, that these animals might advantageously replace the stuffed skins, always injured, which encumber our museums."

In the mid-nineteenth century one writer reports that the glittering dresses that were formerly worn were made of silk and glass threads woven together. The aigrettes also, which adorned ladies' bonnets, and were so fine and flexible that the slightest breeze agitated them, were of spun glass. The flowing black curls which, when worn by a prince, became the admiration of all Paris, were likewise made of spun glass, curled with irons.

In the Viennese newspaper *Hevrnhut* dated January 23, 1879, we find this account of "Glass Clothing" by Herman Frueauff: "At Gudenfrei, the artist and glass-spinner, A. Prengel of Vienna, has established his glass business, offering carpets, cuffs, collars, veils, etc., of glass. He not only spins, but also weaves glass before the eyes of the people. The otherwise brittle glass he changes into pliable threads and uses them for making good warm clothing. It sounds like a myth, but Mr. Prengel introduces certain ingredients, which are his secret, and thereby changes the nature of the glass. He has just finished a white, curly glass muff for a lady in St. Petersburg; he also charges 40 Thalers [$30.00 in U.S. currency at that time] for them. Also ladies' hats of glass, with glass feathers. A remarkable feature of this glass material is that it is lighter than feathers. Wool made of glass cannot be distinguished from the genuine article. Mr. Prengel's glass inventions are something so extraordinary and useful for clothing,

Collection: Toledo Museum of Art
Dress and parasol of spun glass fabric. Made by Libbey Glass Company, 1893.

etc., as glass is a nonconductor, that it will probably cause an entire revolution in dress material."

The following account appeared in a San Francisco newspaper dated February 10, 1879: "There is now weaving in this city the most wonderful fabric of which the voluminous history of unique feminine apparel furnished any account. It is the material (as flexible as the finest of silk and as durable as Blue Jeans Williams' favourite stuff for trousers) for a ladies dress, and it is woven by the world-renowned artist in glass work, Prof. Theodore Grenier, out of innumerable colored strands of glass first spun by himself.

"Compared with the completed garment, the mythical glass slipper of the famous Cinderella will sink into as vulgar an insignificance as an exhausted soda-water bottle. This reporter called on him recently, and he very courteously showed him the entire process. Breaking an extra piece out of the soiled bottom of an already broken tumbler, he submitted it to the heat of a blowpipe until it became incandescent and soft. Then with a 'stick' of glass he touched the molten portion, and with an expert motion which may be described as a flip, he carried a thread so fine that it was almost invisible till it caught on the disk of a slowly revolving wide wooden wheel of nineteen feet circumference. At a certain number of revolutions the strand was complete and the wheel was stopped, and it was removed. It then consisted of innumerable softly-glistening threads, finer than the finest of floss silk. The strands are spun of all colors, and are then washed in a solution of water and beet-root sugar, which toughens them. The spinning is all done, and occupied many weeks. The weaving is done on an old-fashioned hand loom, the warp being nineteen feet long and the woof four feet, so that the material will cut to advantage. Only about ten inches a day can be woven and the whole piece will not be completed until some time in April."

In the *Crockery & Glass Journal*, dated July 22, 1879, there was quite a lengthy article on the use of glass fibers for weaving dress fabrics. It was obviously written with tongue in cheek, but in spite of the many hazards pointed out by the author of this article, glass dresses were most certainly made and for no less personages than a famous stage actress and a Spanish princess.

On September 14, 1880, Hermann Hammesfahr of Pittsburgh, Pennsylvania, assigned his patent for producing glass cloth to James and Thomas Atterbury, proprietors of the White House Glass Works. The

Bird group and fountain of wrought and spun glass.
Spun glass ship in the foreground.

cloth was woven from fine glass fibers which were spun on a large revolving wheel in a manner outlined earlier in this chapter. The Hammesfahr family were the first in this country to produce spun glass cloth on
a large scale. Hammesfahr declared that his glass cloth could be used
to make "shawls, table-covers, neckties, bonnets, and other articles of
fancy clothing."

In a tiny book published by the Libbey Glass Company in 1899,
Kate Field gave an interesting account of how the famous actress Georgia
Cayvan obtained her glass dress. Briefly, it came about in this way. Miss
Cayvan attended the Libbey Glass Company's exhibition at the World
Columbian Exposition of 1893 and saw there lamp shades covered with
a silklike material woven from glass threads. She asked the Libbey Glass
Company if they would weave enough of this material for a dress. They
agreed on a price of twenty-five dollars a yard for the goods and Miss
Cayvan was given the exclusive right to wear such material on the stage.
Libbey sent one of their young women to New York to make the dress
for the actress as the material proved too prickly for her regular seamstress
to handle. Miss Cayvan wore the gown in the first act of Daniel Frohman's
play *The Wife,* and it would be safe to assume that the dress was not
the most comfortable Miss Cayvan had ever worn for the nettlesome
material was not as supple as silk or cotton. Another dress of this same
material was made and placed on view in the Libbey Exhibition Building
where it was seen by the Infanta Eulalia of Spain. The princess was
fascinated by the glass dress and before she returned to Spain she had a
similar gown in her wardrobe.

Most of us can remember with sweet nostalgia the beautiful Christmas
tree ornaments that delighted us as a child; birds with spun glass tails
and angels with beautiful curls and wings made of fine glass threads. The
glass birds with fine spun glass plumage shown in our illustrations were a
favorite Victorian ornament. More elaborate groups were made, some
with as many as twelve birds, all with flowing tails and wings of various
colors. The arrangements included glass flowers and foliage, and usually
fluffy glass cotton about the base; all were completely covered with what
was known as a "French Glass Dome."

What was, in 1713, a contingent possibility for the savant has since
become a reality. Thanks to modern industry, glass is now drawn as fine
and flexible as the finest thread from the silkworm.

English Cameo Glass

THE NORTHWOOD SCHOOL

Late nineteenth-century productions of English Cameo Glass falls into three distinct schools, the first of which is the Northwood School of cameo artists. This was a small, select group of capable glass men to whom John Northwood imparted all the knowledge he had acquired through his many years of experiment and work in this medium.

John Northwood was born in Stourbridge, England, in 1837. He served his early apprenticeship under Benjamin Richardson. Northwood was by no means an ordinary glassman, quite the contrary. He developed and designed many tools and processes, some still in use today. He was one of the most outstanding figures in the history of the English art and table-glass industry.

At the time of his greatest achievements in Cameo Glass he was engaged in a business with his brother Joseph. J. and J. Northwood were decorators and etchers of glass to the trade at Wordsley. John Northwood himself made comparatively few pieces of Cameo Glass. This limitation may have been brought about by the fact that he was having, or did have in later years, some trouble with cataracts of the eyes. Or it may be that he so concentrated on the teaching of his small group of men that he did not find the time for more work of his own hand.

Northwood's first piece of Cameo Glass was produced in 1860. It was a small vase having for its design a depiction of Perseus rescuing the Ethiopian princess Andromeda from a winged monster. It was, unfortunately, broken accidentally a few years later by Northwood's youngest son and namesake, John II.

The second piece was an all crystal vase of Grecian shape with two handles. The decoration is in pure Grecian style, with a frieze running all around the body of the vase and carved in relief, representing two equestrian groups from the Parthenon sculptures generally known as the Elgin Marbles. This work was commissioned by Sir Benjamin Stone. It was completed in 1873 and presented by Sir Benjamin to the Birmingham Art Gallery.

Collection: City of Birmingham Art Gallery
The Elgin Vase by John Northwood. Flint glass; signed and dated 1873 on the base. Height 15 inches.

The Dennis (Pegasus) Vase, carved by John Northwood, 1882.

In 1873, Philip Pargeter of the Red House Glass Works, and a cousin of John Northwood, handed Northwood a blank which, when completed, became the first replica in glass of the famous Portland vase. The carving took three years. The completion of Northwood's copy of the famous Portland-Barberini vase opened another fabulous era in the glass world. After more than fifteen centuries the ancient art of carving cameo reliefs in so intractable a material as glass was again realized. On its completion one of the first to congratulate the artist was Mr. W. H. Richardson, the oldest member of the firm of W. H., B. and J. Richardson, where John had worked as a youth. Mr. Richardson often entered the studio where Northwood was in apprenticeship and holding aloft a Wedgwood copy of the famous cinerary urn would exclaim, "A thousand pounds to him who produces this in glass." The challenge was finally met and won.

After finishing the Portland vase, other notable pieces were undertaken by Northwood. One was the Milton Vase with two handles and figure decoration representing Adam and Eve and the Archangel Michael in the Garden of Eden, as described in Milton's *Paradise Lost*.

Three tazzas were also executed, each having a carved head in the center, the heads being those of Shakespeare, Newton and Flaxman, representing Literature, Science and Art. Earlier prototypes of these busts can be seen in Wedgwood medallions of the late eighteenth century.

Northwood's last and greatest work was the Dennis, or Pegasus, vase. The Pegasus vase was commissioned by Thomas Wilkes Webb, Director-in-Chief of the Dennis Glass Works, a subsidiary of Thos. Webb & Sons. John Northwood was still in the last year of work on his reproduction of the Portland vase and it took some persuasion on the part of Wilkes Webb to convince him that another important piece of cameo glass should be undertaken. Mr. Northwood had already put in three long years of patient, exacting work on his replica of the Portland vase and quite naturally was unwilling to start another such laborious project. Fortunately, Mr. Webb's influence won over John Northwood and he undertook the execution of what was to be his last and greatest work, the Pegasus vase, in 1876, completing it in 1882.

The Pegasus was exhibited unfinished at the Paris Exhibition of 1878. It was hailed as another Northwood triumph and was rather prominently shown in the Thos. Webb & Sons display.

Upon its completion in 1882, the Pegasus vase, now reportedly worth $15,000.00, was sold through Tiffany & Company, New York, to Mrs. Mary

J. Morgan, a prominent collector of the day, for an unspecified amount. On March 18, 1886 the vase was sold at an auction of Mrs. Morgan's vast collection of art objects by the American Art Association in New York City. It brought $5,900.00. At this same auction the sale of a small Peach Blow porcelain vase for $18,000.00 caused a sensation in the art world that oddly enough had repercussions in the glass trade.

The location of the Pegasus vase during the years following its sale in 1886 and its acquisition by John Gellatly in 1928 was for some time a mystery. Ginsburg & Levy, Incorporated of New York City shed some light on this when they revealed to us that they had sold the vase originally to W. D. Breaker. Years later the elder Mr. Ginsburg bought the vase back at a sale of Mr. Breaker's collection. The price Mr. Ginsburg paid for the vase at the Breaker sale was not known, but it was offered to another member of the trade for the trifling sum of $400.00 soon after it was acquired. Its worth now far exceeds its original selling price, and it is now on permanent exhibition as a part of the vast art collection presented to the National Collection of Fine Arts, Smithsonian Institution, in 1929.

In order to appreciate the magnitude of the project an explanation of how the Pegasus vase was made is important. Mr. Northwood modeled in red wax all the figures, the horse head handles and the lid before blanks were made by the glass maker. The colossal task of making the blanks was assigned to the Dennis Glass Works, from which the vase acquired its other name. A gathering of deep blue flint glass was taken up on a blowpipe. The gather was lowered into an opaque white glass cup made to receive it and then pressed down, gradually filling the white cup from the bottom up. This method of casing forced out the air between the outer skin of white glass and the inner casing of blue glass. The gather was then rolled on the marver to weld thoroughly the two layers of glass. After marvering a bubble was blown into the gather through the blowpipe. This bubble was expanded until the blank reached the desired proportions. It was then shaped and the neck formed. A pontil rod was attached to what was later to be the base of the ovoid body and the blank was sheared off at the neck from the blowpipe. Lumps of white glass were attached to either side of the vase for handles. The blanks for the foot and lid were made in somewhat the same fashion. After the separate pieces had properly annealed they were ready for cutting.

The credit for the designs used on the Dennis-Pegasus vase is generally given to John Northwood, although some contemporary writers claimed these were the work of Wilkes Webb. The obvious influences of Josiah Wedgwood's Jasperware productions in the Grecian and Roman taste can be seen in the form of the vase and the Pegasus finial. These designs were blocked out on the outer casing of white glass with a bituminous paint resistant to acids. The white surface was then subjected to hydrofluoric acid until the unprotected parts were eaten away, by the action of the acid, to the deep blue background. A liberal use of the copper wheel, with emory powder and oil as an abrasive, brought the design down to a rough modeling. Using Mr. Northwood's wax models as his guide Mr. Edwin Grice roughed out the horse head handles and the Pegasus finial with files and drills. Mr. Grice was not a cameo artist but a very fine pattern maker. John Northwood II told us that his father was greatly indebted to Mr. Grice for the excellent way he "roughed" these parts and so saved his father a lot of valuable time and work.

Now the long, painstaking task of carving the cameo relief to its last exquisite detail was begun. Using tiny chisels improvised and often homemade, ranging in diameter from one-eighth to one-sixteenth of an inch, Northwood alternately carved and scraped with varying degrees of pressure to bring his masterpiece to completion. John Northwood obviously possessed that "infinite capacity for taking pains" which was Carlyle's definition of genius.

The completed vase, standing twenty-one and a half inches high, depicts stories taken from Greek and Roman mythology: the goddess of love, Aphrodite; Aurora; and Pegasus, the flying horse that sprang from Medusa at her death. These are modeled in opaque white against a glossy cobalt blue background. On one side the beautiful Aphrodite rides the waves in her shell-shaped chariot surrounded by attendants and cherubs. Some of the cherubs are carved from the deep blue background and do not show in most pictures of this famous vase. A close examination brings many more superb details to light.

The obverse side of the vase is expertly modeled and shows the Roman personification of dawn, Aurora, riding across the skies in her chariot, scattering flowers behind her. Aurora is attended by several winged cherubs. This design was borrowed from a fresco painting by Guido Reni, in the Palazzo Rospigliosi in Rome, in which the goddess of dawn is represented as strewing flowers before the advancing chariot of Phoebus attended by the hours. Here again some superb relief details have been

"Aphrodite," a Cameo Glass plaque by John Northwood II.
Diameter 15 inches. Completed in 1905.

lavishly carved on the dark blue background and are only apparent on
close examination.

The lid of the vase, surmounted by a magnificently carved figure of
Pegasus, is in itself a masterpiece in glass sculpture. A classic garland of
laurel leaves encircles the cover. The signature, "John Northwood, 1882"
appears on the underpart in very fine letters. This inscription can also be
found on the body of the vase itself.

The handles are superbly modeled and blend into the body of the vase in an ingenious way. Expertly carved batlike wings seem to emanate from the deep, full chest of the horsehead bust and fasten themselves to the body of the vase. The idea for incorporating the handles into the body of the vase in this manner was indeed a master stroke.

The stem and foot of the vase are a study in beautiful detail. The knop is elegantly embellished with shaded leaves, while an imbricated design known as "fish scale", reminiscent of some early Egyptian works, adorns the wide flaring foot. The body of the vase, the stem and the red velvet cushion on which it stands, are all joined together by means of a steel bolt.

The years of production of English Cameo Glass can be divided into two periods. The first covered a period from 1870 to 1880, when the early pieces were mainly carved by hand tools, the engraving wheel playing a subsidiary part. From the design to the finished article each piece was invariably the work of one individual.

During this early period, craftsmen trained under John Northwood were producing at his works in Wordsley hand-carved cameo vases and other articles. The designs were many and varied, comprising figure subjects, fruits and flowers, and ornamental pieces of various styles. William Northwood, Charles Northwood, W. O. Bowen (whom we shall speak of later), James Hill and others carved some very fine specimens in natural designs. The anatomy and structure of the leaves, fruits and flowers were most carefully and beautifully done, the edges being so skillfully undercut that they gave the appearance of lying on the glass background and not being a part of it. The number produced by this hand work was not great, and those specimens still existing are to be found only in the possession of collectors and museums.

Up to about 1884 a great many of the Cameo Glasses produced had the important parts of the design worked by hand tools. From then onward, as the engraving wheel came to be used more extensively, the character of the work gradually changed. It was a natural development, for the production of hand-tooled Cameo Glass could not supply the public's demand, and the use of the engraving wheel gave much quicker results.

In the second period, from 1880 to 1890, the engraving wheel was used almost exclusively for producing what can be termed "commercial"

"Tailor Bird Feeding Its Young." White cameo design on citron ground. Designed by Frederick Carder for Stevens & Williams, Brierley Hill, England, about 1886. Height 6⅜ inches.

Cameo Glass. It was responsible for a multitude of richly colored vases, bowls, etc., the production being a cooperative one between the designer, etcher and engraver.

This method of working as a team made for more rapid results and accelerated the output. One cannot expect to find the same beautiful finish or the careful attention to detail shown in the best hand-worked pieces. However, in the main, the results were very fine, especially as the engravers became more and more proficient in their treatment of the glass.

During this second period nearly all the manufacturers employed engravers for work on Cameo Glass. The firms which were producing the greatest amount were Stevens & Williams of Brierley Hill and Thos.

Author's Collection
Cameo Glass vase (white on brown). Designed and engraved by William Northwood. Circa 1889.

Webb & Sons of Amblecote. They had many engravers constantly at work to meet the public demand that existed at the time.

A large part of J. and J. Northwood's decorating works at Wordsley were occupied solely with artists working on Cameo Glass for Stevens & Willams. At this works there were some highly trained artists in glass, William Northwood being a well-known designer in all branches of the trade, as well as a very skilled and clever craftsman.

James Hill was another excellent designer and craftsman whose work was remarkable for its great delicacy and beauty of treatment.

Joshua Hodgetts was a first-class engraver, especially of all designs showing flowers, fruits and plants. He was a student of natural forms, and invariably had in front of him while he worked a specimen of the subject he was engraving, whether flowers, fruit or plant. His work was therefore distinguished by its truth to nature.

Frederick Carder, the founder of the Steuben Glass Works in Corning, New York, is another illustrious Northwood Alumnus, and a well-known glass designer and technologist. There are very few achievements in glass manufacture which Mr. Carder has not either pioneered or matched. It was Frederick Carder who influenced John Northwood in accepting the position of art director with the firm of Stevens & Williams.

The list of Northwood pupils reads like "Who's Who" in the glass world. They include George Woodall, Thomas Woodall, Frederick Carder, William Northwood and Charles Northwood (his nephews), W. O. Bowen, James Hill, B. Fenn, Joshua Hodgetts and John Northwood II (his son).

Sometime prior to 1950 Stevens & Williams produced a few pieces of Cameo Glass using old blanks which had been discovered in their warehouse. R. G. Rowley and J. Milward, two of their best engravers, decorated the vases with flower and bird designs. The cameo cutting is not comparable to their earlier productions, but Stevens & Williams felt they were good enough to exhibit during the festivities held in Stourbridge in 1951 to celebrate the coronation of Queen Elizabeth II.

LECHEVREL—LOCKE SCHOOL

The second school of Cameo Glass artists operated under the aegis of Messrs. Hodgetts, Richardson & Company of Wordsley. Its most important artists were Alphonse Lechevrel and Joseph Locke, who later became even more famous for his beautiful "Amberina" art glass.

Alphonse Lechevrel was one of the first to follow John Northwood in this expression of the glassmakers art. A Frenchman, he was engaged by Hodgetts, Richardson & Company to teach a small group of men the fine art of carving glass cameos. Lechevrel had already achieved a name for himself as a medalist, and he was therefore well grounded in figure, floral and geometric designing of all descriptions.

Among the few pieces of Lechevrel's Cameo Glass that have survived the years are two vases, each about sixteen inches tall, in the collection of the Brierley Hill Library. One is entitled "Hercules Restoring Alcestis to Her Husband," the other "Raising an Altar to Bacchus." The design of the former vase has been done in the pseudo-classic style so typical of the late Victorian Era, a style the French Gerome and the English Alma-Tadema were expressing in their painting. The latter design has a whimsical air about it in keeping with its subject.

Collection: Brierley Hill Libraries
"Raising an Altar to Bacchus," a Cameo Glass vase
carved by Alphonse Lechevrel. Circa 1878.

Cameo Glass vase carved by J. Milward, circa 1950. White relief designs on blue ground. Made at Stevens & Williams' Royal Brierley Crystal Glass Works, Brierley Hill, England. Height 12 inches.

Another pair of vases with handles carved by Alphonse Lechevrel, "Venus Rising from the Sea" and "The Birth of Venus," were exhibited at the Paris Exhibition of 1878. For some time the pair was presumed lost, but a few years ago it was discovered by the author that they were given to George Woodall to alter, perhaps in 1923, at which time they were attributed to him. The handles were removed and some slight additional engraving work done on the base and neck of each vase. Lechevrel's cipher "AL" and the date "77" were removed entirely from one and almost obliterated from the other before they were signed "Geo. Woodall."

Author's Collection
"The Birth of Venus," a Cameo Glass vase (white on cobalt-blue) carved by Alphonse Lechevrel in 1877. Altered and signed by George Woodall in 1923 (?).

Alphonse Lechevrel's most promising pupil was Joseph Locke. Locke possessed a pioneering spirit that made him ever dissatisfied with what he had accomplished and forced him to better his work in every field. The result was that he became not only a most accomplished glass technologist, but a finished painter, etcher, engraver, sculptor, and prolific inventor.

Joseph Locke was born in Worcester, England, on August 21, 1846. His father, Edward Locke, was a potter. When he was twelve years old Joseph Locke was apprenticed to his brother Edward at the Royal Worcester china factory where he had the benefit of classes and lectures by the prominent artists of his time who were engaged by the factory to come and demonstrate their arts for the benefit of all the employees. When he was nineteen he won first prize in a competition, held by Guest Brothers, for a design for a fireplace commissioned by the Czar of Russia.

Guest Brothers, who were etchers and decorators of glass in Stourbridge, quickly engaged this talented youth. He later left their employ, being persuaded to leave by Mr. Hodgetts of the firm of Hodgetts, Richardson & Company, much to the chagrin of the Frere's Guest.

While in the employ of Hodgetts, Richardson & Company, Locke produced his masterpiece, the second copy of the Portland vase in Cameo Glass. Of the forty blanks that were made only three finally survived the annealing. The first of the three blanks shattered during the carving because of hidden stresses brought about by faulty annealing. The second remained true throughout the long period of carving and engraving the relief design, and it is still in perfect condition today. Locke's copy of the Portland vase was shown at the Paris Exhibition of 1878 where it won the Gold Medal Award for Hodgetts, Richardson & Company. It was exhibited in several cities throughout Great Britain for many years following this, and is now in the author's collection.

Joseph Locke left the employ of Hodgetts, Richardson & Company and went to work for Mr. Philip Pargeter, proprietor of the Red House Glass Works and owner of the Northwood version of the Portland vase. After a short time he left there and worked for a while at Webb & Corbetts.

Locke finally came to America at some time late in the year 1882. A trick of fate resulted in his being engaged by the New England Glass Company of Cambridge, Massachusetts. He had been offered a position by the Boston & Sandwich Glass Company and was presumably coming

Replica of the Portland Vase (white on cobalt-blue). Signed "Joseph Locke,
Wordsley, 1878." Height 10 inches.

to America to accept this position. The latter firm, however, sent representatives to meet him in New York, but Locke's ship arrived at the Port of Boston, Massachusetts, and he was met there by the agents of the New England Glass Works who quickly signed him up. Amberina, Pomona and Agata are but a few of his many accomplishments in the field of decorative glassware while working for the Cambridge works.

The presence of a small Cameo Glass vase in the collection of the Toledo Museum of Art proves that Mr. Locke continued with his cameo work here in America. It has been attributed to Locke at a time when he was working for Edward Drummond Libbey. Other specimens of Locke's cameo work, some done with exquisite enameling to further embellish them, are in private collections and in the possession of members of his family.

Author's Collection
Head, by Joseph Locke. About 1885. Locke's cipher "J L" scratched on back. White on rose-beige glass. Height 1½ inches.

Collection: Toledo Museum of Art
Cameo Glass vase (white on ruby body). Engraved by Joseph Locke. Circa 1885.

WOODALL SCHOOL

The last of the three great schools of English Cameo Glass, the Woodall school, was by far the most productive, and in the opinion of many connoisseurs George Woodall had few rivals and no equals in the field of Cameo Glass. Born in 1850 in the neighborhood of Stourbridge, a district well known for its superb glass, George Woodall came of a family whose artistic abilities had already been made manifest. His maternal uncle, Thomas Bott, was famous for his painting of figures and natural subjects in Limoges enamels. Thomas Bott encouraged George to develop his natural talent for figure design and was influential in getting both George and his brother Thomas Woodall enrolled in the Stourbridge School of Design.

While Tom Woodall, too, possessed a fine hand for figure delineation, he seems to have found his forte in decorative and floral patterns. At times when he collaborated with his brother George on cameo pieces it was Tom who executed the intricate and beautiful borders. These productions were signed "T & G Woodall."

An exquisitely etched crystal glass tazza was shown at the Stourbridge Exhibition of Glass in 1951 signed "T. Woodall". The tazza was attributed to the year 1874, which would mean that he was employed at John Northwood's etching and decorating works in Wordsley at the time it was made.

Thomas Woodall did other works entirely of his own hand. These reveal a delicacy of design and craftsmanship that can only be expressed by a real artist.

The Woodall brothers received their early training in cameo under the tutelage of John Northwood. George and Tom had the privilege of watching the master craftsman at work on some of his most famous productions. Both brothers were later engaged by Wilkes Webb to work exclusively on Cameo Glass for Thos. Webb & Sons.

George Woodall was a tireless worker. He was constantly improving his skill as an etcher, engraver and sculptor of Cameo Glass. Not only did he acquire a proficiency with the tools he had at his disposal but frequently he improved and invented others. Naturally, he soon was master of his art and second to none.

In his earlier works George Woodall used carving tools to a great extent. But as time went on he used the engraving wheel more and more.

"Aphrodite" (white on puce). Signed "G. Woodall, 1892." Diameter 13 inches.

He carried to a greater extent than any other what might be termed the "pictorial effect" in cameo work.

A background in perspective character was frequently a part of his designs, the effect of distance being obtained by skillfully thinning down the opal glass with an engraving wheel to show a delicate blue opalescent color.

Woodall also worked into his compositions a wealth of detail. Shadings of light and dark, distant perspective and bold relief, the suppleness of rounded flesh and the polished hardness of marble, were all beautifully conveyed in some of Woodall's more ambitious works. Throughout the many years he produced Cameo Glass his best pieces were those of figure design, especially his feminine figures which have a symmetry of form, a gracefulness of pose, and a beauty of feature that has seldom been equaled.

Author's Collection
"Flora" (white on puce). Signed "T & G Woodall." A 9 x 12 Cameo Glass plaque.

Author's Collection

"The Moorish Bathers," signed "Geo. Woodall." 1890 to 1898, Stourbridge, Thomas Webb & Sons. Puce with opaque-white overlay. Diameter 18⅛ inches. (Woodall considered "Moorish Bathers" his masterpiece.)

One of Woodall's early pieces, the "Aurora" vase, went to Australia where it was later destroyed in a fire after having once been rescued from a deep watery grave. This vase was considered to be one of Woodall's best works, and it is unfortunate that, of the many glass cameos produced by Woodall, this one did not survive.

George Woodall's greatest achievement in cameo glass is his placque, "The Moorish Bathers," which he completed in 1898. The placque had been in production since 1890 and was purchased on completion by the Hon. George Brookman of Adelaide, Australia. "The Moorish Bathers" very nearly met somewhat the same fate that befell Woodall's "Aurora" vase when a fire completely destroyed the Brookman home in Adelaide many years ago. In 1912 Woodall stated, in a newspaper interview, that his "Moorish Bathers" placque was the finest thing he had ever done.

Other noteworthy pieces produced by George Woodall were two plaques entitled "The Toilet of Venus" and "The Dance." These two plaques and an exceptionally fine cameo low relief portrait of Lord Kelvin, were destroyed in a fire at the Brussels Exhibition in 1910.

As the demand for Cameo Glass increased, more and more men were employed by Thos. Webb & Sons to work under George Woodall and his brother Tom. Here, as in the case of the Northwood school of artists,

Author's Collection
"A Maid of Athens" (white on puce). Signed "T & G Woodall." A Cameo Glass vase 10½ inches tall.

Author's Collection
"Night," signed "G. Woodall." Thomas Webb & Sons, circa 1900. White cameo relief on puce ground. Height 8⅜ inches.

the work developed from a one-man operation, carrying through from the original design to the finished article, to a group project using the combined skills of designers, etchers and engravers. Quite often this team was enlarged to include a skilled artist in enamels and gold.

The most prominent member of the Woodall school of cameo artists was an Irishman named James M. O'Fallon. Mr. O'Fallon was primarily engaged as art director at the Webb factory, but he did produce a few pieces of Cameo mostly carved by hand in an excellent manner. The designs were usually of flowers and fruits.

Under George Woodall's direction a group of capable artists were producing, as fast as possible, a great quantity of Cameo Glass. The names of some members of this group were, Thomas Farmer, Harry

Author's Collection

George Woodall's "Antarctica Vase." Cameo relief designs of white on citron-colored ground. Height 20 inches. Made to commemorate Admiral Scott's ill-fated expedition to the Antarctic. (Some of the cameo decoration was carved by J. T. Fereday.)

Cameo Glass vase in three colors (blue, white and coral).
Engraved by the Woodall team. Circa 1885. Height 20 inches.

Davies, Frances Smith, Jacob Facer, and J. Fereday. The work produced by this group of men was of a high caliber, although it could not begin to compare with some of Woodall's own original works.

Two more men who worked as a team, and produced many lovely pieces that embodied both the cameo technique and enamel work of the finest kind, were Kretschman (Kritschman) and Barbe. Kretschman did the engraving and hand-tool finishing while Jules Barbe applied his gifted touch with enamels and gold.

In summing up we find the Woodall school of Cameo Glass falls into three categories. The early works of George Woodall, on some of which his brother collaborated, and which were in the main hand carved. Then we have George Woodall's later pieces, mostly worked on the engravers wheel and embodying the pictorial effect to a very large degree. And, finally, the Cameo Glass produced under George Woodall's direction by a large group of workers. In this last category, Tom and George Woodall and James O'Fallon were the designers, although some of the other men were capable of designing as well as executing fine works of their own. Almost all of the cameo pieces produced by this group were marked "Gem Cameo."

In 1910 George Woodall retired from the Dennis Glass Works of Thos. Webb & Sons, and from that date until his death in 1925 he carried on in his home studio at Kinswingford. Here he continued to work in Cameo Glass producing pieces that some consider his finest. George Woodall had devoted his entire working life to his art, and examples of his skill can be found in numerous collections all over the world.

The greatest part of the English Cameo Glass produced between 1880 and 1890 was destined for the American market. About 1890 there was a rapid decline in demand, mainly because of the appearance on the market of a large quantity of cheap imitation Cameo Glass. Henry G. Richardson & Sons, Wordsley, England, advertised "Cameo glass vases, etc. in the most elaborate and in cheaper styles" in the *Pottery Gazette Diary* (1899).

These imitation pieces were articles made with a thin opal casing on the outer side. Their surface had a pattern printed on it with acid-resisting ink. The article was next immersed in a hydrofluoric acid bath, whereby all parts not protected by the ink were dissolved away by the acid. This left a flat opal glass design in very shallow relief on a colored transparent ground.

The firms who produced this cheaper ware gave it the name "Cameo Glass" which it did not deserve, and, because it was less expensive than hand-worked or engraved Cameo Glass, it found a ready market. Experienced buyers would not purchase it, but the publicity it obtained stopped the production and sale of genuine Cameo Glass.

Another type of imitation appeared in the form of a still cheaper product. The "Florentine Art Cameo" and "Lace-De-Boheme-Cameo," pro-

Author's Collection
Cameo Glass pitcher (white design on a ruby ground) with etched background.
English. Circa 1880.

duced by Bohemian factories and distributed in this country by Lazarus & Rosenfeld, had the same disastrous effect on the sale of English Cameo Glass in America and abroad as did their Satin Wares. "Florentine Art Cameo" and "Lace-De-Boheme-Cameo" were produced by painting floral, figure, and lace designs on a colored or Satin Glass body with heavy white enamel. The wares, often copying designs of English manufacture, were usually marked with their respective nomenclatures.

The so-called "Mary Gregory" glassware—transparent colored glassware with white or colored enamel designs painted on their surface, was still another cheap imitation of English Cameo Glass. The production of such wares was more prolific on the Continent than here in America. Much of this glassware is erroneously attributed to the Sandwich factory, and more especially to one Mary Gregory, who is reported to have been employed in the decorating department of the Cape Cod works.

Author's Collection

"Lace-De-Boheme" Cameo Glass vase. Bohemian. Circa 1885. Height 9 inches.

Novelty-Type Cameo Glass

One of the novelty-type Cameo Glasses which appeared in the last quarter of the nineteenth century was made in imitation of old carved ivory. The ware was produced by a process patented in England on November 30, 1887, by Thomas Wilkes Webb. A patent covering this same process was issued to Mr. Webb in America and is dated February 19, 1889. Briefly it was produced in this fashion: A vase, or any other article, of ivory or white opaque glass was first etched with a shallow relief design. The relief design was further worked up with the engraving wheel. The desired pattern thus being produced in outline on the vase it was wiped clean and then rubbed with a brown or other-colored stain. The stain produced a dark tint in the recesses of the design while the high points held just a trace of the color. The result was a piece of cameo glass made in imitation of old carved ivory.

George Woodall and his brother Tom used old specimens of Indian, Chinese and other Oriental and East Indian *objets d'art* as models for this new conception of the cameo technique. Their first productions met with royal favor and were purchased by Queen Victoria. Following Victoria's approval of this new ware production was stepped up considerably to supply the ever-increasing demands of the public.

Several designs for Cameo Glass articles made in imitation of old ivory are shown in the pattern and design books of Thos. Webb & Sons, prefixed by the initial "K." To some it indicates that the designs were the work of Kretschman although it is known that Messrs. Barbe, Facer, and Nash, all members of the Woodall Gem Cameo team, also produced designs for such wares.

Cameo Glass vase imitating old carved ivory, with applied glass windows on both sides. Designed by Kretschman and decorated with gold and enamel by Jules Barbe. Thos. Webb & Sons. Circa 1887.

Evidently glass in imitation of carved ivory remained popular for some years after it was first introduced. The February 28, 1901, edition of the *Crockery & Glass Journal* reported that "John A. Service at the Astor House is showing a novelty in glass which is one of the most elegant and artistic things ever produced in this line. It is like carved ivory."

Cameo Glass pieces made in imitation of eighteenth century Chien Lung Cameo Glass were also made in this later period. An ancient technique known as "padding" produced some interesting and very beautiful effects. On an opaque white or colored ground blobs of glass of different colors were applied where the designs were to appear in relief. These blobs of colored glass were then cut and engraved to resemble flowers, fruits, fish and animal forms, figures, urns, and many other subjects. Gold and enamels accented some of the pieces. Thos. Webb & Sons were the sole producers of this type of novelty Cameo Glass. For the most part they represent a high caliber in design and workmanship.

Another beautiful effect in Cameo Glass, produced by Stevens & Williams and Thos. Webb & Sons, was known as "Dolce-Relievo" (soft relief). A transparent colored glass was plated over a body of opaque white or ivory colored glass. The design was painted on the colored outer skin of the article and carefully etched away, leaving various shadings of

Collection: Brierley Hill Libraries
Ivory-white glass vase with cameo-carved decoration of purple glass in "Dolce-Relievo." Height 4¾ inches.

light and dark in shallow relief on the white or ivory background. All of the merits such pieces have depend entirely on the fine handiwork of the etcher and the beauty of the design. The vase shown in the illustration embodies all the finer points of this technique. It was made at Stevens & Williams circa 1885.

In 1899 Thomas Webb & Sons advertised "sculptured vases and placques in Rock Crystal engraving." The carved crystal productions were made the same way other Cameo Glass objects were made, but the absence of color obviates the three-dimensional effects produced by this firm in earlier days using cased colored blanks for carving.

Author's Collection
Bowl in Chinese "Chien Lung" style Cameo Glass. Celadon colored glass with deeply carved decoration of flowers and leaves. Possibly engraved by Daniel and Lionel Pearce about 1885. Signed "Webb" in base. Height 5 inches.

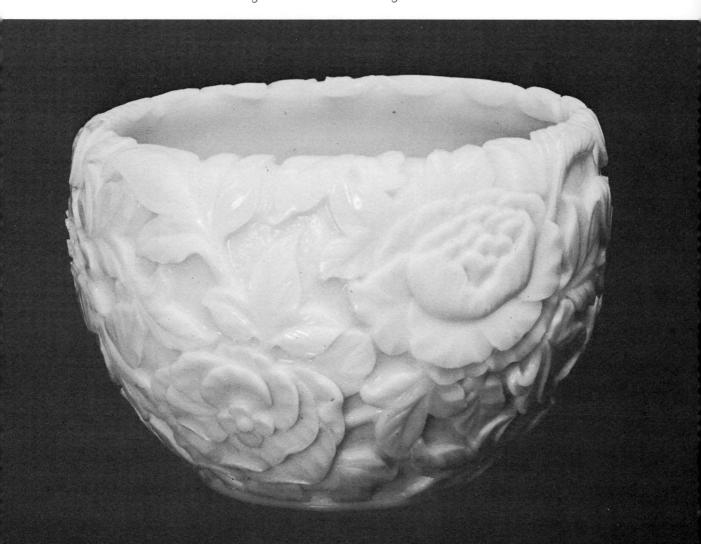

American Cameo Glass

Gillinder & Sons produced a few Cameo Glass vases around 1880, and most of these are still owned by members of the Gillinder family. A few years ago the family pieces were gathered together for a group photograph which we are privileged to illustrate in this book. None of the Gillinder Cameo pieces are marked, and there appears to be very little difference between the Gillinder pieces and the commercial grade of Cameo Glass made in England.

A large counter filled with the Mt. Washington Glass Company's wares was exhibited at the New Bedford Industrial Exposition of 1887. Here and there among the other wares produced by this firm were a few pieces of Cameo Glass. There is little to distinguish them from those Cameo Glasses made in England during the so-called "commercial" period of Cameo Glass production. The pieces shown in an old photograph of this stand have floral decorations about the main body of the vase with some fancy designs about the neck and mouth. Since the English factories had virtually a monopoly on Cameo Glass sold in this country we can assume that the American factories did not manufacture such wares in any quantity.

A Cameo Glass cigar holder with white floral pattern on a blue ground has been attributed to the Boston & Sandwich Glass Company. It was supposed to have been produced during the regime of James D. Lloyd, a former lieutenant and close associate of Deming Jarves. Most certainly the factory did produce a type of Cameo Glass, for fragments have been found of shallow acid-etched colored designs in low relief on a frosted glass ground. The shards proved to be portions of lampshades made at the factory during the last few years of its existence. Whether or not true Cameo Glass was made at Sandwich is still unanswered. Their prolific production of overlaid and cut glassware would certainly qualify them to produce the blanks necessary for cameo work, and it would have been a poor factory indeed if it did not employ men capable of engraving such wares.

On December 5, 1871, William George Webb of Wordsley, England, assigned an American patent for producing etched intaglio and cameo relief designs on glassware to William Langdon Libbey, who at that time was associated with the Mt. Washington Glass Company of New Bedford, Massachusetts. (Libbey later became proprietor of the New England Glass Company, Cambridge, Massachusetts.) Webb's patent covered a means for producing transfer-printed designs with acid-resisting inks and applying these to the surface of the glass before it was subjected to the etching fluids. The etching fluids ate into the unprotected portions of the glass leaving a slightly raised cameo design. This technique was later used by the French Cameo Glass artists of the art nouveau period.

Benjamin Bakewell, Jr., of Bakewell, Pears & Company, Pittsburgh, Pennsylvania, patented a process for pressing glass articles of two or more colors. The result was a glassware that resembled the cameo technique. The patent, dated September 29, 1874, alludes to a type of glass-

Collection: Lowell Innes
"Double Glass" bowl. Process patented by Benjamin Bakewell, Jr.,
Bakewell, Pears & Company, Pittsburgh, Pa.

ware wherein bas-relief glasswork was united to the outer surface of the blown glassware by first pressing articles so as to unite therewith. However, Mr. Bakewell claims in his enumerations that his ware is produced entirely by pressing. Utilizing interchange-plungers and rings, and by varying the inner configuration of the mold, he produced articles of various shapes and great beauty.

On November 23, 1876, Thomas B. Atterbury of Atterbury & Co., Pittsburgh, Pennsylvania, registered a method for producing pressed glassware in which he claimed, "the appearance will be very similar to, and look quite as well as, a cameo." The specifications related two means for producing this effect. The first refers to the article's being made of two different colored metals, the base being of a "jet" colored glass with the central medallion, or medallions, being of "opal or other colored glass," or vice versa. The separately made, closely fitting parts, were joined together either by "friction" or "cement." Atterbury's other method resembles Benjamin Bakewell, Jr.'s means for producing such wares, and suggests that the article be formed with a recess ring in it, and a temporary sustaining ring-plate which would reserve a space for the opal or colored glass medallion to be cast or pressed into place. Dishes, goblets, bowls, buttons, breastpins and some very interesting doorknobs, were among the articles Atterbury mentions as being manufactured according to his process.

Thomas B. Atterbury patented another method on February 1, 1876, for producing hollow glassware composed of two or more differently colored glasses. By utilizing the cupping process practiced by early Cameo

From a negative loaned to the author by J. Fletcher Gillinder
Gillinder Cameo Glass. *Left to right:* White on yellow; white on blue; white on ruby; (the Portland vase is pottery); white on blue; white on yellow; and white on yellow.

Glass makers, Atterbury manufactured a ware very similar to the cameo technique, but more nearly like the cut and engraved overlay glassware popular about 1850.

William L. Libbey of the New England Glass Company patented a process on November 9, 1880, the aim of which was to "reproduce glassware having the general appearance and character of the well-known Portland Vase." Through an ingenious use of manifold molds Libbey was able to press and blow articles of glassware with opaque white designs in bas-relief on a dark colored ground. Production seems to have been on a limited scale since few examples of this ware have been found.

On April 26, 1881, Frederick S. Shirley of the Mt. Washington Glass Works patented a process for producing cameo relief designs on lamp globes. His means for doing this was simple. He blew a gather of glass into an intaglio-cut mold and brought it forth with the design in relief on the blow. Etching and frosting the glass added to the illusion.

The following quotation is taken from an article which was written about John Northwood in an 1883 issue of the *Crockery & Glass Journal*: "Among the few pupils who have enjoyed the advantages of John Northwood's superior instruction is Mr. Wm. O. Bowen, who has recently arrived in this country and established himself in the same line of art, having his studio at 470 Fifth Avenue, South Brooklyn, New York. Some of the cameos carved in glass by Mr. Bowen are simply exquisite, and we have no doubt that Mr. Bowen will find himself in much the same position here as is now filled by his late tutor [John Northwood] in England. A specimen of such work is worth having." Mr. Bowen returned to England a few years later, presumably because of ill health, where he assumed the management of J. and J. Northwood's decorating works.

By the twentieth century the cameo technique had been reduced to shallow acid-etched designs used to some advantage by the exponents of *art nouveau*. Nevertheless, Alfred Henry Freeman of Mt. Vernon, New York patented a process for manufacturing cameo relief designs on ornamental windows and other articles of glass on May 12, 1903. The reliefs were fashioned separately and placed on the flat surface of the glass where spaces of suitable size and shape were cut or etched out. Cement held the applied relief designs in their place.

The American production of true Cameo Glass was limited, but not because we were incapable of producing such wares—quite the contrary. The higher costs of production in this country forced our wares off the market.

Venetian Cameo Glass

*W*hen this book was first released in 1959 we reported the discovery of several pieces of Cameo Glass said to have been made in Italy in the last quarter of the nineteenth century. This collection, which we viewed in 1956 in the company of Professor Aldo Polato, manager of the famous Pauly & Cie. glassworks in Venice, Italy, was housed in a large sixteenth-century pallazo on one of the many crooked little streets which abound in Venice.

Since 1959 we have come across a report published in 1880 concerning the glasswares exhibited by several European and American manufacturers at the Paris Exposition of 1878. This report revealed that the Venice and Murano Glass and Mosaic Company, Ltd., of 731 Campo San Vio, Venice, Italy, and 30 St. James Street, London, England, were exhibiting, among other things, some fine examples of Cameo Glass.

Collection: Pauly & Cie., Venice
Cameo Glass vases and cups (white on cobalt-blue). Venetian. Last quarter of the nineteenth century.

The Venice and Murano Glass and Mosaic Company was formed in 1866 by a few English gentlemen whose interest in Italian art induced them to subscribe the capital necessary to give the proper artistic and commercial direction dedicated to the revival of an industry for which Venice and Murano, in their palmy days, had acquired worldwide celebrity.

For help and guidance with their tremendous task of reviving the "lost arts" of Venetian glass, these Englishmen turned to Signor Alessando Castellani. Armed with fragments of some of the more remarkable ancient productions, which he carried with him and exhibited to the workmen, Signor Castellani retaught the glass workers to reproduce some of the celebrated objects preserved in museums throughout the world. His success was crowned at the Paris Exposition of 1878 where the firm won several awards for their productions in glass and mosaics.

Most important among their many artistic achievements was their Cameo Glass, some of which we are able to show in our illustrations. It

Collection: Pauly & Cie., Venice
Cameo Glass vase (white on dark blue). Venetian. Last quarter of the nineteenth century.

will be apparent to students of ancient glass that many of these objects were copied from ancient specimens to be found in great museum collections all over the world—the Portland vase being the most noteworthy. Some of these objects have since found their way into public and private collections.

Instead of a heavy flint glass, a light soda metal, typical of most Venetian products, was used for both the body glass and the outer skin. This softer metal gave the engraver a freedom of movement he could not have had with the tougher and harder flint glass used by the English and American factories. This ease of movement in working was manifested in each of the designs, all of which were beautifully carved with figure and floral patterns. The only failing point in these Venetian productions is in the small details, which in English and American Cameo Glass are well defined. Facial features and other small details were not easily achieved in the softer metal used by the Venetian craftsman as it would not stand up to much engraving of an intricate nature.

Recently Pauly & Cie. experimented with cameo engraving using some old blanks left over from the nineteenth century. The few pieces produced convinced them that it would be far too expensive to put on a commercial basis.

Author's Collection
Venetian Cameo Glass vase. Made by the Venice & Murano Glass and Mosaic Co. Ltd., 1878. Height 4½ inches.

French Cameo Glass

The French technique of acid-engraving cameo relief designs on blanks of cased colored glass was but one facet of the trend in glass manufacturing known as *art nouveau*, which became popular in France about 1890 and continued in favor until just before the First World War in 1914.

Cameo Glass in the French tradition was not intended to rival the meticulously engraved English Cameo Glass. It was, instead, a new conception of glass design, utilizing color and form in what was originally intended as a subtle Oriental style, and very handsome and artistically executed examples were developed. French glassmakers were proud of their work and almost all of their pieces bear a signature. Toward the end of the *art nouveau* era, this Cameo Glass, of such merit in earlier years, deteriorated into grotesquely formed pieces of garish colored glass.

Joseph Brocard, artist, glass technologist, and early disciple of *art nouveau*, exerted a strong influence on the work produced by such men as Galle, Rousseau, Marinot, De Latte, De Vez, and many of his other contemporaries. Primarily, though, Brocard was noted for his enameled glassware, made in imitation of Oriental and mid-eastern wares. Best remembered of these are his lighting fixtures, resembling enameled mosque lamps.

The most renowned of the French masters of Cameo Glass was Emile Galle, who was born in the important glass center of Nancy, France, in 1846. Galle started his first glass factory in Mysenthal (Meisenthal), a small glass manufacturing center in the Moselle Department, in 1879. The blanks made at Mysenthal were decorated under his personal supervision in a small studio which he established in Nancy. His work gained

Cameo Glass pitcher by Emile Galle. Circa 1900. Height 10 inches.

public recognition at L'Exposition de l'Union Centrale des Arts Decoratif in Paris in 1884. Galle's fame became such that he was appointed head of the school of arts at Nancy. He developed to be the foremost exponent of the so-called *art nouveau,* the modern style in glass in his time.

Galle took for his subjects flowers and landscape designs instead of the figure subjects favored by English artists for Cameo Glass. By the use of varied colored casings of glass upon a base of either transparent or translucent metal, he obtained new and artistic effects. Some of these casings of colored glass were obtained by picking up powdered glass from the marver as the hot glass was being rolled to give it shape, reheating the whole—in some instances this color was locked in by casing another layer of a different color over the entire mass—and finally blowing it into the shape desired. Galle utilized these masses of color underneath and on the surface of the glass by designing subjects to suit the object in hand, using the various layers of color in his flowers, insects and landscapes. When we consider that all of this work was done in relief, by first etching out the mass with acid and then engraving the detail with a wheel, the craftsmanship underlying such beauty of individual work is apparent.

Galle's work, bought by museums and people of good taste in Europe and America, placed glass upon a high artistic plane.

Principal among Galle's collaborators and workers were Louis Hertaux who created several designs for him at Nancy, the decorator Paul Nicolas, and August Herbst and Daigueperce, two of the most accomplished etchers and engravers in Galle's studios. Paul Nicolas in later years worked for L'Verrerie de la Compagnie des Cristaleries de Saint Louis, a branch of the Baccarat firm, and also under his own name in Nancy as a decorator of glass, exhibiting in the expositions of 1927 and 1937 and winning awards both years for his glassware.

After the death of Galle in 1905, the factory was under the direction of Victor Prouve until 1914. The wares produced during Prouve's management are marked with a star preceding the name "Galle." (This refutes undeniably the erroneous assumption by some dealers and collectors that pieces so marked were made by the hands of the master, Galle.) Following the First World War, in 1918, the firm carried on production at Epinay in the Vosges. The works changed hands in 1921, continuing for a time, but the glassware became increasingly poor in quality.

Eugene Rousseau (1827–1891) worked originally in ceramics; later he manufactured artistic glassware. He and Galle were the principal apostles of the new conception of glass design inspired by Japanese art forms, Japan being at that time just recently opened to the West. Among his other commendable wares were Craquelle Glass (crackled glass), Marble Glass, Agate Glass and imitation gems. Rousseau incrusted his models

Cameo Glass vase (*left*) in shades of light to dark blue on a white ground. Signed "Emile Galle." Circa 1895. Signed "Galle" vase (*right*) in the Chinese style. *Art nouveau* cameo relief design of orchid flowers and leaves in various shades of terra cotta and gray on a crystal ground. Height 6½ inches.

Collection: *Smithsonian Institute*

Collection: *Richard Cole*

with gold and introduced gold and other metallic oxides in his melts (glass batches). His productions—and some consider these his best—date from 1867 when he was employed by the Appert Brothers of Clichy. After gaining recognition at the exposition of 1884, Rousseau sold his establishment to Leveille in 1885.

M. Leveille directed and operated a decorating establishment for glass and porcelain in 1869. In 1885 he acquired Rousseau's glassworks and continued to make glass, as Rousseau had done, along the lines inspired by Japanese art. About 1889 he produced glassware employing acid etching and wheel engraving in the style of *art nouveau*. At the beginning of the twentieth century the business was taken over by Harant & Guignard of Paris, who were primarily decorators of glass.

Maurice Marinot, an accomplished painter, entered the glass trade in 1911 at Bar-sur-Seine an ancient town pleasantly situated on the left bank of the Seine, about 125 miles southeast of Paris. His first productions were decorated with colored enamels; usually in designs of decorative flowers, birds, or feminine heads. From enamels he turned to deep geometric engraving, using blanks that were, to say the least, uninspired in form and color. In his third period, Marinot renounced exterior decoration for his glassware and, like Rousseau and Galle before him, sought colorful effects with the aid of mineral stains, oxides, and cased colored glass.

In later years Marinot developed a style all his own. Handling the blowpipe himself, often in the very doors of the furnace, he made those glass productions that won him honors during the Exposition of Modern Art in 1925, and won him the reputation among his countrymen of possessing the greatest genius of any of the craftsmen in glass.

The Daum Brothers, Auguste and Antonin, were originally from Lorraine, which explains the Cross of Lorraine, used in their monogram. They founded their first factory in Nancy in 1875, producing bottles. Their earliest efforts in artistic decorative and tableware were with gold ornamentation; they turned from this to glassware inspired by Arabian designs and decorated with scrolls and leaves. Shortly after the introduction of this "Egyptian" glass, they began to produce colored glass by the "flushed" process. Their cameo and enamel glasswares, produced about 1890, rank among the best representations of these types. The Daums were active in the School of Art in Nancy during Galle's direction of that institution and also under the new staff formed in later years by Marinot. As time went on they developed techniques of their own which are familiar to us today. Currently the Daum glass works is producing decorative crystal glassware in the modern vein.

There were many lesser known craftsmen-artists who worked in what is now termed "French Cameo Glass." Pieces signed "De Vez" and those bearing the mark "Mont Joye," were produced by Saint-Hilaire, Touvier, de Varreaux & Company, successors to Monot & Stumpf, at

Author's Collection
Cameo Glass inkwell. Daum Brothers, Nancy, France. Circa 1895.

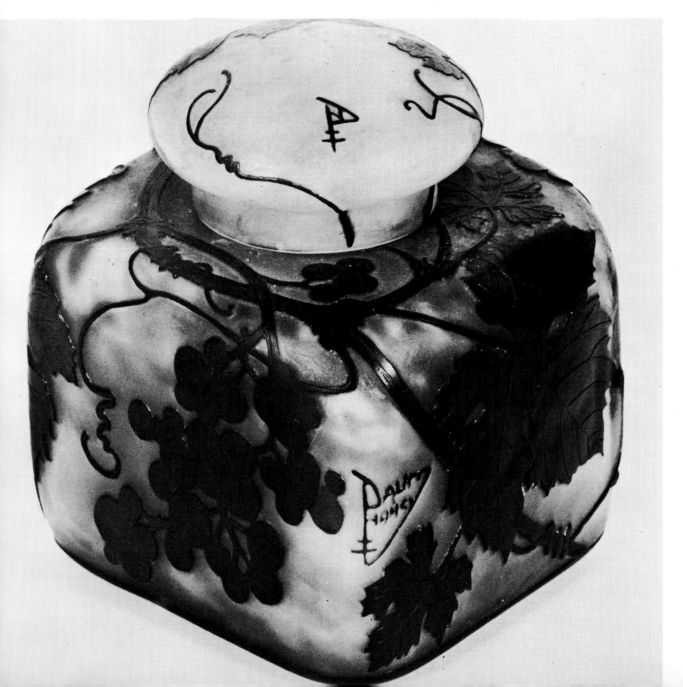

their glassworks in Pantin, just north of Paris. M. de Varreux was the firm's art director and signed many pieces of Cameo Glass with the alias "De Vez." Still other pieces of this firm's Cameo Glass were signed with the firm's initials in an elaborate monogram. The trade mark "Mont Joye" was used mostly on lightly etched Cameo Glass pieces which are in many ways similar to etched cameo glasses produced by Baccarat in France, and Val St. Lambert in Belgium.

Le Gras was noted for his imaginative glassware and bottles until he ceased production about 1914. He started work in Saint-Dennis, a suburb north of Paris, in 1864. Especially laudable are his scenic productions.

Muller Brothers of Luneville began their careers working for Emile Galle. They founded their own factory in the vicinity of Luneville, just south of Nancy on the Moselle River, afterwards moving it to Crois Mare. Cameo pieces made at Luneville are signed "Muller," "Muller Luneville," or simply "Luneville." Those made at Crois Mare bear the name of the town in connection with the name Muller or just "Crois Mare." Their most active period was between 1905 and 1937.

J. B. Williaume (Villaume) of Pantin was noted for his acid-engraving on cased glass blanks, especially portraits, about 1878. Very few of his early portrait pieces have been found.

Andre De Latte established his works in Nancy in 1921. the principal output being lighting fixtures and opaque glassware in imitation of the Bohemian Opaline. Among his best wares were his cameo productions, often done with a sensitive combination of graceful design and vibrant color effects.

Edward Michel was the finest engraver of glass in France in his time. (He was a direct descendant of Nancy-born Claude Michel, 1738–1814, known as "Clodion," whose ceramic figure modeling was world renowned.) Towards the end of the nineteenth century, Edward Michel worked for Rousseau and later Leveille. Examples of his cameo work are very rare. The quality of Michel's engraving rivals that of his English contemporaries, Woodall and Northwood.

M. Walters of Nancy began working about 1925 in Cameo Glass and artistic productions of Pate de Verre. His cameo pieces are not always fine in color or design but, happily, there are plentiful exceptions.

Alphonse G. Reyen, one of the most able engravers and decorators of

Sculptured Cameo Glass vase by Edward Michel. Late nineteenth century.
Height 10 inches.

glass, worked for Eugene Rousseau about 1877. Many examples of his cameo work were exhibited at the exposition of 1889.

Tessire du Motay, Kessler and Mareschal were three artists who utilized the etching needle in making shallow cameo relief designs on glass, working from about 1862 until the end of the nineteenth century.

Cameo Glass in the French style was produced in most of the countries of Europe contemporaneously with the birth of this expression of *art nouveau* in France. Benjamin Richardson, of the Wordsley Flint Glass Works near Stourbridge, patented a method for producing cameo relief designs on a cased glass blank on June 20, 1857. Mr. Richardson coated the surface of a cased blank with gutta-percha or India rubber, both of which are resistant to acids, and removed some of the pelicle with a suitable tool before dipping the article in acid to remove those portions of the outer casing not protected by the resist. The article, being composed

Cameo Glass covered pot.
Etched by Benjamin Richardson.
Circa 1857.

of two or more casings of colored glass, when finished, displayed a design of one color in shallow relief on a ground of another hue. Mr. Richardson maintained in his specifications that the use of fluoric acid would leave a mat finish on the design, while a combination of fluoric and sulphuric acids would leave a bright finish.

On June 19, 1885, Archibald Cochran of the Saint Rollex Flint Glass Works in Lanark, North Britain, patented a similar method for producing

Collection: Richard Cole
Signed "WEBB" vase with *art nouveau* cameo relief design of tulips and leaves on an etched crystal ground. Made at Thomas Webb & Sons by Ludwig Kny, circa 1910. Height 6 inches.

Russian Cameo Glass vase. Dated 1909. Height 6 inches.

Collection: Richard Cole
Signed "WEBB" vase with *art nouveau* cameo design of lilies and leaves in amethyst on an etched crystal ground. Made by Ludwig Kny at Thomas Webb & Sons, circa 1910. Height 8¾ inches.

cameo relief designs on the colored inner casing of his lamp globes, leaving the outer surface smooth to the touch.

On November 9, 1885, a patent was issued in London to Lewis John Murray of the Soho and Vesta Glassworks, Birmingham, England, for a means of producing shallow cameo relief designs on a cased glass body. The method was very similar to Richardson's except that Murray suggested the use of a sandblasting machine in connection with acid engraving to produce his effects. He also recommended the use of gold or bronze to accent his designs.

Ludwig Kny, the son of Frederick Kny, a celebrated engraver of glass in the Stourbridge district in England, also worked in etching cased glass articles in the French style of Cameo Glass. He designed and executed many such pieces for Thos. Webb & Sons about the beginning of the twentieth century. Kny's style differs greatly from the Continental Cameo Glass in color composition and design. When Kny's pieces are found, they are more likely to bear the Webb trade mark or name than his own signature, since his brother, Frederick Kny, told us he signed very few of his works.

The Cameo Glass productions of the Val St. Lambert factory in Belgium are well know to collectors. Their cased glass bodies were lavishly cut with the wheel and acid-engraved into beautiful expressions of art Cameo Glass.

In the heyday of *art nouveau,* Loetz of Austria produced a few cameo pieces of real distinction, although they were primarily known for their iridescent glass which was contemporary with Tiffany's similar lustered glasses.

The overlaid and decorated vase, pictured in the illustrations as an example of Russian Cameo Glass, was obviously inspired by the Galle group of French glass artists. Its attribution presented a problem before the monogram on the base was identified as that of Czar Nicholas II, the last of the Romanov dynasty. It is dated 1909.

To some extent acid-etched relief designs on cased glass blanks were used by the Tiffany Furnaces and the Steuben Glass Works. Both the padding technique and shallow acid engraving were ably used by both factories in their efforts to produce interesting glasses for the early twentieth-century devotees of *art nouveau.*

Cut, Engraved, and Etched Overlay Glassware

$\mathcal{E}$ngraved cased colored glassware as we know it today was produced in England in the eighteenth century, and in other parts of the world, too. On November 22, 1780, William Peckitt of York received a royal patent from King George III for manufacturing cut and engraved cased colored glass. Peckitt's specifications required that "the glass maker gather, either crown, flint, or any other sort of glass, from the melting pot while it is flexibly hot, which glass must then be marbled (rolled on a marver) level and smooth; then immediately he must gather upon that, over the whole or any particular place or places, a quantity of colored or stained glass of the same temper from another pot, which in like manner he must marble, blow, and spread level and smooth, heating in again the same as often as occasion shall require." Peckitt also claimed that the colored bulb could be gathered first and coated with uncolored glass in the same manner.

"The glass cutter," continued Peckitt, "by his apparatus of wheels and other instruments (as commonly used), with water, or oil and emery, must grind off so much of the colored glass from the uncolored glass, which must appear in ornamental devices in parts, polishing the same with oil, tripoli, and putty, as his ingenuity shall dictate." The finished product must have looked very much like the engraved beaker of ruby overlay glass shown in our illustrations.

On November 25, 1853, Emanuel Barthelemy, Tony Petitjean, and Jean Pierre Bourquin, all of London, England, patented their means for etching through cased colored glass to various depths to produce a

Engraved cased colored-glass pokal, blue over white over crystal. Made in Bohemia,
circa 1865, by Karl Pfohl. Height 30 inches.

Overlaid and cut covered sweetmeat jar, sapphire-blue on crystal. Cut crystal foot and finial. Possibly American; circa 1850. Height 7¾ inches.

shaded colored design. By using cut-out stencils a design was painted on the colored surface of the glass article with resists. Hydrofluoric acids etched away the exposed portions of the glass (those parts not protected by the resist) leaving a colored design in relief. Portions of this raised colored design were thinned down with acids, producing shaded colored patterns on a background of clear crystal or glass of another color. (This is very much like the process patented by Benjamin Richardson, June 20, 1857.)

Stevens & Williams of Brierley Hill, England, manufactured beautiful intaglio engraved cased colored glassware in the last quarter of the nineteenth century. The small vase with engraved mushrooms shown in our illustrations was produced from a blank of ivory-colored glass cased over with rose and purple glass. Similar wares in transparent rose, blue, and

Brierley Hill Library Collection
Engraved overlay compote by F. Zach. Height 13 inches.

green over ivory-colored glass were also produced by this firm. Joshua Hodgetts was the engraver most prominently associated with this type of engraved colored glassware at the Brierley Hill Glass Works.

Bohemian glass manufacturers were responsible for some very choice pieces of cut, etched, and engraved cased colored glass. The art developed in this area of Europe about the middle of the seventeenth century and continued to be a favorite type of glass embellishment far into the nineteenth and twentieth centuries. There is little to distinguish Bohemian cut overlay glassware from those made in England, France, and America from 1830 to 1880, and collectors will always be at variance with one another over a correct attribution.

Some of the most artistically engraved pieces of overlay glass came from the factory of F. Steigerwald in Munich, Germany, about 1855. The principal artist engaged in this factory was F. Zach. Zach's designs were engraved in colored relief, usually a deep blue, on crystal glass. The outer casing of blue glass was so skillfully thinned down that the subtle color gradations produced superb pictorial effects. Examples of Zach's work are to be found in the Brierley Hill Library collection, the Victoria and Albert Museum, and in many public and private collections all over the world.

The monumental covered pokal shown in our illustrations was engraved by Karl Pfohl, a Bohemian, about 1865. The triple cased glass—blue, over white, over crystal—has been expertly engraved with Pfohl's favorite subject, horses, in a style very similar to Zach's. However, Pfohl's works lack the superb details found only in Zach's productions.

Cutting and engraving cased colored blanks was more or less a universal art practiced in European and American glass factories between 1830 and 1880. Much of this kind of decorated glass was produced at the Boston & Sandwich Glass Works, but we can be certain that other American glass factories manufactured this same kind of decorated glass. Lura Woodside Watkins mentioned the beautiful work of Louis Vaupel and Henry Leighton, as well as others prominent in this field at the New England Glass Works, in her *Cambridge Glass*, published in 1930. Mrs.

Collection: Royal Ontario Museum, Canada
Cut and engraved overlay beaker. Ruby on crystal glass. Early eighteenth century. Height 5 inches.

Watkins also quoted from a letter written to Thomas Garfield by William Leighton, Jr., describing in detail a magnificent vase composed of four layers of glass that was cut and engraved by his father at the "New England."

Collection: H. S. Williams-Thomas
Cased colored-glass vase, purple, rose, and opal, with intaglio decoration. Engraved by Joshua Hodgetts at Stevens & Williams, Brierley Hill, England, circa 1885. Height 6 inches.

The Diatreta Technique

Diatreta vases, or "cage cups" as they are sometimes called, represent a group of Roman glasses which are covered with a network of thin glass supported by small glass struts. The few pieces known to us date from about the third or fourth century A.D. That part of the world in which most pieces have been found is known as the Roman-Germanic Cologne area. The latest find occurred at Niederemmel in 1950, and is now housed in the Landesmuseum in Trier, Germany.

At first examination these glasses seem to be essentially of the same kind, but there are variations which make it possible to classify them in three distinct groups:

(A) Diatreta which are completely covered by a network of glass.
(B) Diatreta with letters on the upper portion and an ornamental network on the lower portion.
(C) Diatreta with ornamental figure reliefs and a network of glass.

While the ancient Diatreta vases may differ in coloring they have certain characteristics which can be found in all vases.

(1) The basic form is that of a bell.
(2) The network is opened at the base.
(3) There is a padlike swelling at the rim of the vase.
(4) There are rosette ornaments at those points where the struts join the outer network with the body of the vase.

These four characteristics formed the basis for conclusions reached by several glass technologists and antiquarians. The famous eighteenth-century German archaeologist, art historian and antiquarian, Johann Joachim Winckelmann (1717–1768), discussed the Diatreta technique in his *Annotations on the History of the Arts among the Ancients*, suggesting that the cage cups were actually cut from a thick bodied beaker. This theory was championed by F. Fremersdorf in his article "Die Herstellung der Diatreta," published in Mainz in 1930. H. Eiden, the curator of the lately-found Trier Diatreta, agrees.

Practically speaking, it is difficult to reconcile oneself with Herr Fremersdorf since this theory presupposes that the ancients had access to drills and engraving tools similar to those used in modern dentistry. We are inclined to discount this, since we have no corroborating evidence to prove that implements as fine as these existed at such an early date.

Furthermore, it is unlikely that the ancients would choose so difficult a form as the bell shape to cut with their straight wheels. The traces of cutting found under the net and on the body of the ancient specimens referred to by Fremersdorf, in supporting his theory, would appear to be nothing more than attempts at correcting the fit of the two casings. Very few traces of grinding are evident on the outer wall of the inner body, and none are on the back of the network attached thereto.

Unless we are willing to agree that the ancients were capable of polishing these seemingly inaccessible areas we are forced to conclude that a Diatretum was formed by two cuplike bodies, joined together with small glass struts, instead of being cut from a thick-walled beaker.

Carl Friedrich published some papers on the Diatreta theory in the magazine *Sprechsaal* (1881 and 1882). Besides his own theory, which incidentally coincides somewhat with the Winckelmann-Fremersdorf observations, he advanced an idea sponsored by H. W. Schulz and de Rossi, who explained the manufacture of cage cups by stating that the body and net were made separately and afterwards fused together. This opinion is not shared by other glass technologists.

Reviewing the book *La Verrerie Antique* by W. Froehner (1879) in the *Bohner Almanach* (1882), Carl Friedrich wrote: "It seems to be difficult indeed to convince a nonexpert eye of the application of the production technique, whereas all experts who had the opportunity to see a Diatretum immediately agree on the production technique. Producers, makers, and grinders of glass who saw the Diatretum at the Antiquarian in Munich were convinced at first sight that it had been manufactured by the use of the grinding wheel. The work is said to be too time-consuming and impossible!

"I have published a few articles about the Diatreta in *Sprechsaal* (1881, No. 1, 4). These articles came to the eyes of a manager of a glass factory located in the Bavarian forest. Challenged by the fact that the ancients were credited with more achievements in some techniques than we ourselves, he went to Munich in order to inspect the Diatretum concerned. He then immediately initiated the undercutting and grinding through of pieces of glass in his factory.

"Thus, within the shortest time some brilliantly achieved pieces, completely undercut and ground through, were completed which are in no way inferior to the ancient Roman achievements. One such piece, a beer stein cover, could be seen at the Bavarian Exhibition of Industry, Trade and Art in Nuremberg where everybody could admire it as a masterly achievement. The factory concerned plans to produce an accurate copy of an old Roman Diatretum in the near future and believes to be able to do this for a few hundred marks since it requires hardly half a year to produce it. Therefore, away with the talk that it takes a whole lifetime to produce a Diatretum.

"Since so far all the experts agree on the manufacture of the Diatreta, this latest achievement is hoped to also dissuade scientists like Herr Froehner from their doubts. More details about the glass involved were reported by me in the *Ausstellungszeitung der Bayrischen Landesausstellung*, No. 71, and in *Sprechsaal*, 1882, No. 27."

The man who undertook the cutting of the pieces mentioned by Friedrich was Anton Roeck of the Ludwig Stangel Fabrik, at Spiegelau.

In 1932, O. Knapp proposed a theory which was later put to the test by W. von Eiff, a prominent glass engraver of our day. Knapp suggested the Diatreta were made by first forming the inner body of the cup, attaching rings of glass at equidistant points about this body, and then placing the inner body in a cup of glass made to receive it. After proper annealing the blank was cut through.

While this method approaches a more practical view of the manufacturing technique necessary to produce a Diatreta vase it was nevertheless reported a failure by Karl Weidmann, the man who collaborated with von Eiff in these experiments.

In his report to the Glastechnischen Gesellschaft (Frankfurt am Main, 1953), Karl Weidmann cast some doubt that a "real Diatretum" was ever made by Anton Roeck and further stated that he believed these attempts were limited to a revival of the ancient cutting technique, rather than to the making of a real Diatretum. This author has been unable to find any visible evidence of the wares made at Spiegelau, though certainly at least a stein cover was produced.

Having worked closely with von Eiff for some time during his Diatreta experiments, and finding these attempts to be a failure, Weidmann decided to approach the problem on his own, he produced a few examples one of which we illustrate.

Forming a double-walled cup of glass, Weidmann placed at regular intervals on its outer surface blobs of molten glass. He then pushed through the outer shell, at those points made soft by the blobs of hot glass, small glass rods which passed through the outer shell and attached themselves to the wall of the inner shell. The outer shell was again made smooth by grinding off the projections. Filling the aperture between the two shells of glass with wax, Weidmann was able thereby to lend the needed stability to withstand the pressures of the cutting operation.

Collection: Württembergische Metallwarenfabrik
Diatreta vase by Karl Weidmann. Circa 1939.

After closely examining the Trier Diatretum found some twelve years after he patented his process (Germany, July 28, 1939) Weidmann concluded that this specimen corroborated his interpretation of the ancient manufacturing process.

In more recent years Fred Carder of Corning, New York, produced several Diatreta vases by the ancient cire perdue or "lost wax" method, a predecessor of "investment casting." (See chapter on "Cire Perdue.")

In 1953 one piece of Mr. Carder's Diatreta was sent to Germany, along with an extensive collection of American glass, where it was seen and admired by Karl Wiedmann.

The noted Spanish-French glassman, Sala, has also produced modern Diatreta, but by what process is unknown to us. Mr. Sala prefers to keep his manufacturing methods a secret, a prerogative often exercised by artists.

The author has drawn a few conclusions of his own concerning the possible method of manufacture used by the ancients. The precise spacing of the supporting struts leads us to believe that the inner body was formed by blowing a gather of glass into a mold, the sides of which were fitted with indentations to form the supports on the outer surface of the blow. The blow, now studded with projections would then be lowered into a cup of glass of suitable size and shape and expanded by blowing until the supporting struts came into contact with the inner wall of the outer shell. Filling the space between the outer and inner shell with wax could be accomplished by cutting one or two preliminary holes in the outer shell and pouring the liquid wax between the walls of the blank. This method would seem practical to us today, a view shared by those technologists with whom we have discussed such a possibility.

Diatreta vase (translucent green and blue). Signed "Fred Carder, 1953."
Height 10 inches.

Vasa Murrhina, Spangled Glass and Spatterglass

One of the most colorful glasswares produced in the nineteenth century was named for the fabled "Vasa Murrhina". It was a ware in which the body was transparent and showed imbedded pieces of colored glass and mica flakes. Striking effects were obtained with opaque and transparent colored casings; the colored crumbs of glass and metallic flakes, picked up by rolling the plastic gather on a marver covered with such materials, sparkled through the outer skin of transparent glass, brightening the atmosphere of Victorian homes.

John Charles De Voy, assignor to the Vasa Murrhina Art Glass Company of Sandwich, Massachusetts, and Hartford, Conn., registered a patent on July 1, 1884, for a process of ornamenting glassware which consisted, essentially, in coating sheets or particles of mica with silver, gold, copper, or nickel, incorporating the coated mica with a ball of glass and subjecting the same to heat to cause the glass to flow over and adhere to the mica. The bulb of glass, thus treated, was then formed into a vase or other article of glassware. De Voy was associated with Dr. R. C. Flowers at this time, but in 1882 he was in business with Theophilus D. Farrall in the Farrall Venetian Art Glass Manufacturing Company of Brooklyn, New York. It is possible that some of De Voy's decorating techniques were originally produced by Farrall.

Diggings at the site of the Vasa Murrhina Art Glass Company in Sandwich, Massachusetts, which was originally built by Deming Jarves after his separation from the Boston & Sandwich Glass works in 1858, un-

Vasa Murrhina jug (multicolored and splashed with green Aventurine).
Circa 1884. Height 5 inches.

earthed a multitude of shards proving that this factory produced Vasa Murrhina Glassware in quantity. The shards all showed splotches of vivid colors and crumbs of Aventurine and mica flecks throughout the metal. Some were heavily cased with dark colored glasses against which the brilliant splashes of color and spangles sparkled like jewels. Shards of gayly colored Vasa Murrhina Glassware were found on the old factory site of the Boston & Sandwich works; some gave evidence of having been pattern-molded in the Venetian Diamond pattern.

Between 1878 and 1882 the following patents for producing a type of Vasa Murrhina Glassware were registered in England: No. 314, to William Webb Boulton, dated January 25, 1879; No. 2880, to Theophilus D. Farrall, dated July 1, 1881; also No. 2913, dated July 4, 1881 (patented in the U.S.A. on August 8, 1882) to Mr. Farrall; No. 5737, to Rice William Harris of the Islington Glass Works, Birmingham, England (he was then residing in Calais, France), dated December 31, 1881; and No. 5324, to Arthur John Nash (later associated with Louis C. Tiffany), dated November 8, 1882. At that time Nash was living in Wordsley, England, and was employed by Sir Edward Webb as manager of the Whitehouse Glass Works in Stourbridge, England.

January 29, 1884, a patent was issued to William Leighton, Jr. of Hobbs, Brockunier & Company covering his method of manufacturing "Spangled Glassware." Leighton's process was a simple one and consisted in rolling a bulb of opaque white or transparent colored glass over a marver covered with metallic flakes (biotite or mica). The flakes adhered to the plastic glass. Next the parison was dipped into a pot of fluid, transparent metal locking in the spangles. It was then ready to be blown and shaped into the article desired. Spangled Glass was produced in "Turquoise, Ormolu, Lazuline and Indian," all trade names for the various colors Hobbs, Brockunier & Company employed for this ware at that time. Full-page color advertisements appeared in the *Crockery & Glass Journal* late in the year 1883 offering various table and decorative wares to the trade, including the small spangled jug shown in our illustrations. Spangled Glass became one of the most popular art and tablewares produced by the Wheeling works.

Contemporary to Mr. Leighton's "Spangled Glassware," Sowerby's of Newcastle-upon-Tyne, England, produced a spangled ware which they termed "Blue Nugget." It differs but a little from Leighton's colorful

Spangled jug (cobalt-blue body plated with amber glass).
Hobbs, Brockunier & Co., 1884. Height 6 inches.

glassware. Taking up a bulb of colored metal, usually a dark cobalt blue, the worker rolled it over a marver that had been previously sprinkled with biotite or mica flakes and then plated the bulb with a layer of transparent crystal or colored glass. The article was then blown into a full-size mold to shape it. If the article was plated with amber glass the spangles appeared to be small nuggets of gold; if crystal glass was used the natural silver color of the biotite or mica flakes showed through the outer casing. Other transparent colored platings produced different effects which were very pleasing.

John Samuel Irwin of Saltsburg, Pennsylvania, registered a patent for producing a type of Spatterglass on August 1, 1893. Irwin's method was not much different from any other in use at that time, but it appears to be one of the few patents for Spatterglass production recorded in America. We found no association between Irwin and a glass factory in Saltsburg, but it is quite possible that the Spatterglass technique he patented was used in a glass factory in nearby Pittsburgh, Pennsylvania.

Collectors have given the nomenclature of "Spatterglass" to glassware with variegated colors applied to a body of opaque white or colored glass but not having either metallic flakes or aventurine crumbs added thereto. These wares were simple to manufacture and it would only be repeating the same process used to manufacture Spangled Glassware if we were to relate it here.

Several factories in Europe produced Vasa Murrhina Glass, Spangled Glass, and Spatterglass during the 1800 to 1890 period. The J. B. Graesser glass factory in Zwickau, Germany, published a catalog of such wares which they made in the form of vases, baskets, and bowls with applied thorny and floral decorations.

Collection: Lang Art Gallery Committee, Newcastle-upon-Tyne
Molded "Blue Nugget" vases. The fourth from the left is molded "Vitro Porcelain" (mottled blue and green). All made by Sowerby's, Newcastle-upon-Tyne. Circa 1880.

Splashed pattern vase (red, white and yellow). First century A.D.

Variegated, colorful glassware of the type we have had under discussion has a very ancient ancestry. The splashed pattern vase shown in our illustrations is attributed to Syria in the first century A.D.

Clutha Glassware

Shortly before the turn of the century, about 1895, James Couper & Sons of Glasgow, Scotland, produced a glassware which they marketed under the trade name "Clutha." The name was derived from an old Scottish word meaning "cloudy."

To produce Clutha glassware a worker took up a light gather of pale ruby or pale yellow colored glass and rolled it over a marver lightly strewn with bits of colored glass and mica flecks. The gather was reheated at the glory hole and blown and tooled into the finished form. Couper's Clutha glassware is full of character and quaintness, with little specks of color, bubbles, and a general contour which tends to render the shape visible.

James Couper & Sons employed the well-known English designer Christopher Dresser to design several of the forms in which their Clutha glass was made. Dresser's designs are identified by the initials "C. D." which are incorporated with the manufacturer's mark for Clutha glass. Most of Dresser's designs were registered at the Patent Office in London.

James Couper & Sons' mark for their "Clutha" glassware.

Another designer, George Walton of Glasgow, also supplied Couper & Sons with designs for Clutha glassware, and his initials will probably be found on pieces of this ware in connection with the maker's mark and the name "Clutha" etched lightly in the base of the object.

About 1930 the Steuben Glass Works produced a somewhat similar ware which they named "Cluthra." A. Douglas Nash Corporation (successors to Tiffany Furnaces), and the Vineland Flint Glass Works of Victor Durand also made glass of this character.

Collection: George Welch
Clutha vase designed by Christopher Dresser; body of glass of transparent gold-colored glass with streaks of ruby, opaque white, and mica flecks dispersed throughout the bubbly glass.

Onyx Glassware

On February 1, 1889, George W. Leighton of Findlay, Ohio, "Assignor to the Dalzell, Gilmore & Leighton Company, of the same place," filed a patent application for the manufacture of a decorative glassware which was sold under the name "Onyx." The patent was awarded Mr. Leighton on April 23, 1889, and it would be safe to assume that production was in effect about this date.

The method of manufacture was ingenious and could be expected of a man whose family tree boasted many enterprising and adroit glassmen. No illustrations accompanied Mr. Leighton's patent application, but the text of his specifications leaves little doubt as to how his invention was carried out.

Briefly, the specifications bring out the following points: Onyx Glassware was made from a sensitive mixture containing metallic constituents capable of producing silver, ruby and other lusters; the coloration came about when the still glowing mass was subjected to heat and gaseous fumes. Two molds were used, one to produce the raised ornamentation, the other to bring the article to full size and ultimate shape. The enumeration of particulars would lead one to believe that Onyx was made from a homogeneous stock since no mention of casing or plating is made by Mr. Leighton. This, however, was not always the case.

Patents, we must remember, especially those dealing with the effects obtained by chemical aids, are purposely worded so that the important details of the process covered are hidden; the style of presentation being

207

such as to prevent a copying of the exact method of manufacture and at the same time forming a deterrent to would-be infringers. To a degree this was the case with Mr. Leighton's account of his formula for producing Onyx Glassware.

There are many varieties of lusters and effects produced by the action of gases upon metal impregnated glass mixtures, not only by sulphurous fumes but also by reducing gases which bring the metals in the glass to the surface where they mass and give off metallic effects. The degree of heat alters and varies the effect of color, and also the mixture and the strength of the gases will modify the color shades. John Northwood II and his father experimented with such mixtures and found it often difficult to obtain consistent and similar results. This problem was also faced by Dalzell, Gilmore & Leighton in producing their beautiful Onyx wares.

A chemical analysis of finished glassware often reveals more of the processes of manufacture than patent papers. The following summation of such a chemical analysis of numerous shards of various types of Onyx glassware, obtained from the glasshouse site in Findlay, Ohio, proves how true this is in the case of Leighton's Onyx patent.

Silver (Platinum) Luster: Although it was possible to produce a silver luster on this ware, utilizing the method suggested by George Leighton in his patent specifications, this was not the means whereby this effect was produced. Instead, Silver Onyx was produced in this way. The body of the article, ranging in hue from a creamy opaque white to a clam-broth color and sometimes approaching a pale orange, was produced from a sensitive opal glass melt. It would appear to be cased or plated glassware but is in reality homogeneous. The illusion of plating or casing is the result of imperfectly turning or developing the opalescence in the metal. The gaffer dipped his blowpipe into a pot of fluid glass and developed the opalescence slightly by quickly cooling the bulb and reheating it at the glory hole. Two, and sometimes three, additional platings were taken up over this original bulb of opalescent glass, all from the same pot of metal, and each in its turn developed in color as the first was. In this way the several platings were developed to different degress of opalescence. Since the inner casing, or the original bulb, was reheated more than the successive platings, it developed a denser color. The pattern-molded article, when it had properly annealed, had its raised floral design painted with a platinum luster, after which it was fired in a muffle to fix the stain. The degree of color in these silver pieces of Onyx was governed by the amount of platinum luster applied.

Collectors would be well advised not to clean their silver luster Onyx pieces with household abrasive cleaners or steel-wool pads, since these will easily remove the applied stain. Constant washings will no doubt have an adverse effect on the lustrous decoration and should be avoided whenever possible.

Author's Collection
"Onyx" cream pitcher. Platinum luster on cream ground. Height 5 inches.

Ruby (Pink) Onyx: The ruby pieces found to date are all cased with opal glass. The outer plating is composed of a sensitive, transparent gold-ruby metal. After the article was pattern molded, and before it was blown to full size in the second mold, the bulb was quickly cooled below a glowing red heat with a blast of cool air and then reheated at the glory hole. The sensitive outer skin struck a red color on the raised ornamentation. The original idea was to produce a raised motif in ruby-red on a white ground; but, since it was difficult to control the coloring, some articles are a more vivid red than others, and many times the entire piece struck a ruby-red. The raised ornamentation stands out on these latter specimens because more ruby glass was collected at those prominent points. This difficulty in controlling the color was one of the primary factors accounting for the discontinuance of this ware by the manufacturer.

Amber Onyx: Again, only cased pieces of this ware have come to light. The opal lining makes a good background for the beautiful shades of transparent amber developed in this variant with the aid of heat and gaseous fumes. The outer plating or skin of glass, containing an oxide of uranium, produced a rich amber color, especially when a small amount of iron oxide was also added to the batch. In treating the pattern-molded bulb in the heated vapors to develop the color resident in the glass, the problem of control was again encountered. When the desired hue was obtained with caloric and gaseous aids it was "frozen in" by rapid cooling; but the worker could not always determine when this desired color had been attained, the mass being in a still somewhat glowing red state. In arresting the coloring operation by rapid cooling, the danger of fracturing the article was always present. These thermal changes were particularly hazardous in the plated wares, and the resultant losses were another factor that put an all-too-soon end to the production of Onyx.

Orange Onyx: By adding larger amounts of iron oxide to a uranium amber melt, a rich orange color, sometimes approaching red, was developed. This applied skin against an opal lining was, when developed with heat and gases to a rich color, easily one of the most pleasing effects ever produced in Onyx Glassware. The mechanics of its manufacture are similar to, or the same as, those employed in making ruby and amber Onyx.

Orchid and Purple Onyx: To a transparent white metal (crystal), manganese and a small amount of cobalt were added, producing a sensitive plating for the orchid and purple pieces of Onyx. Again the color was developed through thermal and gaseous reaction on the metals colloidally dispersed throughout the glass. So far only cased specimens of this ware have been discovered, and few of these at that. The opal lining of the articles is a wonderful foil for the jewel-like coloring of this variation.

Green Onyx: We have heard of this color, but have not seen any examples. Since we have not had a piece in hand to examine, we can only form a conjectural opinion as to the basis for this green color. It is probably a chrome oxide, although iron and nickel oxides could also produce a green color.

Author's Collection
"Onyx" tumbler (orange-amber glass cased with white).

Opalescent Onyx: Opalescent Glassware was produced long before Onyx came into being, even before William Leighton, Jr. patented his process on June 1, 1886, for manufacturing opalescent hobnail glassware for Messrs. Hobbs, Brockunier & Company.

The shards of Onyx we have examined indicated that a bulb of colored transparent metal was plated with a transparent white metal made sensitive to thermal changes. This sensitive skin, after being pattern molded, was quickly cooled below a glowing red and reheated at the glory hole till it struck opalescent white on the raised pattern. So far the author has found only acidized pieces of this ware, although it is quite probable that some articles were left in their original glossy condition.

The Onyx molds were used to produce articles in homogeneous, transparent ruby (cranberry-red) and opaque black glass. These wares are in scant evidence and could be considered rare, though they run a poor second in appearance to those variants discussed in preceding paragraphs. The black glass was sometimes used in a pedestal base for Onyx oil lamps, the bowl or font being composed of silver Onyx glass. Shades for these lamps were probably of etched crystal.

Although we have not seen other colors in this variant, it would be reasonable to assume that such might exist but have not yet been brought to public attention.

The raised ornamentation on the pattern-molded Onyx Glass is well known to collectors. It has been described in many ways; for the sake of conformity we suggest it be called a floral pattern or design. We have heard of another pattern in this ware, described as "Snowflake," but seemingly no one has had a piece in hand.

The concentric rings found on the bottom of some Onyx pieces were an integral part of the pattern molding designed to add stability.

Because of the difficulties in controlling the colors of these wares—in particular those produced by an application of heat and gaseous fumes—several shades of rose, amber, orange, orchid and purple will be encountered. The question, "Is this another variant" may arise. We say, "No, basically it will be the same as its near brothers and sisters in color, due to the fact that its coloring was produced from the same ingredients and under the same conditions, sometimes from the same melt."

Rough rims are the rule and not the exception with Onyx Glassware, especially those pieces made from opalescent or other sensitive metals.

Fire polishing these extremities would have resulted in a change of character or color, therefore they were simply cut off where the mold-line indicated the rim should be and ground down on a wheel to a tolerable smoothness. An interesting fact encountered by the author is that whereas chips or small damages to other nineteenth-century glasses, free-blown, pressed, or pattern-molded, decidedly affect the article's value such is not the case with Onyx Glass. Rim chips, minute or not, are more or less the rule and considered of no real importance by collectors of this beautiful glassware.

Collection: Mrs. Robert Neiman
"Onyx" covered sugar bowl (white opalescent design on ruby ground). Height 5 inches.

Two very interesting reports were found in contemporary newspapers published in Findlay, Ohio, concerning Leighton's Onyx ware. The first appeared in *The Findlay Daily Courier*, September 30, 1889. It stated: "George W. Leighton, who has been a metal worker at the Dalzell, Gilmore & Leighton Company glassworks, has resigned that position, but still retains his interest in the firm." The reference to Leighton as a "metal worker" implies that he made glass molds, and more than likely he made the molds used to manufacture his Onyx Glass.

The second report was published in the *National Glass Budget* on October 3, 1889. "Just as we go to press," it said, "we are informed that Dalzell, Gilmore & Leighton of Findlay, Ohio, has given their men a week's notice preparatory to closing down the whole factory. This action is said to be necessitated because the famous oriental ware, in which they heavily invested, is found to be as brittle as it is beautiful, and the heavy breakage makes it unprofitable for dealers to handle it. It is hoped, however, that the stop is only temporary and that the firm will recover from this misfortune." The reference to "oriental ware" is obviously a mistake on the part of the reporter, and we feel certain that he was referring instead to Dalzell, Gilmore & Leighton's Onyx Glassware. Leighton may have resigned a few days before this second report was published because of the manufacturing difficulties his firm incurred with the production of his Onyx Glass.

One of the rarest forms of Onyx Glassware is the small compote shown in our color illustrations. It is made of light opaque pink glass, pressed and hand-tooled to form a frilly edge. Rococo silver lustre designs decorate the inside top of the compote, while the underside, stem and foot, have been treated with an Agata-like mottling of light green metallic stain. The compote is signed on the underside of the foot: "Onyx/ Pat./1889." Since this compote is so unlike the other Onyx wares mentioned earlier it has probably gone undetected by many dealers and collectors.

Silveria

$\mathcal{A}$ ware akin to the Fondi d'Oro, or Gold Sandwich Glass of ancient times, was produced by Stevens & Williams, of Brierley Hills, at the turn of the century. Its inventor, John Northwood II, named it "Silveria." In our talks with Mr. Northwood in his home at Brierley Hills in 1956, he told us that he developed this type of silvered glassware about 1900; his father was not in good health at the time, but nevertheless was present in the shop during the experiments, lending encouragement and offering helpful suggestions.

Silveria was made by sandwiching silver foil between two layers of transparent crystal or colored glass. The trick of production lay in the fact that the primary bulb was blown to almost full size before the foil was picked up by the plastic glass from the marver. A protective film of glass was then placed over the foil by dipping the bulb into a pot of fluid metal. Trailings of colored glass were dripped here and there on the surface of the article, sometimes haphazardly, sometimes with purpose of design.

Mr. Northwood's Silveria would seem not to have been a unique type of glassware, for as early as February 13, 1878, Paul Raoul de Facheux d'Humy, of Litchfield Street, Soho, County of Middlesex, England, patented a somewhat similar means for decorating glass. This method differed from Northwood's in that the primary bulb was not blown to full size before picking up the silver or gold foil from the marver; consequently, when the parison was expanded to full size the foil imprisoned

215

Collection: Brierley Hill Libraries
"Silveria" vase (silver leaf ground with trailings of bright green glass).
Height 5 inches.

between the two layers of glass tore apart giving a somewhat different effect than Silveria.

Still another patent for applying metals in the manufacture of glassware was registered in England on November 29, 1878, through a patent attorney, under the name of Messieurs Monot, Père et Fils, & Stumpf, of Paris, France. This invention related to a process of applying a layer of gold or other metal foil either between two layers or thicknesses of glass or crystal, or on the exterior thereof, for the purpose of producing the ornamental effect known in France as "Chine' Metallique."

Several methods for the manufacture of this ware were suggested in the patent specifications. The only real difference between Messrs. Monot & Stumpf's and d'Humy's processes was that the former suggested making the outer shell first and coating the inside of this "envelope" or "cap" of glass to seal the metallic substance between the two layers of glass. Further expansion of the metallized bulb resulted in the tearing of the metallic sheet or coating between the layers of glass, producing the effect mentioned in d'Humy's specifications.

The decorative techniques suggested in the d'Humy, and Monot-Stumpf patent papers were used to some extent by the exponents of *art nouveau*. Galle, Rousseau, the brothers Daum, and others introduced sheets of silver and gold foil within the walls of their many-skinned glasses with some very interesting and beautiful results.

One factor on which all of these various wares depended for their lasting beauty was airtightness. No cracks could occur in the outer or inner skin of the article; if they did the exposed metallic foil, especially the silver foil, would oxidize and discolor. A small experimental piece given to the author by Mr. Northwood has many such fissures in its outer surface; consequently it is now somewhat discolored wherever these crackles appear.

Pieces of Silveria are sometimes found marked "S & W" for Stevens & Williams. Mr. Northwood never patented his Silveria. In spite of its necessarily high production cost, Silveria was a good seller and collectors should have no trouble in finding specimens of this handsome glassware.

Silvered Glass

In the waning years of the seventeenth century Silvered Glass balls of Continental origin were used to brighten the atmosphere of English and Continental houses. The hollow interiors of the glass balls were silvered with a solution containing bismuth, lead, tin and mercury. The solution was poured into the receptacle through a small aperture, sloshed around to coat the interior, or inner surface, of the glass object, and then the excess liquor poured out. The opening was plugged or otherwise sealed to protect the inner surface coating from the ruinous effect of atmospheric conditions.

Several patents for silvering glass were registered in England in the middle of the nineteenth century, but not all of them were applicable to art-glass forms. Thomas Drayton, a London chemist, registered a patent for a silvering process that he used on glass blanks purchased from Bohemian sources. He protected the silvered surface of his glass from atmospheric influences by coating it with varnish, by which a certain amount of dullness was communicated to the reflecting surface. Even so, the silvering deteriorated rapidly and Drayton was forced to seek another means for producing silvered glassware. On December 11, 1848, he filed another patent for silvering glassware, but this, too, proved unsatisfactory.

Frederick Hale Thomson and Edward Varnish registered a joint patent for silvering glassware on December 19, 1849, which was not only successful, but extremely beautiful, too. These wares were manufactured by Varnish & Company of London using double-walled vessels made expressly for their use by James Powell & Sons' White Friar Glass Works in London.

218

Two methods for producing the double-walled vessels were outlined in the Thomson-Varnish patent. The first called for the double-walled vessels to be blown all in one piece; the second outlined a means for joining the inner and outer walls of a double-walled vessel with a metal ring or rim which was fastened to the two pieces with plaster of Paris. One of the more important elements of the patent referred to cased colored blanks—red, blue, green, purple, and yellow glass plated over the outer casing of crystal glass—which were cut intaglio to produce interesting colored and silvered patterns in the finished article.

Almost exactly the same processes for the manufacture of silvered glassware with colored and cut decorations was patented by Frederick Hale Thomson and Thomas Mellish on August 22, 1850. The *London Illustrated News* (July 6, 1850) reported that examples of this silvered glassware could be seen at Mr. Mellish's offices, 48 Berners Street, London, and that "many of the ornamental examples are relieved and enriched by cutting and engraving and in those in which the glass is colored the result is exceedingly beautiful and quite novel. The ruby is particularly rich in effect, while some of the greens forcibly remind us of the colored metallic brilliance of the wing-cases of certain tropical beetles." Mellish exhibited some very beautiful examples of this richly colored and cut silvered glassware at the Crystal Palace in 1851.

George Dodd, the author of *The Curiosities of Industry and the Applied Sciences* (London, 1857), had this to say about Thomson's silvered glassware: "The silvered glass produced by the method of Mr. Hale Thomson is a product of singular beauty. Whether in the form of cups or goblets, of tazzas or wine-coolers, of epergnes, ewers, candelabra, inkstands, salt or sugar-boxes, of flat mirrors or of mirror globes, it exhibits a brilliancy of hue that can hardly fail to arrest attention. It is to the combination of colour with silvering that we owe this result. Some months ago, Mr. Donaldson, in advocating the use of this material for architectural decoration, especially in the adornment of shop-fronts, stated that the influence of the silver on the colour gave rise to tints almost unknown before, and such as no combination of the ordinary colouring ingredients could imitate. It may, in this respect, be compared to the Diorama, which differs from other pictures in being viewed by reflected and transmitted light conjointly; the glass presents the reflective power of the silver with the transmissive or transparent power of the coloured

Courtesy of The Henry Ford Museum, Dearborn, Michigan

Engraved Silvered Glass goblet (*left*) plated with green glass. E. Varnish & Co., London. Circa 1850. Silvered Glass vase (*right*) blue overlaid on crystal and cut through in a design of flowers and leaves. The inner and outer sections of the vase have been joined together at the rim with a metal seal in accordance with the method outlined in a patent issued to Frederick Hale Thomson and Edward Varnish, dated at London, England, December 19, 1849. Height 7⅞ inches.

medium. The most conspicuous products, perhaps, are the mirror globes, which present every variety of brilliant colour, and have a size of from two inches to thirty inches in diameter, but, excellently as these illustrate the combination of effects just alluded to, they are not so delicately beautiful as articles of more diverse form, where endless nuances are produced by the different angles at which the light is reflected to the eye. So much more brilliant is the argentine reflection than that produced by the mercury-amalgam at the back of a looking-glass, that it is contemplated to employ this glass in many useful ways for optical and scientific instruments."

Some very interesting effects in Silvered Glass were invented by a man named Kidd. In this method, devices or patterns were cut on the under surface of the glass and the small facets were silvered; the result was that innumerable tiny mirrors threw up reflections in every direction. This was the case where colored or colorless transparent glass was employed. When multicolored glass was used many novel combinations presented themselves. Sometimes Kidd used first a primary layer of transparent glass; then an opaque layer of white glass was poured over this; and, lastly, a layer of ruby glass on the white. The many-skinned glass article was then cut to various depths and in many designs, and, whether silvered or not, a rich color effect was produced. Specimens of Mr. Kidd's "Embossed Glass," as well as his "Silvered Glass" were exhibited at the great Exhibition of 1851.

Glittering Silvered Glass Christmas tree ornaments were made in France and Bohemia around the middle of the nineteenth century, as well as other articles for decorative and table use. Some of the French

Silvered Glass jug with sterling silver top. Boston Silver-Glass Co., Cambridge, Mass., 1865. Height 7 inches.

pieces are marked "Depose" indicating that the process for silvering was registered in France.

Silvered Glassware was made by the New England Glass Company of Cambridge, Massachusetts, whose William Leighton patented a means for producing fine Silvered Glass door knobs on January 16, 1855. The patented means was applied to other articles for table and decorative use.

Tony Petitjean, of Tottenham Court Road, London, registered a patent in England (July 24, 1855) and in America (October 21, 1856) for silvering glass sheets and hollow-wares.

John W. Haines of Somerville, Massachusetts, who was associated with the Union Glass Works in Somerville, Massachusetts, and the Boston Silver-Glass Company in Cambridge, Massachusetts, registered a process for producing hollow glass vessels with an inner compartment for silvering. The Silvered Glass jug with sterling silver top and engraved

A group of Silvered Glass articles, possibly of Continental origin. Circa 1850.

vintage design bears the date of Mr. Haines' patent about the silver fitting, April 4, 1865.

Henry Balen Walker of New York City filed a means for silvering glassware at the patent offices in Washington, D.C., on December 14, 1869. The formula closely follows the original Drayton process, adding a heavy coating of litharge, red lead and oil to seal in the silvering compound and protect it from the damaging effects of the atmosphere.

On January 30, 1872, Dominique Durand registered his process for silvering glassware and mirrors. It parallels Petitjean's formula, adding a protective sealant to cover the Silvered Glassware and protect it from atmospheric damage.

Some other American factories producing Silvered Glass in the last half of the nineteenth century were The Boston & Sandwich Glass Works, Cape Cod; The Mt. Washington Glass Company, New Bedford; The Brooklyn Flint Glass Company, Brooklyn, New York; and Dithridge & Company of Pittsburgh, Pennsylvania.

Surface decorations on Silvered Glass were confined mostly to shallow engraving, colored enamels, and sometimes the articles were painted with gold or other colored transparent stains, usually on the inner surface of the article to simulate a gold-wash or silver-gilt.

There seems to have been no limitation put on the possibilities for Silvered Glassware, for the articles made range from large gazing balls to tablewares, candlesticks, statues, door knobs and curtain tiebacks. Ornaments of almost every description were manufactured by several factories both in America and abroad. Sometimes the articles are marked, revealing the manufacturer's name and location, as, for example, are those fine wares made by Varnish & Company, but most are unattributable because they lack this factor.

Silver Deposit

Silver Deposit, or "solid deposit" as it was known to the trade, was accomplished by putting a base for the metal on the glass and burning it onto the glass. The base was a powdered flux containing a large proportion of silver. After firing the article in a kiln to set the flux, the silver base was scratch-buffed with a brush and water. The article was then suspended from a negative copper wire in a silver plating solution in which pure silver anodes were suspended. A current of two volts, or thirty amperes, was used for a period of six hours and a heavy coating of the silver was deposited upon the silver flux base. The deposit was then buffed and polished with rouge to a bright finish and sometimes engraved with beautiful designs.

In his patent specifications for decorating Lava Glassware, dated September 30, 1879, Frederick Shirley suggests the electro-depositing of metals on the surface of the glass to produce the illusion of "cloisonné." This means of decorating glass with metallic deposits is spoken of in a familiar way by Mr. Shirley, indicating that the process had long been a well-known means of embellishing glassware.

There are several means for depositing silver and other metals on glass and china patented in the last half of the nineteenth century. The principal ones were registered by Oscar Pierre Erard (England) and John H. Scharling (U.S.A.).

On May 9, 1889, Oscar Pierre Erard and John Benjamin Round, both of Birmingham, England, registered a simple and effective method for

Silver Deposit jug by Erard. Circa 1889.

electro-depositing gold, silver, copper and other metallic designs on glass, porcelain and earthenware. Forming a flux of seven parts of calcined borax, three parts of sand, four parts of oxide of lead, one part of nitrate of potash, one half part of phosphate of lime and two parts of white arsenic, which was crushed and washed after it had melted and cooled, they added to this powdered flux silver in the proportions of ten parts of silver to four and one half parts of flux powder. These ingredients were ground together to effect a thorough mixture. This was then formed into a "wash" by being mixed with turpentine. This wash was applied with a brush over the particular parts of the article which were to be covered with the deposited metal so as to form the required design. The article was then burnt in a kiln and after being thoroughly cleaned was placed in a solution of the particular metal required to be deposited, which deposit was effected by the aid of a dynamo or any cell battery.

In cases where a raised or incised ornamentation was required, it was either formed by the article being first prepared with the ordinary raised paste known to the trade, prior to being covered with the wash, or the metal could be engraved after it had been heavily deposited on the surface of the glass. The small jug with a silver deposit design shown in our illustrations is an example of Erard's work, done about 1889, from the collection of Messrs. Stevens & Williams of Brierley Hill.

John H. Scharling of Newark, New Jersey, registered two means for producing raised metallic designs on glassware. The first was dated March 7, 1893. The article to be decorated was first covered entirely with a thin film of silver deposit in the usual way in an electroplating bath. A design was painted on the silvered surface of the article with a resist and the article subjected to an acid bath which dissolved away all the metal not protected by the resist. A continuous piece of rubber, formed to the contours of the article, was slipped over the said article and then vulcanized so that it carried the raised design of the silver deposit on its inner surface. This rubber covering was removed from the article, reversed, and the portions not carrying the raised design were cut away. This formed a mask that could be slipped over similarly shaped articles after they had been covered with a metallic deposit. The articles so masked were then subjected to acid baths to dissolve away all the exposed metal showing through the perforated rubber mask, or they were sandblasted to remove the exposed metallic surfaces from the object.

Scharling's second patented method was dated September 26, 1893. It was a much simpler operation and produced a richer looking article of glassware. The glass article to be decorated was first wholly coated with a silver deposit by repeatedly flowing thereon an easily decomposable silver solution by means of a pump, while slowly turning or moving the article during the process. The thin layer of silver so deposited on the article formed a base for electro-depositing a layer of gold and another layer of silver, thus sandwiching a layer of gold between two layers of silver. The designs were painted on the surface of the multiplated article with a resist varnish and the unwanted portions of silver and gold deposits were etched away. Beautiful designs were engraved on the intermediate layers of gold and silver producing a rich ornamental glassware.

Silver Deposit continued to be a favorite means for decorating glass and pottery until just after the First World War. It has made an appearance on and off the market since that time, the more recent productions being made tarnish-proof by plating over the silver deposit with rhodium.

Metal Encased Glassware

$\mathcal{F}$or many centuries glass workers have enhanced their works of art with mountings of gold, silver, pewter, lead, and other metals—the glass articles being made to the desired shape and the metal fixtures or mounts fashioned to fit its form.

On August 18, 1884, an easier means for producing a similar effect was patented by Fritz Heckert of Petersdorf, Germany. For this purpose Mr. Heckert employed open metalwork ornaments formed by stamping, casting, pressing, or by galvanic deposit. These he placed in a mold so as to lie close against its sides. A gather of glass was introduced into the mold and blown to fill it entirely, thereby coming into contact with the metalwork structure and adhering to it. After the article was released from the mold, the "blow-over" (that part of the bulb which came above the desired height of the article) was removed and the rim fire-polished to a smooth finish.

When ornaments consisting of separated pieces of metal, porcelain, glass, mosaic, beads, precious stones, and the like were to be used, they were cemented with their faces to some material or fabric that would be destroyed by heat. The matrix was placed in a mold so as to present the back surfaces to the glass when it was blown into the mold. The ornaments were thus embedded in and, in some cases, cemented or melted onto the glass while the backing to which they were attached was either destroyed by the heat or subsequently removed by solvents.

In Heckert's patent illustrations Figure 1 shows the metal framework in the mold and the gather of glass already blown into it. The "blow-

Author's Collection
Ruby glass vase encased in gilded metalwork frame. (See text for full description and an explanation of the manufacturing process involved in this interesting work of art.)
Height 10 inches.

over" is seen extending above the mold. Figures 2 and 3 show other types of metalwork, used here in making tumblers. Figure 4 represents a cloth matrix on which beads of glass were cemented in fancy patterns. This matrix was placed inside the mold; the glass blown into the mold picks up the design of beads on its outer surface, as shown in Figure 5.

After the articles were formed, it was a simple task to plate base metals like copper, brass, or lead, with gold or silver deposit.

On June 28, 1901, the Faulkner Bronze Company of Birmingham, England, headed by Thomas Birkett and Frederick George Faulkner, patented a process for Metal Encased Glassware which more or less duplicates Heckert's methods. The main feature, as outlined in the Faulkner patent specifications, provided that the glass be blown into a perforated metal shell so that it projected through the openings, producing a very beautiful ornamental effect.

Heckert's method for producing Metal Encased Glassware soon came into universal use. Stevens & Williams of Brierley Hill, England, manufactured Venetian-style lamp globes—large bulging bubbles of colored glass protruding through a simple metal framework. Glass factories in Bohemia made decanters and steins with pewter or German silver frameworks. As early as 1878 such wares were being exhibited at the Paris Exposition by Salviati & Company of Venice, Italy. Tiffany Furnaces produced metal encased glassware for many purposes for their subsidiary, Tiffany Studios of New York City; at Tiffany's works it was known as Reticulated" ware.

The illustrations from Heckert's patent papers. (See text for explanation.)

Lava Glassware

On December 12, 1878, an article entitled "Aetna and its Lava Streams" appeared in the *Crockery & Glass Journal*. The story rather dramatically introduced a new kind of glassware made by the Mt. Washington Glass Company. The glass was composed primarily of volcanic lava. According to some accounts related in this journal the variety of effects produced were very attractive and graded from a soft velvety porphyry finish to a brilliant mosaic, making it difficult to decide which was the most beautiful.

"Sicilian Ware," as the new material was called, in view of its chief element being obtained from "the lava flows of Mt. Aetna," was introduced in all the leading stores where it attracted considerable attention, some of the ornaments being "very grotesque and pleasing."

Prior to its introduction to the trade, Frederick Shirley patented two means for producing his Lava Glassware. The first patent, dated May 28, 1878, covers a compound that was capable of being blown, pressed or otherwise fashioned, and which consisted of seven parts of clear flint batch, one part carbonate of potash or its equivalent, and two parts of lava or volcanic slag. The slag, being mixed with vitreous impurities, mixed with and colored the mass, producing various tints and colors, which were varied as the proportions of the ingredients were changed. When the melted mass was in the proper condition for working, it was blown or otherwise molded into any shape desired. Shirley emphasized that this melt was especially adapted for making copies of antique urns and vases and copies of works of art.

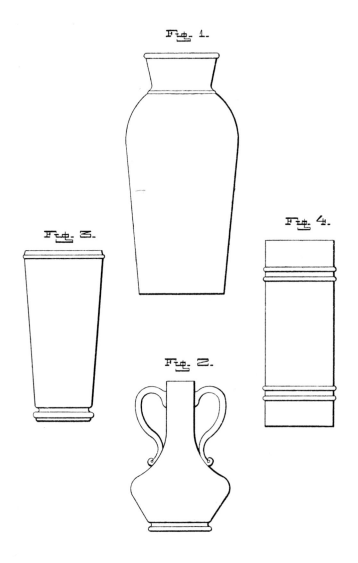

Witnesses.

J. W. Garner

Will H. Kerr

Inventor.

F. S. Shirley

per

F. A. Lehmann,

atty.

Drawings from F. S. Shirley's patent specifications (May 28, 1878).

If desired, regular glass, except clear flint and plain white or opal glass, which decolorizes the coloring mixture, could be used and colored with the necessary chemicals to produce the required colors and to render them opaque, either by coating or backing with such dense coloring matter as vitrified cobalt, taffee, calcined vitriol, or their equivalents for the several colors required. These substances were used as a substitute for the lava.

Shirley suggested in his patent specifications that the articles made from this Lava Glass melt could be left in their original glazed finish, or they could be wholly or partially treated in an acid bath to give the articles a dull lusterless appearance.

Drawings from F. S. Shirley's patent specifications (June 18, 1878).

The second patent, acquired by Shirley on September 30, 1879, referred primarily to methods for decorating his Sicilian Ware. Preferring to use glass having lava mixed with it, so as to have a dark, perfectly black, or colored background to make a stronger contrast, he imbedded in the surface of the article colored glass or other vitreous material. The pieces inserted for the sake of decoration were of an analogous material to the material out of which the article was made. If this was not possible, the pieces were backed with a coating of suitable fluxing, so that they would more readily be absorbed into the surface of the glass. Colored beads of glass and pieces of metal were picked up from the marver by rolling the plastic parison over it; reheating and warming-in followed to further amalgamate the article and its applied decoration.

Where irregular designs, such as mosaic or marble patterns, were desired, pieces or plates of glass or lava of various colors, usually opaque, were broken or cut into the required shapes, and then inserted or imbedded into the surface of the glass article. By making the flux of a dense white or a brilliant color, and having it flow around the edges of the pieces inserted, a fine finish was secured, especially effective on a black or dark-colored ground.

Where grotesque figures or ornamentations were desired, the pieces to be inserted, of different colors, forms and sizes, were "floated" on the glass and after the article was finished an artist took his brush and added parts of the figures in gilt or color, transforming them through his imaginative touch into figures of animals and human beings of the most grotesque forms. Where metallic figures were added, gold traceries or designs were painted all around it. When it was desired to form figures of these pieces without outlining them in gold and adding parts of the figures to them, the pieces were cut through to the dark backing of glass by means of the etching process, copper engraving wheels, or other similar methods.

Where special designs were required the glass worker formed the pieces that were to be attached or inserted in special molds or formers. These pieces, in whatever form or color preferred, were fluxed over and then applied to metal plates having indented lines or figures therein. A hot mass of glass was then worked over the same, so as to attach them to the plate, thereby producing figures in relief or cameo effect.

F. S. SHIRLEY.
Ornamentation of Glassware.

No. 220,038.   Patented Sept. 30, 1879.

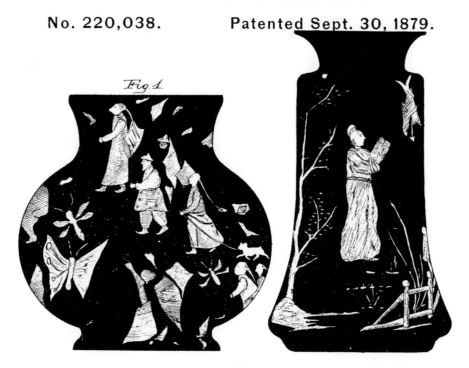

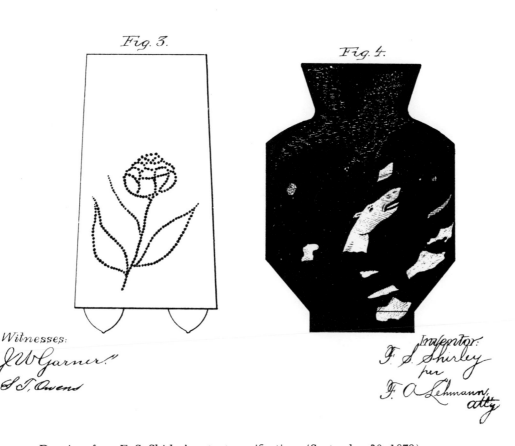

Drawings from F. S. Shirley's patent specifications (September 30, 1879)

Perforated metal shells or pieces of metal could be attached to the glass article that was being formed while the glass was yet soft, and the glass was then blown and finished. All the glass points projecting through the metal plates or network could be cut away and polished down to the metal surface, thereby producing the same effects as those in the Japanese metal-enamel ware called cloisonné.

In the late nineteenth century archeological explorations at Troy, Mycenae, and other sites unearthed strange and wonderful forms of art that excited and influenced the public's taste in decorative wares. Lava Glass lent itself well to the grotesque forms and copies of ancient glass and pottery which were in vogue at that time. Articles in the Chinese taste were also manufactured, as is indicated in the patent illustrations for September 30, 1879. This awareness of ancient art forms resembles somewhat the Greek Revival of an earlier period.

While it appears to be in scant supply today Sicilian Ware was most assuredly manfactured and sold through the Mt. Washington Glass Company's New York City showrooms at 20 College Place, which at that time was under the direction of William H. Lum. In subsequent issues of the various trade journals Mr. Shirley advised the trade that his works were filling their orders for the new glassware just as quickly as they could, which would indicate that it was a commercial success.

Frederick Shirley's Sicilian Ware had many prototypes. As early as 1771, the famous chemist le Sage discovered that one could bring black lava, as well as basalt, into fusion again.

Carolina Maria, the cruel and dissolute Queen of Naples, was probably the first to give instructions to her glass works to make glass out of lava in the manner outlined in the published course of experiments by the great French chemist and statesman, Jean Antoine Chaptal, Count de Chanteloup (1756–1832).

In more than one French glass factory thereafter substantial use was made of Chaptal's discoveries. In 1780 a French bottle manufacturer named Ducros, following the suggestions of Chaptal, used basaltic earth (volcanic ash) and lava in his melts. He produced a good metal, well suited at that time for bottles. The well-known glass manufacturer, Giral, produced black bottles from a melt composed simply of three parts lava and one part river sand. Giral also made beautiful glass articles out of a melt of pure lava, without any alloy or admixture of any kind. Among the articles produced by Giral were stoves, tables, mantelpieces, tiles for flooring and many other decorative and useful items.

Soon after Ducros' experiments, the French chemist Alliot made trials with Lava Glass, producing several interesting color effects.

At Göttingen, in 1811, Johann Heinrich Moritz Poppe published a report in *Geschichte der Kunst und Wissenschaften*, concerning the experiments in Lava Glass made by le Sage, Chaptal, Giral and the Englishman, Sir James Hall. Poppe also reported that in Bohemia, "already for more than a few years," glass utensils—chiefly boxes, candlesticks and such wares—were manufactured out of a blackish basalt glass. He also informed glass manufacturers that, because of the fluidity of the basalt melt, it should not be blown as an ordinary glass mass and that the metal would not lend itself well to cutting and polishing.

Black (lava) glass bottle dated 1831. Stippled Biblical and Masonic designs produced with a sharp-pointed hammer. A peasant work attributable to the Alloa Glass Works, Alloa, Scotland.

Collection: Lang Art Gallery Committee, Newcastle-upon-Tyne
The first and second vases shown are "Jet" Vitro-Porcelain. The third is a molded "Malachite" Vitro-Porcelain, disc-shaped vase. The fourth and fifth are molded blue and green mottled Vitro-Porcelain.

About 1884, Sowerby, of Newcastle-upon-Tyne, made a type of Lava Glassware utilizing the blast furnace slag to which was added cryolite. Sowerbys called this ware "vitro porcelain." The glass was a streaky green with purple veins of opaque quality running throughout the metal. They also produced other color effects similar to Challinor, Taylor & Company's "Mosaic" glassware in an opaque glass simulating marble or agate stones and in "jet" black.

On May 26, 1893, Count Solms-Baruth of Klitschdorf in Silesia, patented a method for producing glassware resembling agate. A mixture of basalt or lava, soda, borax, carbonate of lime, and sand with a small quantity of silver chloride was finely pulverized and fused in a melting pot. Small pieces of lava, about the size of a walnut, were gradually added, and finally dichloride of tin was stirred in. After purification the glass was ready for working. Count Solms-Baruth explained that the glass articles should be cooled irregularly, thereby making the more quickly cooled parts appear darkest. The incomplete dissolution of the basalt, lava, or slag from glass or welding furnaces, produced a turbidity throughout the metal, creating effects resembling agate stones. By using other metallic salts as fluxes, the color was varied, for instance copper suboxide and tin monoxide gave a red or black color against which the splotches of variegated color showed to advantage.

We should mention that in 1875 S. Troutmann & Company of Philadelphia, agents for A. Tschinkel of Bohemia, offered the trade a lava pottery known as "Sydrolite." Troutmanns were also the sole agents for the Phoenix Pottery Company, a subsidiary of Schreiber & Company, who were domestic manufacturers of lava pottery. The John B. Connally Company of New York City also produced a "lava pottery with a vitrified surface" according to their advertisements in the trade journals, and the Mettlach factory in Germany produced a type of lava pottery too. The basalt and stonewares of Josiah Wedgwood were a form of lava pottery and these black wares and agate and granite wares influenced the designs and decorations Shirley used for his interesting Sicilian Ware.

Stone Glasses

*G*lass has been made to imitate stones from early Egyptian times. Stratified and marbleized glassware made in imitation of chalcedony and jasper was a popular item in ancient Rome. The technique was revived by the Venetians in the late fifteenth century, and references are made to the manufacture of "jasper," "chalcedony" and "schmelzglas" in many sixteenth and seventeenth century glass recipes.

One of the most beautiful Stone Glasses made in the nineteenth century was produced by Friedrich Egermann (1777–1864), the famous Bohemian glass manufacturer. In *Chemistry Applied to the Arts and to Manufactures* (London, 1848) Dr. F. Knapp states that the hyalith or "jasperwares" were produced by fluxing slag with basalt. The black jasper being prepared by adding forge scales, lava or basalt to the ordinary materials for making glass. A yellowish bronze-colored jasper glass was produced by substituting lead-slags for forge-scales, and a red by oxide of copper, etc., etc. Knapp explained that a deficiency of carbon caused the fractured or laminated effect in the glass presenting a marbled appearance. The blanks were cut and polished with broad, flat facets which

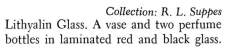

Collection: R. L. Suppes
Lithyalin Glass. A vase and two perfume bottles in laminated red and black glass.

revealed the laminated or marbleized structure of the glass, producing the effect of carved chalcedony or other stratified or multicolored stone.

Egermann gave his glassware the name "Lithyalin." It was first produced by him at his works in Haida in 1830. He also made a jet black stone glass which he decorated with *chinoiserie* designs. This ware, produced about 1820–1830, he named "Hyalith." Egermann's Stone Glasses no doubt influenced Count Solms-Baruth's agate wares (see chapter on Lava Glassware).

Josef Rindskopfs Sons of Kosten, Germany, produced a ware very similar to Lithyalin which they called "Diluvium." Several examples of Diluvium glass with cut and carved decorations, either intaglio or cameo, were illustrated in Gustave Pazaurek's *Moderne Gläser* (Leipzig, 1901).

Another beautiful Stone Glass was produced by Stevens & Williams. It was named "Moss Agate," and was originated by John Northwood. Fred Carder, who at that time worked at the Brierley Hill Glass Works as head designer, created the designs for the many forms of vases and bowls made in Moss Agate.

Collection: Brierley Hill Libraries
"Moss Agate" vase. Stevens & Williams. Circa 1888.

Lithyalin Glass vase in striated green, brown, and yellow. Circa 1830. Height 12 inches.

The manufacturing process was unusual. First a light bulb of soda glass was blown and then coated with a gathering of heavier lead glass. The parison was rolled on a marver that had been previously covered with powdered glasses of different colors. After the "splosh" had been picked up off the marver by the plastic bulb it was pulled into form with a pointed hook. The parison was reheated and coated again with a layer of lead glass; handles and rings were added while the article was still on the punty. When the piece had been shaped, and before it was removed from the punty, water was poured into the interior and quickly thrown out. This last operation caused crackles in the soft interior soda glass. Upon reheating, the cracks on the inside closed and gave the crackled quality associated with moss agate.

The body glass being made from a melt containing a supersaturation of lead is yellowish in color, a quality which has been erroneously associated with early Waterford Glasses. The abundance of lead in the metal makes the glass not only slightly yellow, but very heavy too. The white, orange, yellow and black-colored splosh gave texture to the glass, at the same time recreating the natural coloring of the moss agate.

After the article had annealed the body, rim and handles were beautifully cut and polished. The small vase shown in the illustrations is an excellent example of this ware.

David Challinor of Challinor, Taylor & Company, Pittsburgh, Pennsylvania, patented a process for manufacturing a type of glass in imitation of stone or marble on June 1, 1886. Challinor first prepared various colored opaque glasses in separate pots or tanks. He then took a suitable portion of each different color and placed them in a single crucible or pot. These variously colored metals were stirred together and intermingled. Articles were then formed from these mixed glasses in the usual way—as, for example, by blowing or casting. Challinor's "Mosaic" glassware was followed by several others similar in appearance. It became quite popular in the late nineteenth century, both in America and abroad, and continues in favor with many collectors of old glassware.

A method for manufacturing Marble Glass was patented in England on April 25, 1892, by C. F. E. Grosse. Glass of any color, preferably addled or opaque, was worked on a pipe and then sprinkled over with finely pulverized, colored glass flux by blowing, sieving, etc. The mass was reheated in the furnace to fuse the flux and then finished in the usual way.

In the early twentieth century, Arthur Nash of the Tiffany Furnaces and Martin Bach of the Quezal Art Glass and Decorating Works produced some beautiful examples of stone glassware. The opaque, multicolored glass, which incidentally predates the luster or iridescent glasses made by these two firms, was strikingly handsome, but, being difficult to make, only a little of this "laminated" glassware was produced.

Author's Collection
The second piece of Favrile "Laminated" glass made by Arthur J. Nash prior to 1900.
Height 5½ inches.

Iridescent Glassware

Surface shimmering with rainbow hues
Purple and crimson and turquoise blues,
Ruby and orange, yellow and green;
Each of them decked in glorious sheen.
(From *Royal Lancastrian Pottery*
by A. Lomax)

*M*any people have asked the cause of iridescence on old pieces of glass and glazed pottery; here is the answer. Iridescence on glass is caused by the action of carbonic acid or ammonia salts contained in the air or the earth, which in the presence of moisture decomposes the glass, forming soluble carbonate of soda or potash. As this is washed from the surface of the glass there remain scales, or laminae, of an acid silicate of lime, alumina or lead, as the case may be, which breaks up the rays of light, thus giving the iridescent effect. These conditions are admirably met when glass lies buried in humid earth at high temperatures, such conditions being often found in Roman, Egyptian and Greek tombs. The conditions having been met, the deterioration or decomposition of the glass can begin in a comparatively short time, as is evidenced by the iridescent film found on many bits of glass exposed to the elements which one can find along the roads and highways.

It has been generally thought that the glassmaker sought to produce on the surface of the glass an exceedingly thin metallic film. This is not wholly true, for a film of some metals is not iridescent (e.g., platinum).

244

Instead the glassmaker sought to produce a finely-ridged metallic film that would split ordinary daylight into its constituent colors. Ordinary daylight, or white light, under certain conditions becomes separated. This happens when light is bent or refracted, as for instance in a thin layer of oil on the surface of the water. It is this assemblage of many colors that produces iridescence on the surface of the glass.

In *5000 Years of Glass-Making*, the author, J. R. Vavra, suggests that the ancient glassmakers frequently iridized glass: "The Romans," Mr. Vavra writes, "knew how to give glass a metal sheen. It was not identical with that found in old glasses after they had been buried in earth for hundreds of years. This we call 'incandescence.' The Romans added a certain resin to the salts and made their glasses iridescent 'golden' by the use of silver, and 'blue' by the use of bismuth. Franchet asserts that he gained similar results with Roman recipes."

At the 1873 Exposition in Vienna, Ludwig Lobmeyer exhibited the first Iridescent Glass to be commercially produced in the nineteenth century. He was followed in short order by Count Harrach of Neuwelt, Bohemia. The British trade journals gave such an accomplishment little notice, but later in 1878, when Lobmeyer's iridescent wares were exhibited in Paris along with similar wares produced by Thos. Webb & Sons, these same journals had much to say about the "new" Iridescent Glasses. In the American trade paper, *The Crockery & Glass Journal*, for January 9 1875, mention was made of an iridescent glass tumbler, manufactured in Hungary and bought there by Mr. N. M. Lowe of Boston, Massachusetts for two florins (about $1.00 at that time). The iridescence was due to a surface treatment which was supposed to be a closely guarded secret, but, as Mr. Lowe commented, "it could be had in America."

To gain a better understanding of what these early artificially iridized glasswares looked like let us read some contemporary reports taken from several English and American trade journals: In May, 1879, C. F. A. Hinrichs of 31 Park Place, New York City, wholesale distributors of Bohemian glass products reported that they had "just received from Bohemia the finest selection of iridescent glass and Bronze glass ever assembled under one roof." The list included many articles of use as well as ornamental pieces. "In the Bronze glass the Pompeiian and antique styles prevail. These are interesting as well as beautiful, specially so as being exact copies of relics rescued from the ruins of the buried city.

The iridescent glass goods are of the most perfect finish and graceful shapes, and glitter in the light with all the hues of the rainbow. Here are vases and bouquet-holders of unique forms, and of all sizes, mingled with more practical articles of tableware, such as goblets, finger bowls, wines, etc. A table furnished with these last-named must have a dazzling effect. Among the vases in iridescent glass are a number of elegant ones decorated with engraved and cameo work, with medallions rich with beautiful birds and flowers. The Bronze vases are also, many of them, finely ornamented. A superb line of bouquet-holders have the vase and base in iridescent, the body, representing a tulip, being in bronzed glass. The combination is in admirable taste, and the result is strikingly rich. The iridescent crackle ware is another attractive novelty which must take with people of good taste."

In the winter of 1878, Charles K. Ovington had the following report to make on Iridescent Glass for one of the American trade papers: "Modern chemists and glassmakers have long been trying to discover the art of making glass iridescent by some more speedy means than that of burying it in a damp soil for the benefit of a thankless posterity. With all the progress made in kindred branches of the art, nothing of note was done in this direction until two French chemists quite recently succeeded in artificially producing this iridescence. The process they make use of is said to consist essentially in submitting the glass under a considerable pressure, and at an elevated temperature, to the action of water containing fifteen per cent of hydrochloric acid. Only certain kinds of glass are suitable for this operation. The action of this acid is thought to be analogous to that of the elements upon older glass, in dissolving the alkaline silicates and leaving the surface of the glass finely ridged or corrugated, and thus capable of refracting the light with prismatic or rainbow colors, like those of mother-of-pearl." (Ovington was no doubt referring to a method patented by Louis Clemandot, a civil engineer of Paris, on March 9, 1877.)

Mr. Ovington continued: "Peligot, the celebrated French chemist, speaking of ancient glass, says, 'The iridescence is caused by fine scales or laminae which may be removed by gentle rubbing.' The modern glass stands any amount of rubbing or cleaning without losing this curious property; but if the exposed surface be cut or ground off, the iridescent effect is instantly lost, showing that its cause is merely superficial and not structural.

"The Bohemian glass, so far, seems to be the favorite for embellishing with the new iridescence. Bohemian glass will resist a much greater heat than any other kind, and it is made in graceful shapes and is clear and transparent. At present the leading Bohemian factory" [Lobmeyer's works at Zlatno, Hungary] "is producing a good deal of this iridescent glassware, principally for the European market, as the American public is hardly as yet acquainted with this novel and beautiful glassware.

"One of the greatest charms of this new glass is its infinite variety and freshness. No two pieces are alike in color [mainly because the manufacturer had difficulty controlling this particular factor], and no piece remains the same when placed in a new position, or regarded from a different point of view. All show a greater or smaller range of the spectrum, curved or bent according to the shape of the glass, but while some pieces flash with red and yellow, others are tender, with silvery blue or a rich gold-gray, and still others exhibit all the colors of the rainbow.

"As to the articles of glassware to which this enrichment may be applied, there seems to be almost no limit; but to certain pieces it is especially appropriate. Large crystal balls, highly iridescent, and resembling soap-bubbles in everything but frailty, are very beautiful; and glasses intended to hold white or light-colored wines give a piquant color to the contents by the sparkle of the rainbow hues upon the cup. But nothing has such charm as delicate crystal copies of the old Roman and Cypriote glass urns and vases glistening with iridescent colors more brightly than their ancient models, upon the dusty shelves of some museums."

In an English trade journal date-lined "London, August 29, 1878" the following commentary by Her Majesty, Queen Victoria, with specific reference to Thos. Webb & Sons "Bronze Glass" appeared: "On a recent visit to Mr. Goode's attractive galleries at Audley Street" (Thos. Goode & Sons are still doing business at the same place), "we noticed a fine selection of the new Bronze Glass, discovered and made by Messrs. Thomas Webb & Sons, of Stourbridge. Its purple bronze surface shines with the hues of the rainbow, such as they appear on molten lead, or on pieces of steel which have been tempered in gradually diminishing degrees of heat, in fact, the appearance of these jars, vases and bowls is such as if they had been made of oxidized steel or copper, and their remarkable weight and solidity makes us believe that some metallic preparation is used for coating or impregnating the surface. The shapes are in preference borrowed from Dr. Schliemann's finds at Troy and Mycenae, owl-faced

"Bronze" glass vase; dark green glass, heavily lustered, and with gold, purple, and green highlights. Signed "Webb's / J. T. H. R. / Patent." Height 4 inches.
Collection: L. A. Randolph

and curiously-lipped vessels predominating. Although the specimens we have seen combine the character of curious and ornament, the manufacturer might apply their process with equally good effect to vessels which in shape belong to more advanced periods of Greek and Roman culture, and therewith meet the taste of a refined public. Like the iridescent glass, an invention of the same firm, bronze glass will find admirers, and be utilized in many ways for the purpose of ornament. It has already attracted considerable attention at the Paris Exhibition [1878], likewise at the Grosvenor Gallery, where Mr. Goode placed some of his finest specimens."

The bronze glass of which Queen Victoria speaks has a mirrorlike, metallic sheen upon its surface brought about by subjecting the dark body glass used in this ware to the fumes of metallic chlorides. As Victoria pointed out in her press release, the bronze glass does have the appearance of tempered steel, bluish purple, with highlights of coppery-red and gold.

Its mirrorlike surface is slick instead of velvety smooth like the finely puckered surfaces of the iridescent wares of a later period (i.e., Tiffany, Aurene, etc.).

From the pages of the *Crockery & Glass Journal*, dated October 31, 1878, we have this informative, contemporary account of the iridescent glasses made in America in the late nineteenth century entitled "Rainbow or Iris Glassware": "This ware, which is now much used by the public, and is daily growing in popularity, is comparatively of recent origin; and it is only lately that the manufacture has been what may be called successful. New results are constantly being attained, particularly by glass manufacturers, but so carefully guarded are they in their experiments that valuable developments are frequently obtained before even an intimation of discovery is disclosed to the trade. This is probably because they fear that rival manufacturers will take advantage of their efforts towards developing this particular ware. This seems to have been equally the case in regard to the production of 'Iris' or 'Rainbow' glassware; for from information received from various sources it appears that desultory efforts to obtain hues on glassware and similar substances" (glazed pottery and tiles) "have been simultaneously carried on by several parties in districts entirely remote from each other, as in France, Bohemia and England, and also in this country. Each indeed with greater or less success until entire perfection seems attained, at least until something surpassing all present results is produced. The accidental production of these colors has been long known and often proved a source of serious annoyance to manufacturers, and was considered a detriment even to the articles themselves, occurring as it did in a haphazard way and not producible at will, while the colors generally lacked the intensity and brilliancy desired and produced in present manufacture. The cause of these colored surfaces were generally attributed to sulphuring, at least so known to the trade." (Sulphurous fumes from the furnace frequently escaped and formed what is known as a "sulphur bloom" on glassware, usually while the articles were being worked or shaped at the glory hole. The "bloom" was sometimes an iridescent discoloration.) "Whether this was the cause may be deemed an open question, in view of the means adopted to successfully obtain results. Several vague descriptions have been given methods by which colors are said to be produced, but the explanations are of such a nature that only those who give them hold the key to solve what they doubtless intended to remain a mystery; for success in attaining the desired end is only gained by practice, and in the combination of the proper elements at the right moment and by observing the greatest nicety in the mixing of the compounds used. Doubtless there are several ways to iridize surfaces, each method requiring a needed combination of certain elements according to the constituents of the material to be acted on, while the color itself can only be produced under certain conditions. Two processes recently patented in this country, though pointed to the same end, are entirely different in their elements and methods of working. As it may be interesting to our readers we will describe the processes as practiced.

"In one of these the article is taken and submitted to a degree of heat sufficient not alone to insure freedom from moisture but also to expand the surface, rendering it susceptible of absorbing vapours or gases in which it may be enveloped; these gases being produced by the vapourizing of mixtures of Iodide of Bromine or solutions of them or their equivalents in alchohol, petroleum, etc. By these means articles which have in themselves little or no color acquire a surface tint with every variety of color and shade, from the lightest silver yellow to the deepest wine color; and brilliantly illumined with iridescent reflecting surfaces, the depth of color being dependent on the time the article may be exposed in the muffle or oven and the amount of impregnating material absorbed by it.

"By another method the articles are taken while still in the course of manufacture and submitted to the action of a gaseous vapour which acts on the surface of the material exposed to it; this, however, must be done at the precise moment when the gas contains the correct proportion of free acid, which is instrumental in depositing the tinted coating, and to this end it becomes a necessity that the constituents of the chemical compound should be adjusted with the greatest nicety and these even require alteration and regulating according to the article it may be wanted for; and where the nicest results are desired it is preferable to develop the compounds into gases and mix them when subjecting the articles to their action. This is done by heating a closed receptacle having a slide door or some ready means of closing and inserting the article at the requisite heat and filling the chamber with gas. Though this method is by far the most certain and greater brilliancy is obtained, the greatly increased expense in operating renders it less desirable for common use than that by which the article is exposed to the gaseous vapour as directly produced from the compound.

"From the results already obtained by these processes it is beyond a doubt that still further progress and new discoveries will develop themselves by continued efforts in this direction. Though the inventor, whoever be the fortunate one, may not discover the philosopher's stone he will certainly find a most profitable reward for his researches. Already the manufactures of this country are being brought into comparison with the wares of the leading European producers, and the day does not seem far distant when the artistic products of America shall be as freely handled on the other side of the ocean as they are in this country."

In the fall of 1878 the Mt. Washington Glass Company ran this advertisement in various trade journals:

NEW HOLIDAY GOODS!

The NEW BRONZE GLASS in all the Original Grotesque Forms, as discovered at Ancient Troy and Mycenae.
SOLE MANUFACTURERS OF THE NEW "RAINBOW" or "IRIDESCENT" GLASSWARE IN THE U.S.
N.B. The patent on this glass has been for a long time in interference and is now declared and issued giving the ENTIRE CONTROL of the manufacture and sale of these goods to this company. To meet the wants of the trade, we shall keep a large variety of styles in these goods, both of our own manufacture and imported.

A short time later, in the early part of 1879, the following item was published in the *Crockery & Glass Journal*: "We learn that the U.S. Patents controlling the manufacture and sale of iridescent glassware in this country has been just sold for $5000.00; the present owner assuming all suits on the same, and looking for his returns in the royalties to be collected on the manufacture."

Shirley patented two methods for producing his "Rainbow" or "Iris" Iridescent Glassware on August 13, 1878. The specifications are very much the same as those registered in England by Thos. Webb just one year earlier. We will discuss these later on in the text on foreign patents.

The only indication we could find of any other American firm manufacturing Iridescent Glass that early was this excerpt from a lengthy discussion of Hobbs, Brockunier & Company's display at the Mechanics Fair in Boston on October 14, 1878: "The goods shown by this firm are displayed on a handsome table, and consist of blown, pressed and etched ware in crystal and in colors, and in *iridescent glass*." Reviewing Wm. Leighton Jr.'s poem "Change; The Whisper of the Sphinx" the January 2, 1879, issue of the *Crockery & Glass Journal* had this to say: "Like the many-hued and beautiful *iridescent glass* which comes from his glowing furnace to grace our tables, and the exhibition of his wares in our stores, so in the offspring of the poetic fire burning in his soul shine forth the manifold beauty and brilliance of his thoughts and words." Certainly iridescent wares were made at Hobbs, Brockunier & Company, still no mention of them could be found in their many full-page and half-page advertisements in the trade journals. It is quite possible that the Mt. Washington Glass Company exercised their patent rights.

Some time later, on August 4, 1887, Bohemian Iridescent Glass was advertised in the trade papers under the name "Nacre de Perle" by Messrs. Hinrichs & Company of New York City, a wholesale distributor of imported glass and china—the nomenclature being a phrase borrowed from antiquarians who refer to the iridescence found on some ancient glass as "nacre de perle," or sometimes just "nacre."

Author's Collection

Nacre de Perle beaker.

Bohemian. Circa 1875.

Collection: Stevens & Williams Ltd.
Iridescent Glass bowl decorated by Erard. Circa 1890.

An occasional advertisement in the American trade papers by Salviati & Cie. of Venice, Italy, informed the trade of their iridescent wares. The Iridescent Glass bowl with enamel decoration shown in our illustrations was produced by Stevens & Williams in the late nineteenth century. It would appear that most glass factories throughout Europe were manufacturing Iridescent Glassware at this time.

The following methods for producing iridescent effects on glass and pottery were registered abroad: On July 8, 1857, Jules Joseph Henri Brianchon of Paris, France, registered a method for producing "the rich tint of shells, or the reflections of the prism" on glass and china.

The first portion of Brianchon's patent relates to a flux which is prepared as a base and to which are added various elements, each calculated to produce a differently colored iridescent luster. The first of these lusters was a combination of the flux-base with nitrate of uranium. This produced a brilliant yellow tint. The second coloring matter was a combination of the flux-base with nitrate of iron, which, after being baked in a kiln, produced a red, orange or "nankin" color with prismatic effects. The third coloring matter was made by preparing the flux-base with three parts of the uranium compound and one part of the iron preparation.

The metallic color produced, after baking in a kiln, imitated the various tints of polished gold. A fourth preparation using gold or mercury as a colorant with an added coating of uranium solution, produced variegated colors of the prism. Still another preparation produced what Brianchon termed "mother-of-pearl" tints; this last lustrous treatment was strongly recommended as being particularly effective on crystal glass.

Besides the chemicals mentioned specifically as producing various lustrous effects Brianchon also suggested the use of platina, silver, palladium, rhodium, iridium, antimony, tin, zinc, cobalt, chrome, copper, nickel, manganese, etc., etc.

On March 9, 1877, specifications for imparting to glass, etc. iridescence were patented by Louis Clemandot, Paris, France. Clemandot's means for producing this iridescence was to employ under pressure of two to five or six atmospheres water acidulated with hydrochloric acid in the proportions of 15 per cent of acid, which resulted in his obtaining nacreous and iridescent effects which were analogous to those produced by time and atmospheric agents on antique glass.

On August 29, 1877, a method for producing iridescent colors on glass was issued to Thomas Wilkes Webb of Stourbridge, England. The process called for the use of a closed muffle or chamber wherein the fumes from the evaporation of tin and other metallic salts were made to play directly upon the surface of the glasses which were enclosed in this chamber; the acids involved having an affinity for the molten surface of the glass remained permanently attached thereto, thus producing rainbow or prismatic tints upon the surface of the glass. On October 12, 1878, an amplification was made to this process and added to the former patent specifications by recommending a fine crackled effect on the surface of the glass in connection with the iridescent colors.

On November 29, 1877, provisional protection only was given to a method for iridizing glass surfaces discovered by Sidney Wittmann, an importer of goods of all types whose shop was located on Great Marlborough Street in London. The glass in this case was boiled in a solution of muriatic acid under pressure of several atmospheres. The iridized material was used primarily as inlay in ornamental furniture, such as ebony and other fancy woods, probably in imitation of Chinese inlaid furniture. Nevertheless, it could have applied to hollow wares of all kinds.

On November 29, 1878, Messieurs Monot Père et Fils & Stumpf of Paris, France, were issued two patents covering processes for metallizing and iridizing glassware. The metallic oxides in the glass itself were subjected to a reducing flame which produced a metallized or bronzed effect on the surface of the glass. Specifically mentioned was oxide of copper, which the first patent states will produce this bronzed or golden sheen on the glass. The second patent dealt with a crackling process used in connection with the first process to produce a different effect. Both patents resemble the methods used by Thos. Webb & Sons mentioned earlier.

On May 27, 1882, John Charles De Voy, Alfred Trumble, and Frederick M. Johnson incorporated the Farrall Venetian Art Glass Manufacturing Company in New York City; the factory was located in Brooklyn, New York. All kinds of fancy glassware in the Venetian style was produced by this firm, and also a type of iridescent glass which they manufactured according to Theophilus D. Farrall's process first patented in England on July 4, 1881, and later in America on August 8, 1882. Farrall's patent called for the application of heated crystals or chlorides of metallic nitrates to glass while it was in a heated state, and subjecting the glass to the action of coal or illuminating gas, and carbonate of strontia. By this method Farrall produced a multi-colored ware with iridescent tints.

On December 31, 1881, Rice W. Harris of Calais, France, registered a patent somewhat similar to that issued to T. D. McDermott Farrall. It too suggested the use of carbonic acid fumes on the surface of the glass and very likely produced the same mirrorlike effect.

On October 5, 1889, a patent was issued to Franz Emil Grosse of Berlin, Germany, and referred to an iridizing effect he produced on glass with use of the fumes from "pink salts."

On February 27, 1892, John Jacobson of Boston, Massachusetts, registered a method in England for producing iridescent effects on glass by imparting to its surface a finely ridged effect which would bring about an iridescent or scintillated effect, very much like that found in mother of pearl shells.

Contemporary reporters and most all patent specifications omit certain pertinent elements necessary to the manufacture of colored Iridescent Glassware. Most important is that to a large degree the tints produced on the glass are decidedly influenced by the color of the body glass. For instance, Tiffany's iridescent "Mohammedan Blue," known to collectors as "Butterfly Blue" depended greatly on the fact that the body glass was a deep, transparent blue, purple or green color. The light, golden iridescent wares had a body glass of transparent or translucent amber or yellow. Opaque glasses did not lend themselves well to iridizing processes.

For a short time Iridescent Glass and pottery ceased to be of interest to the buying public and its manufacture was discontinued except for sporadic attempts by some factories to revive interest.

Tiffany Furnaces: After one abortive attempt to establish a glass works, Louis Comfort Tiffany engaged the services, on a shareholding basis, of Arthur J. Nash. Later, Mr. Nash was joined in the business by his son, A. Douglas Nash; ten years afterward another son, Leslie Nash, was taken into the business. The Nashes operated the glass factory at Corona, Long Island, New York, and were responsible for most of the glass formulas and decorating techniques, but the designs for the most part were supplied by Mr. Tiffany and a staff of artists working under his direction.

Several trade marks were registered by Tiffany between the years 1894 and 1920. The first trade mark was granted the Tiffany Glass & Decorating Company of Jersey City, New Jersey, and New York City, New York, November 13, 1894, and enumerated the following descriptive terms for their glassware: "Tiffany Favrile Fabric Glass," "Tiffany Favrile Sunset Glass," "Tiffany Favrile Horizon Glass," "Tiffany Favrile Twig Glass," and "Tiffany Favrile Lace Glass." In each case the names were applied to certain colors, or textured surfaces used by Tiffany in the production of stained glass windows, lamps shades, and so on. Leslie Nash was awarded some stock in the company as a reward for developing a "peacock green" color which was especially pleasing to Mr. Tiffany. At a time when Tiffany was introducing copies of ancient glass objects the Nashes developed an ingenious imitation of the nacreous and pimpled surface texture sometimes found on ancient specimens which they called "Cypriote" glassware.

The Nashes, because of their superior development of iridescent and other fine glassware, brought the Tiffany Furnaces to first place in the production of artistic glass in America in their time. At first, they encountered many adversities, and for years the glass works had to be subsidized by Mr. Tiffany. Later on, the Nashes developed several very beautiful products which enjoyed great favor with the public. Unfortunately Mr.

Favrile "Cypriote" Glass—a rare technique. Circa 1900. Height 4½ inches.

Tiffany was opposed to what he believed was "commercialism," and he withdrew his support at a time when the glass factory was just beginning to stand on solid ground. A. Douglas Nash purchased the factory and its equipment, and with the financial aid of some of his close friends he managed to carry on the business for a few years. The depression was fast taking its toll of many luxury industries in the early 1930s, and within a very few years—three at the most—the A. Douglas Nash Corporation was forced to close its doors.

Steuben Glass Works: "Aurene" was the registered trade name for the iridescent wares produced at the Steuben Glass Works of Corning, New York. It was granted on September 6, 1904. Fred R. Carder signed the papers as "Secretary" of the firm with Samuel Hawkes and W. H. Hawkes as witnesses. These two last named gentlemen were both financially and actively connected with the firm at its inception. In the course of our extensive research into the field of Iridescent Glass we had several talks with Fred Carder, whose beautiful "Aurene" and "Verre de Soie" rank

Author's Collection
Tiffany vase of multicolored iridescent design. Circa 1900. Height 6 inches.

among the best Iridescent Glassware ever made in America. Mr. Carder spoke of Lobmeyer as being the first in his opinion to make Iridescent Glassware. Lobmeyer, he said, would introduce tin crystals into a muffle and the fumes from these oxidizing crystals attacked the surface of the glass subjected to them causing a coruscated effect. Fred Carder produced the same effect by spraying the heated glass with a solution of tin crystals dissolved in distilled water.

Quezal Art Glass & Decorating Company: Blown Iridescent Glassware was made by the Quezal factory, located at Fresh Pond Road and Metropolitan Avenue, in Brooklyn, New York. Its founder, Martin Bach, was once a trusted employee at the Tiffany Furnaces working directly under Arthur Nash. Leslie Nash told us that some of the techniques used at the Quezal factory were those practiced at the Corona plant. In our files we have the trade-mark papers issued to Martin Bach for the name "Quezal" as applied to fancy glassware of all descriptions. It is dated October 28, 1902, and signed by Bach as president of the firm. The

Author's Collection
Aurene vase (red, iridescent greeen and gold design on white ground). Circa 1900. Height 7 inches.

Iridescent Glasses produced by this firm are of a fine quality in both form and color.

Durand Art Glass Company: This factory, owned and operated by Victor Durand, was located in Vineland, New Jersey, and produced beautiful Irisdescent Glassware, as well as other fine decorative glasses. Pieces of his ware were signed with his monogram, "Durand" within a large "V," or simply marked in script "Durand." The works operated contemporarily with Tiffany Furnaces, Steuben and Quezal.

Colonel Ewan Kimball also operated a glass works in Vineland, New Jersey. We were unable to unearth any trade-mark papers issued to either Kimball or Durand but this is not unusual where family names are used to identify a product.

At one time Messrs. Kimball and Durand are reported to have operated jointly as "Kimball & Durand," but with little success.

Union Glass Company: The Union Glass Works of Somerville, Massachusetts made Iridescent Glassware and named it "Kew Blas." These

Durand covered jar. Red body with gold lustre decoration in the King Tut pattern. Jar and cover lined with gold lustre. Height 7 inches. *Chrysler Art Museum of Provincetown*

A group of Iridescent Glass vases manufactured by the firm of J. Lötz Witwe
of Klastersky Mlyn (Klostermühle). Circa 1900.

wares are contemporary with Tiffany's. The name "Kew Blas" is very likely
derived from the words "Keweeanawite," which is an arsenide of copper,
nickel and cobalt, the fumes of which were used in making Iridescent
Glassware, and "blas" which Webster defines as "an emanation from the
stars—coined by Van Helmont." The Union Glass Works' iridescent wares
differ little from those manufactured by other firms and unless they are
signed with their identifying mark it would be impossible to distinguish
them from other iridescent wares made in the early part of the twentieth
century.

Lötz' Witwe, Klostermühle (Loetz of Austria): A fine quality Iridescent Glassware was made by this firm. The group of vases shown in
our illustrations resembles in many ways those wares made at the Tiffany
Furnaces. Loetz of Austria was also noted for its fine cameo effects produced on cased glassware and inspired by the French productions of the
art nouveau period.

While we were in England we spent a great deal of time talking with
John Northwood II about the glasses made in the Stourbridge district.
Our talks embraced iridescent wares and Mr. Northwood spoke of the
extensive experiments he and his father conducted in this field shortly

before the turn of the century. They learned during the course of these trials that while each kind of metallic salts used resulted in a somewhat different iridescent tint, chloride of iron in a low state of fusion could be made to produce more colored iridescent effects than any of the other oxides.

Mr. Northwood remembered, too, that sometime after the turn of the century his brother Harry, who operated a factory in America, sent him a piece of pressed Iridescent Glass and asked him to analyze the surface coating for him. Harry Northwood told his brother John that this iridescent ware, produced by a rival company, was making serious inroads on his trade and he would have to learn how to produce these effects if he was not to lose considerably for the lack of it. After much tedious work John Northwood II finally isolated the material and determined that it was chloride of iron. A few months after he made his report to his brother in America a shipment of Harry Northwood's pressed Iridescent Glassware was delivered to him in England. He remarked how peculiar it was to find that "Harry's glass is now considered antique."

Prominent in the field of late pressed Iridescent Glassware were the Fenton Art Glass Works of Williamstown, West Virginia; the Imperial Glass Company of Belaire, Ohio; and, of course, the Northwood Company of Wheeling, West Virginia, and Indiana, Pennsylvania.

Pottery with an iridescent glaze was also produced in the late period. The pitcher shown in our illustrations bears an original paper label identifying it as a Tiffany product. The Royal Lancastrian Potteries of Messrs. Pilkington of England stands out as possibly the most artistic lustered or iridescent pottery of our time (1900–1938). In Germany, the Zsolnay factory was the major producer of fine iridescent pottery.

Pate de Verre

$\mathcal{I}$n the field of decorative glassware very few artisans have attempted to produce glass articles in accordance with the technique known as "pate de verre." The key to understanding the method by which this kind of glassware was produced lies in a literal translation of the French term into English.

Pate de Verre, or "paste of glass," is precisely just that. Colored or white glass, either transparent, translucent or opaque, is ground into a very fine powder in a ball-mill and mixed into a thick paste with an adhesive medium, usually just plain water. This paste is shaped either free-hand on a wheel like pottery, or in a mold, and then fired. In firing the metal is fused sufficiently to preserve the shape of the article and keep it fit for use when it has cooled and hardened. Such articles have a finely-pitted, mat finish and are easily distinguished from blown glasses.

The ancient Egyptians first used the Pate de Verre technique, and, judging from the scarcity of existing specimens, articles so produced were not made in quantity. Small vessels, amulets, miniature figurines, beads and masks are found in but a few museums and private collections throughout the world.

Early in the seventeenth century (1618) Guillaume Bicheaux, a Frenchman, rediscovered the technique of molding glass articles from Pate de Verre. His works were confined to the production of intaglio seals for impressing ciphers and initials in wax. For some unknown reason it seems not to have been used for anything else, probably because it was so much easier to remelt the cullet and blow into shape the articles needed.

264

Credit for the nineteenth-century revival of the Pate de Verre technique is given to Henry Cros (1840–1907) who, with his son, used this method to make fairly large panels in relief. The blending of colors used in these panels gave the works distinction. Cros' first attempts in Pate de Verre were successfully carried out in 1884. Many of Henry Cros' productions in this medium can be found in the Musée des Arts Modernes, and the Musée des Arts Decoratifs, in France. During the *art nouveau* period such prominent artists in the field of glass as Galle, De Latte, Rousseau, Walters and Lalique produced fine artistic works in this medium.

In the beginning of the twentieth century Francois Decorchemont took the technique a stage further and modelled bowls and vases in which a design of birds, flowers and other forms were done in low relief. Decorchemont's use of soft, misty colors added much to his works. Needless to say, many examples from his workshop can be found in Museums devoted to art and crafts.

In the United States Fred Carder worked, on a limited scale, with Pate de Verre. A piece in the author's collection was Mr. Carder's first experiment with this technique and was produced some forty years ago. Pink and white opal glass was used in powdered form for a cameo profile of a Grecian head. The paste was prepared from refuse scraps of glass of which Steuben was then producing fancy glass articles. In this lies a clue to its origin in ancient Egypt.

Pate de Verre head by Fred Carder.
(Photo: The Corning Museum of Glass.)

Pate de Riz (Pate d'Albatre) literally translated means "paste of rice" or "paste of alabaster." The translation implies that the glass was of a translucent quality and of a white, or near whitish, color. The process followed for producing Pate de Riz was exactly the same as that prescribed for making Pate de Verre, but in making Pate de Riz an opaline metal of a greyish tint was always used. The production of articles in Pate de Riz was limited to small bottles, vases and such trifles. The glass left much to be desired in color and consequently a great deal of it was decorated with enamels and gold. Pate de Riz was made in France sometime after 1843 in imitation of the Bohemian Opaline Glass.

In short, the technique of Pate de Verre is clearly a case of reversion to the exactly similar methods of ceramics.

Cire Perdue

Cire Perdue, or the "lost wax" process of casting practiced simultaneously in all parts of the world some three thousand years ago was originally used to form articles of metal. The object to be cast was first modeled in wax and then coated with a ceramic paste. When the paste had hardened the form was heated and the wax melted out. The ceramic mold, thus formed, was filled with pulverized glass, or molten glass, and placed in a kiln to fuse. When the article was formed and had sufficiently cooled, the ceramic mold was broken away leaving a single copy of the object which originally had been modeled in wax.

In recent years Fred Carder produced some extremely intricate and beautiful "Diatreta" vases utilizing this ancient technique.

"Aphrodite," a sculpture cast in glass by the "lost wax process" (Cire Perdue) by Fred Carder, 1950. (Photo: The Corning Museum of Glass.)

Tortoise-Shell Glass

A German chemist, Francis Pohl of Silesia, received provisional protection only on a patent registered October 25, 1880, covering his process for manufacturing glassware in imitation of tortoise shell.

To produce this novelty glassware Mr. Pohl first blew several bulbs of different shades of brown glass. These were broken into fragments. A bulb of plain glass was then blown, and the upper part cut off from the lower portion which adhered to the blowpipe, forming a cup of glass. While this plain glass bulb was being blown another worker blew another bulb of plain glass and rolled it among the fragments of brown glass, which adhered to said bulb. The bulb with fragments adhering thereto was then inserted in the cut off portion of the first bulb and the two were blown together. The whole was then rewarmed and swung and drawn

Author's Collection
Tortoise-shell finger bowl and plate. Circa 1880. Height 4 inches.

out as one bulb and treated in the manner ordinarily practiced in preparing glass articles.

When the fashioning of the vessel or article was completed it was coated or painted with a solution of chloride of silver and yellow ochre, or with other suitable materials for producing a yellow color, and afterwards fired in a muffle to fix the stain.

Provisional protection being all that was provided it stands to reason that glass made in imitation of tortoise shell could have been manufactured by any glass factory in the world, providing they circumvented the Pohl process in any way. For instance, should a manufacturer blow one or both of the glass bulbs used in forming the body from a yellow glass, thus making the staining of the glassware unnecessary, he would have sufficiently changed the process patented by Mr. Pohl to get around his coverage. And this was exactly the case.

Decorative articles, boudoir accessories and tablewares of all kinds can be found in this ware. Sometimes gold and enamel decorations were added or mica flecks dispersed throughout the metal, but these latter features added little to the beauty of the glass. Unless such articles have an identifying mark or label attached to them it would be almost impossible to attribute them to one particular source.

Author's Collection
Tortoise-shell glass covered bowl. Circa 1880. Height 6 inches to top of knob.

Applied Glass House Decoration

*T*hroughout the centuries glassmakers have been applying glass decorations to a glass body. The manifestations of this means of embellishment appear in the form of glass threads, trailings, blobs, prunts and many other devices. The late nineteenth-century glassmakers utilized all the known techniques to satisfy the taste for elaborately decorated glassware.

To attach applied decorations to a glass body the worker gathered on the end of an iron a quantity of metal. This he applied to the body of the article and by stretching and pulling the plastic glass laid it thereon in the design he wished to follow. Using his tools he alternately pinched, shaped and applied the glass into the desired forms. In this way branches, leaves, flowers, quilling, and other such decorations as were wanted were made right on the body of the article.

Some means for decorating glass articles were patented in the nineteenth century. A few of the more interesting techniques are worth mentioning here.

On June 9, 1876, Thomas Wilkes Webb patented an invention for an improvement in the manufacture of ornamental vases and other articles of glass which consisted in the production of designs in leaves, ribbons and other forms on the surface of vases, etc. of glass during the process of blowing thereby making it unnecessary to enamel or paint the article, as usual, after it was formed.

For this purpose pieces of glass of varied forms and lengths to suit the required design were applied in a heated state to the surface of the ball of glass intended to form the vase or other article. While the mass of glass was in this ball form the applied external pieces were drawn, with a tool, in the directions required for the particular design intended to be produced, the ball of glass was then blown and shaped into the desired article. During the process of blowing and expanding the ball of glass the externally applied pieces, now in a semifluid state from being reheated at the glory hole, expanded, forming the desired designs on the surface of the glass.

On February 1, 1884, John Northwood patented a simple gadget for crimping ornamental designs on glass articles. The device was a board on which pegs had been arranged so that when the glass bowl or other object was pressed onto this contrivance it produced an attractive fluted edge. This same device was patented in America on September 29, 1885.

On October 18, 1884, Stevens & Williams registered a beautiful design for applied glass decoration which they named "Matsu-No-Ke." The

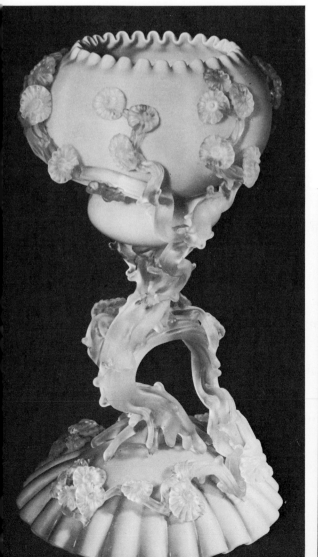

Collection: Stevens & Williams Ltd.
Satinglass vase with Matsu-No-Ke decoration; circa 1885. Height 13 inches.

Collection: Stourbridge Corporation
Satinglass vase with glassmaker's applied acanthus leaves decoration.

decoration consisted of twisted, rustic treelike stems trailing around a glass body. Superimposed daisy-shaped flowers or rosettes—one overlapping the other—were applied in small clusters along the stem or branch. Such articles usually had the registry number "Rd. 15353" etched or engraved in some place on the body.

On November 21, 1884, William Watson of Glasgow registered a means for producing enlarged reproductions of microscopic organisms in glass and other substances for decorative purposes. The process consisted of forming these organisms in glass or pottery from microphotographs enlarged several times, utilizing molds especially made for this purpose.

Some very beautiful applied decorations were made using two patented tools registered by John Northwood, August 12, 1885. The simplest device was a combination press and spring-action print for stamping or impressing a flower patterned prunt to a glass body. The second device was a

By courtesy of the Stourbridge Corporation
Rose-colored "Verre de Soie" bowl with applied crystal decoration.
Stevens & Williams. Circa 1885. Height 5½ inches.

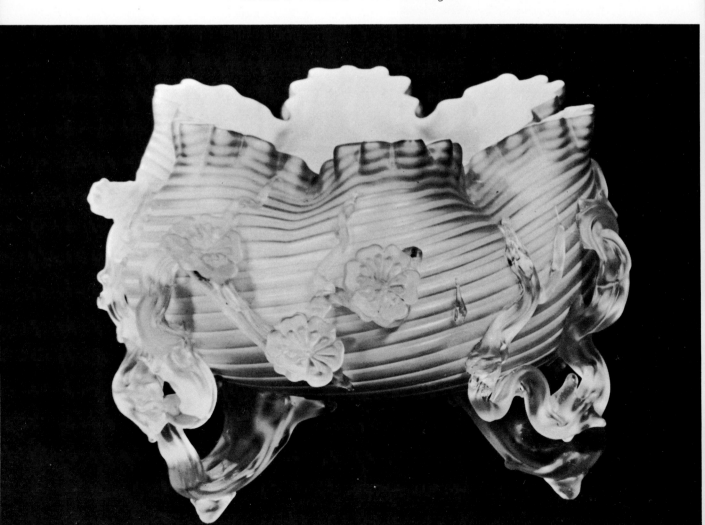

combination of two tools which both stamped out the desired floral prunt and allowed it to be applied in a raised position on the body of the article.

On June 29, 1886, William Leighton, Jr. of Hobbs, Brockunier & Company patented a rather elaborate glass crimping machine. The mechanism was worked by a foot press which shaped the article both inside and out into the desired patterns.

On November 6, 1888, a patent was issued to Harry Northwood, son of John Northwood, then residing in Wheeling, West Virginia, for an unusual type of applied glasshouse decoration. The invention consisted of glassware having an exterior coating of unvitrified sand, acid roughed or etched.

To produce this unusual type of ornamentation on glassware the worker gathered on an iron blowpipe a quantity of either crystal, colored, flashed,

Author's Collection
Footed basket with applied glass decoration of fruits and leaves. Height 7 inches.

or sensitive glass. After giving it a preliminary shape he rolled the parison into a quantity of fine sand until the sand adhered to the surface of the gather. The article was then blown and formed. Acid-roughing or etching completed the operation, producing an article of glass with "lusterless surface similar to a peach-skin" according to Northwood's patent enumerations.

Northwood pointed out in his specifications that if the article was subjected to a high degree of heat the sand would melt or vitrify, forming small globules of glass on the surface of the article.

By courtesy of the Stourbridge Corporation
Bowl with applied decoration, blackthorn spray on threaded body.
Stevens & Williams, 1886.

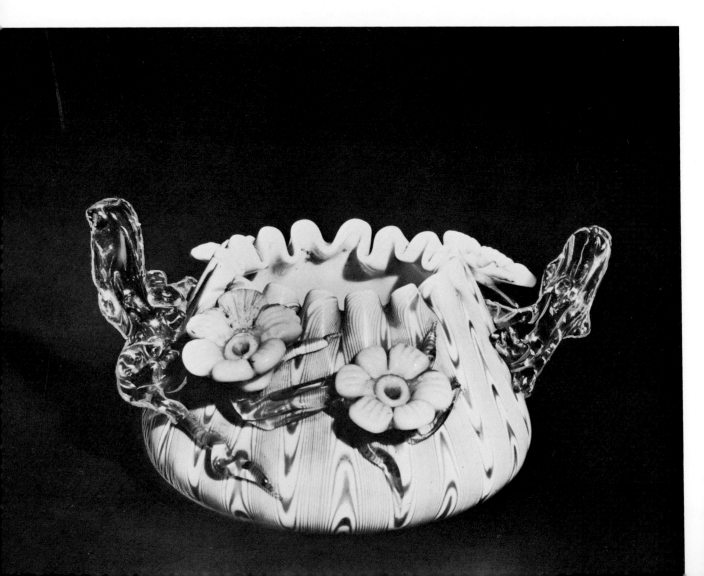

Collection: Richard Cole
Footed bowl of transparent olive-green glass with applied crystal decorations and gold and silver enamelwork. Signed with spider's web mark and the letter "E.". (This is the mark of the Whitehouse Glass Works, Stourbridge, England, operated by Sir Edward Webb; circa 1885.) Height 5½ inches; length 9 inches.

Cameo Incrustations
(Crystallo Ceramie)

*A*rticles made of flint glass were sometimes very tastefully ornamented by inclosing within their substance various objects formed from bodies which, being less fusible than glass, would not alter their form or nature by the heat contained in the glass at the moment of their insertion. Some writers have attributed this art of cameo incrustation, sometimes called "Crystallo Ceramie," to Bohemia in the thirteenth century; some to Bohemia in the sixteenth century; and still others to Bohemia in the late eighteenth century. Those specimens found by collectors today are, for the most part, products of the first half of the nineteenth century.

The Rev. Dionysus Lardner, in his treatise on glass dated 1832, has this to say about cameo incrustations: "The art was first attempted about fifty years ago" (circa 1780), "by a glass manufacturer in Bohemia, who sought to incrust small figures made with a grayish kind of clay. His success in this attempt was but moderate; the material of which he made choice for his figures, expanded and contracted very unequally with the surrounding glass, and their adhesion to it was consequently imperfect."

Further on the Rev. Lardner speaks of the success of the French Saint Amans and Desprez', father and son; and Apsley Pellatt in England.

Pellatt patented his methods for producing cameo incrustations on June 17, 1819. Three different approaches were made to the production of this type of decoration in a glass body; the most successful one is worth quoting here: "The figure intended for incrustation must be made of materials that will require a higher degree of heat for their fusion than

276

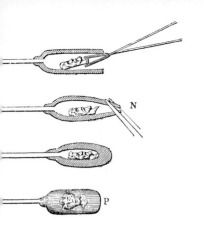

Illustrated explanation of the Crystallo Ceramie technique from Apsley Pellatt's *Curiosities of Glass Making*. (See Text.)

the glass within which it is to be incrusted; these are china clay and super-silicate of potash, ground and mixed in such proportions as upon experiment harmonize with the density of the glass; and thus, when molded into a bas-relief or bust (in plaster of paris molds) should be slightly baked, and then suffered gradually to cool; or the cameos may be kept in readiness till required for incrustation, for which purpose they should be carefully reheated to redness in a small Stourbridge clay muffle. A cylindrical flint glass pocket is then prepared, one end adhering to the hollow iron rod, 'M,' with an opening at the other extremity, into which the hot composition figure is introduced; the end, 'N,' is then collapsed and welded together by pressure, at a red heat, so that the figure is in the center of the hollow hot glass pocket or muffle. The workman next applied his mouth at the end of the tube, 'O,' while rewarming the glass at the other extremity; but instead of blowing, he exhausts the air, thus perfecting the collapse, by atmospheric pressure, and causing the glass and composition figure to be of one homogeneous mass, as 'P.'" (See illustration.)

Numerous examples of the Crystallo Ceramie technique are manifested in nineteenth-century glass articles of French, Bohemian and English manufacture. A wonderful example of eighteenth-century work is exhibited in the Sevres Museum. It is a pillar of crystal glass within which is imbedded a diamond-shaped Wedgwood Jasperware medallion. Superbly modeled busts of personages of eighteenth and early nineteenth century fame are found in paperweights, plaques, pendants, scent bottles and covered boxes. Tumblers, goblets, vases and many other articles have been decorated with cameo incrustations of various kinds and in several colors, including lavender and black. The decorative uses of this artful and beautiful way to embellish glass objects were numerous.

Collection: The Corning Museum of Glass
Tumbler with applied cameo incrustation. Bohemian or French.
Mid-nineteenth century.

The Satinglass bowl shown in our illustrations was produced by Thos. Webb & Sons in 1887 to commemorate Queen Victoria's Diamond Jubilee. Beautifully modeled busts of Victoria are attached to the front and back of this signed "Webb" rarity.

Pellatt also patented a means for decorating glassware which he named "Crystallo Engraving." It consisted in taking a facsimile of casts or dies from intaglios, and compressing them in intaglio on hollow glass vessels. This process was conveniently adopted where numerous copies of elaborate devices were required, such as badges of regiments, or arms upon decanters or table glass. The die or cast was sprinkled over first with Tripoli powder, then with fine dry plaster and brick dust, and then with coarse powder of the same two materials; it was placed under a press, and at the same time exposed to the action of water, by which means the sandy layers became solidified into a cast. This cast was placed in an iron mold in which the glass vessel was to be made, and became an integral part of the piece so produced; but by an application of a little water the cast was separated, leaving an intaglio impression upon the glass as sharp as the original die. The cast or cake thus used seldom sufficed for a second impression.

Author's Collection
Satinglass bowl in rose-beige with applied cameo incrustations.
Thos. Webb & Sons, 1887. Diameter 6 inches.

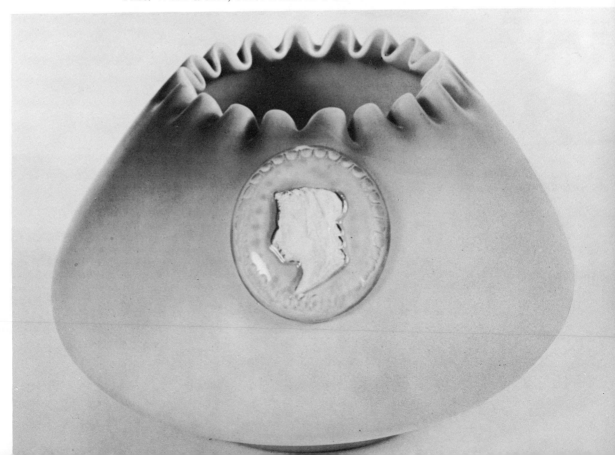

Messrs. Powell & Company took Pellatt's invention a step further, producing a most novel and beautiful glassware. After impressing a device
or design in intaglio on the surface of the glass, melted glass of another
color was poured into the cavities, and, when cold, the surface was properly
ground and polished.

James S. and Thomas Atterbury patented a method for pressing glassware having busts or figures of any desired kind impressed permanently
in their bottoms in such a manner that these figures, when painted with
a white color, would have the appearance of cameo incrustations set into
the glass. The patent specifications were filed on October 17, 1865. The
Atterburys' political feelings at that time are reflected in their choice of
illustration—they often used a likeness of Abraham Lincoln.

Author's Collection
An extremely rare Clichy Sulphide paperweight of the death mask of Napoleon Bona-
parte resting on a cushion. French; circa 1850.

Paperweight Patents

*P*rior to 1900 there were several designs for paperweights filed at the Patent Office in Washington, D.C., but the patent that would be of most interest to collectors is that one filed by Henry Miller of Pittsburgh, Pennsylvania, "assignor of three-fourths to Thomas Miller, Daniel H. Stoehr, and Alva A. Moore, all of the same place," May 27, 1890. Miller described his paperweight design thus: "My invention has relation to designs for glass paper-weights; and it consists of a sphere flattened on one side and containing an image of a bouquet or group of flowers composed of a large central flower surrounded by flowers of smaller size arranged somewhat below the central flower, each flower being provided with a bulbous pistil, in conventional representation or imitation of a drop of dew.

"In the illustration accompanying this specification I have shown a paper-weight consisting of a sphere. (A), flattened on one side, as at (a), and containing an image of a bouquet of flowers consisting of a large central flower (B) and smaller flowers (b b b) grouped around and below the flower (B), each flower of the bouquet being provided with a bulbous pistil (C)." On July 1, 1890, Miller registered design patents for a paperweight door knob and a flower vase, in which his original paperweight design was incorporated.

On September 5, 1882 William H. Maxwell of Rochester, Pennsylvania, "Assignor to Brown, Maxwell & Company (Limited) of same place" filed specifications for manufacturing glass paperweights.

On October 2, 1866, Thomas Rollason Hartell, co-owner of Hartell & Letchworth, glass manufacturers of Philadelphia, Pennsylvania, patented another means for making pressed cameo incrustations. Hartell's firm produced knife-rests and other objects in pressed glass with intaglio designs impressed in the bottom of the object. These intaglio designs were filled with plaster of Paris, and when viewed from above they had all the physical characteristics of a real cameo incrustation.

On January 16, 1888, Jonathan Haley of Ravenna, Ohio, registered a patent in England covering a process for producing pressed-glass tiles having the appearance of being backed with gold or silver foil. Colored glass was pressed in molds of various designs to produce configurations in intaglio on the underside of the tile. The tile was backed with plaster of Paris which gave off a silvery sheen (like a cameo incrustation). Haley patented this same technique in America on October 25, 1892, adding further to his claims by stating that the thick and thin portions of his pressed-glass tiles would reflect various shades of the color used and contribute greatly to the decorative effect.

DESIGN.
—o—
H. MILLER.
GLASS PAPER WEIGHT.

No. 19,858.   Patented May 27, 1890.

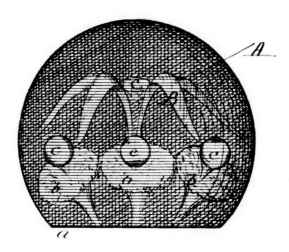

Witnesses
V. E. Hodges
E. H. Bond.

Henry Miller
Inventor
by Connery Bros
attys

Illustration from design patent issued to H. Miller, May 27, 1890.

(Model.)

W. H. MAXWELL.

MANUFACTURE OF GLASS PAPER WEIGHTS.

No. 263,931.   Patented Sept. 5, 1882.

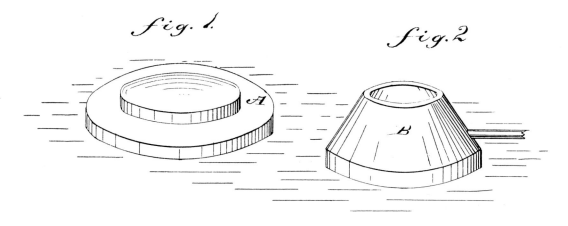

fig. 1.

fig. 2.

A

B

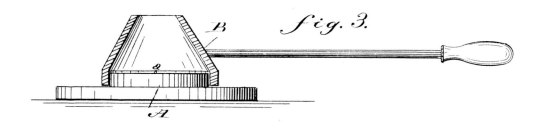

B.

fig. 3.

A

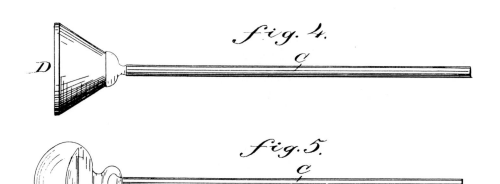

D

fig. 4.

C

D.

fig. 5.

C

WITNESSES :

Geo. Beyer

C. Sedgwick

INVENTOR :

W. H. Maxwell

BY Munn & Co

ATTORNEYS.

"My invention," writes Maxwell, "consists in a new process for the manufacture of paper-weights and other articles from glass, and containing names, designs, or pictures in color.

"The essential feature consists in the covering of paintings or designs made in vitrifiable colors with molten glass, as hereinafter described and claimed, reference being had to the accompanying drawings, wherein I have illustrated the apparatus used in carrying out the process.

"The process is as follows: Upon a thin plate, (a), of white glass, or glass of any color, and of a circular or other shape, are first painted or printed names, monograms, or designs of any kind, as may be desired, and in vitrifiable colors. This plate is then placed in a mold (A) shown in Fig. 1 of the drawings, which mold is made with a concave or flat surface, according to the form it is desired to give to the painted plate, and the mold and glass plate are then placed in the fire until the glass is sufficiently heated. The ring (B) shown in Fig. 2 is then placed over the plate (a) and around the mold, as shown in Fig. 3, and into this ring glass in a molten state is dropped, so that it covers the back and one side of the painted plate. The glass thus molded is then removed and 'stuck up' on a 'punty' or pipe, as illustrated in Fig. 4, and the other side of the painted

Author's Collection
An example of William H. Maxwell's patented paperweight; rust and blue design on opaque-white glass disc-base. Signed "Manufactured by Brown, Maxwell & Co., Ltd., Rochester, Pa." Diameter 3¼ inches.

J. REDER.
MANUFACTURE OF ORNAMENTAL GLASS ARTICLES.

No. 389,595.   Patented Sept. 18, 1888.

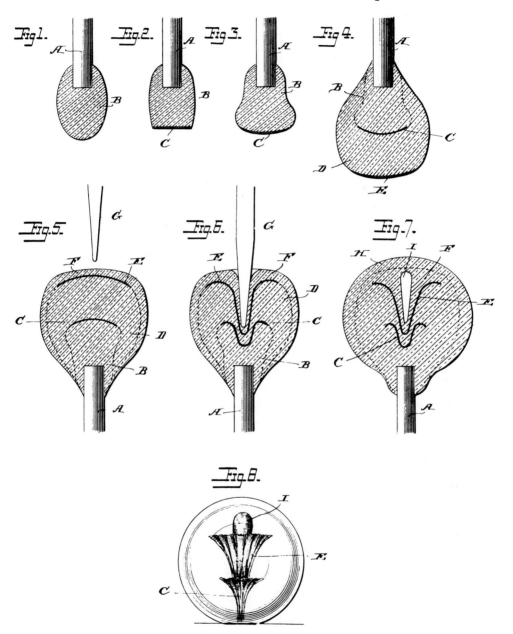

Patent illustration (sheet 1) issued to J. Reder, September 18, 1888.

plate is then covered, either by 'casting on' the glass or 'gathering it' on in the pot. I then cut down behind the plate with ordinary glass-working tools until it is small enough to be knocked off, as in Fig. 5."

In an attempt to broaden his coverage William Maxwell further stated in his enumerations: "I do not limit myself to any particular shape, form, or size, nor especially to the manufacture of paper-weights, as door-knobs, curtain-pins, door-plates, and other articles can be made by the same process." Even so, Maxwell's son reported the venture was unsuccessful.

Some of the most unusual paperweights were manufactured according to methods related in the patent enumerations of Joseph Reder of Creighton, Pennsylvania, dated September 18, 1888; I quote:

"My invention relates to the manufacture of ornamental glass articles, consisting, mainly, of a transparent glass having ornamental effects produced therein by the novel arrangement of colored glass and by cavities formed therein; and it consists, besides the novelty in the articles themselves, of certain improvements in the process whereby they are manufactured.

"In the drawings, Figures 1 to 7 illustrate the various steps in the process of making the article shown in Fig. 8. Figs. 9 to 12 show steps in making the article shown in Fig. 13, and Fig. 14 shows an article somewhat differently ornamented from that shown in the other figures used in connection with a burner.

"In carrying out my invention the clear or transparent glass which forms the main body of the article is kept in a melted condition in a crucible or suitable receptacle in the usual manner. The colored glass or other suitable material by which the ornamental effects are produced is reduced to a powder or to small grains, and in this condition is thinly spread upon a slab. When the clear glass is in condition to be worked, a metallic rod, preferably of iron, about six feet long and three-fourths of an inch in diameter and heated to redness at one end, is dipped into the molten glass and a small portion of the latter is withdrawn from the crucible. By rotating the bar the glass is formed into the shape shown in Fig. 1, where (A) represents the rod, and (B) the mass of glass thereon. After the mass of glass upon the end of the rod has sufficiently cooled the end thereof is pressed upon the slab covered by the finely-divided colored material, which, being loose, will adhere to and be taken up by the mass of glass on the end of the rod, thus forming a coating, (C), which has been flattened by contact with the plate. This coating may be either a film of fine powder or of separate particles of larger size, more or less closely arranged, this step of the process being illustrated in Fig. 2. By rotation of the rod and the use of a flat iron the glass is formed into a pear-shaped mass (illustrated in Fig. 3), the colored glass covering the outer curved end thereof. The ball or mass of glass thus formed is now dipped again into the molten clear glass, some of which is taken up, incasing the mass or ball already formed. This entire mass is now rotated by the rod in proximity to the fire to render it soft and plastic. The second addition of glass is represented by the letter (D), Fig. 4, so that the film of colored glass is embedded in the larger body of glass, (B) (D). Having been sufficiently heated, it is removed from the fire, and when at the proper temperature it is pressed softly upon a slab covered with colored particles, forming a coating (E), thereof in the same manner the coating (C) was produced. The mass is then shaped as shown in Fig. 4. This is next dipped into the molten glass and another transparent coating (F) applied thereon, and the rod with the body of glass thereon is rotated in the presence of the fire until the entire mass assumes the form shown in Fig. 5. The mass thus formed is now brought to such a temperature that it may be indented by a round-ended tapering rod (G), preferably of copper, without breaking the surface of the glass. This action in pressing down the central portion of the glass carries into a funnel form both the layers, (E C), of colored glass, as shown in Fig. 6. The rod (G) is now withdrawn, leaving the mass of glass centrally indented almost to the supporting-rod (A). The mass is then dipped into molten glass and the entire mass again coated and enveloped by a layer (H) of transparent glass, the cavity formed by the rod (G) being closed and forming an air-cavity (I), centrally arranged relatively to the colored funnel-shaped figures. The clear glass last added is kept from filling the aperture (I) by inverting the mass during the coating process. The mass shown in Fig. 7 is next thoroughly heated and then placed in a wooden former having a spherical or other shaped cavity, wherein it is pressed or molded into any desired shape. The completed article is then cut off just above the rod (A), and, if desired, is annealed in any suitable manner. This process produces an article like that shown in Fig. 8, the colored ornament in the center of the ball being in the art termed a 'flower,' of which the part (E) is the 'calyx' and the cavity the 'stamens.'

J. REDER.
MANUFACTURE OF ORNAMENTAL GLASS ARTICLES.

No. 389,595. Patented Sept. 18, 1888.

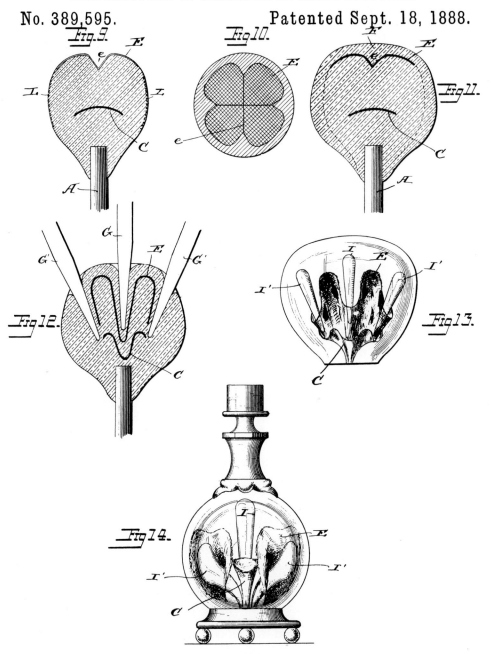

WITNESSES:

Jno. G. Hinkel Jr.

J. S. Barker

INVENTOR:

Joseph Reder,

BY

Foster & Freeman

ATTORNEYS.

"The ornamental portions (C) and (E) may be of glass of like colors or of different colors, as taste may dictate, or formed of particles of any suitable material. It will also be understood that my invention is not limited to the two colored portions (C) and (E), as one or more might be used and still the essential features of the invention be preserved.

"In Fig. 13 is shown a somewhat more elaborately ornamented ball than that shown in Fig. 8, there being besides the central air-cavity (I) a number of other air-cavities (I') arranged outside the central one (I).

"In making the ball shown in Fig. 13 the steps of the process are identical with those described for making the ball shown in Fig. 8 up to the point illustrated in Fig. 4. At this point of the process I cross, crease, or channel by means of a blunt-edged knife the end of the ball with the colored glass (E), thereby forming grooves or channels (e), crossing each other centrally, as illustrated in Figs. 9 and 10. If at this step in the process I proceed in the manner already described and penetrate only centrally the article produced will resemble that shown in Fig. 8, except that the edges of the funnel-shaped calyx will be waved or fluted; but in making the article shown in Fig. 13 the next step in the process is to coat

Author's Collection
Footed mantel ornament or paperweight. Mottled red, white, and green decoration, with air-cavities. American; circa 1888. Height 6¾ inches.

the end thus creased with a layer (F) of clear glass, as shown in Fig. 11. When this mass of glass has arrived at the proper temperature, it is centrally indented at different points by a number of rods (G G'), as shown in Fig. 12. The article is then finished in the manner described for finishing the ball shown in Fig. 8, forming an article like that shown in Fig. 13.

"In Fig. 14 an article having somewhat different ornamentation from that shown in the other figures is illustrated as forming part of a stand for a burner. In this instance the leaves or colored portions (E), which surround the cavities (I'), are separated from each other, their edges being turned or bent outward somewhat, instead of being united, as in Fig. 13. This effect I may produce by coating the glass with the colored material upon the sides, as shown at (L L), Fig. 9. The separate portions of the colored glass (E) are then punctured by the rods (G'), which in the article shown have broken and passed through the colored glass (E), while at the same time it has folded the same, as well as the glass (C) to a certain extent.

"It will be readily seen without further description of various articles produced by my invention that it admits of much variation in detail, whereby a great number of differently ornamented articles may be produced.

"The articles thus produced are suitable for many ornamental purposes, according to their sizes and shapes—as, for instance, paperweights, parts of brackets or stands for lamps, &c., or in use in decoration in connection with other materials."

Paperweights produced according to the two methods explained in Reder's specifications have a marked similarity to the lily-type weights attributed to the Whitall, Tatum Company of Millville, New Jersey, and the Crown Flint Glass Company of Ravenna, Ohio. The pedestal paperweight, or mantle ornament, shown in our illustrations is a superb example of Mr. Reder's patented method, the manufacturing technique of which is outlined in figures 9 through 13 of his illustrations.

Glossary

Air traps: A pattern of air blebs imprisoned between two walls of glass (*see* Pearl Satinglass and Vetro di Trina).

Anneal: To temper glassware immediately after its manufacture by a controlled and gradual cooling. This is accomplished by placing the article in a Leer (lehr).

Aqua regia: A mixture of nitric and hydrochloric acids which will dissolve gold or platinum.

Batch (noun): The mixture of chemicals formulated for use in a single glass-melting operation.

Batch (verb): The putting of the raw materials into the glass pot.

Blank: An article of plain glassware, before decorating by cutting, engraving, enameling, etc.

Blowpipe (*blowing-iron*): A hollow iron tube, two to six feet in length, made much wider and thicker at the end on which the gather is collected than at the blowing end or mouth piece.

Bobêche: A saucer-shaped disk to catch candle drippings; a drip cup.

Bosses (*nodules*): Knob-like ornamental designs (trade names for this type of decoration were Dewdrop, Spot, and Raindrop).

Caloric (noun): Meaning heat.

Cast (verb): To form glass into a particular shape, as by pouring it into a mold and letting it harden.

Castor hole: An aperture in a glass furnace through which large articles of glass can be reheated, as needed, during the processes of manipulation or fire polishing.

Comb (verb): Pulling threads of glass with a hooked tool into decorative patterns while the glass is still in a plastic state.

Cullet: Scraps of refuse glass suitable for remelting.

Cullet heap: A pile of refuse glass.

Enamel: A hard, glossy vitreous coating or paint—in opaque white or in colors—which can be fused onto glassware for decorating purposes. The term is sometimes applied to opaque white glass.

Fire polishing: The reheating of a glass vessel to bring about an incipient surface melting, thereby removing marks left by molds or tools and providing a smooth even surface.

Flashing: A means of covering plain uncolored glass with a thin layer of colored glass, often done with intense colors like ruby, or cobalt blue.

Flushed process: The use of various colored platings on a glass body which are afterwards etched and engraved into designs (*see* French Cameo Glass).

Free-blown glass: Glass formed by blowing and manipulating the metal with the tools of the trade and without the use of molds.

Full-size mold (*contact mold*): A mold composed of two or more sections of the approximate size of the finished article.

Gather: A gob of molten glass secured on the end of the blowpipe.

Glory hole: A small aperture in a glass furnace through which the worker can reheat a glass article, as needed, during the processes of manipulation or fire polishing.

Hobnail: A six-sided, flat-topped motif resembling the hobnails used on heavy boots.

Humpen: A drinking vessel in the form of a large brimmer or bumper.

Imbricated design: A design consisting of overlapping edges, like that of tiles, scales or shingles.

Intaglio-cut: An incised figure or design depressed below the surface of the glass so that an impression from it yields an image in relief.

Interchange plungers: As used in the manufacture of pressed glassware, the vertical plungers of a press-mold. Each plunger fitting the recess of the mold, and therefore being interchangeable, but having different patterns thereon wherewith to impress different designs on the glass article formed in the mold.

Investment casting: An American refinement of the ancient cire perdue, or "lost wax" process of casting. The refinement being a reusable mold capable of casting precision parts from glass or metal.

Leer (lehr) : An annealing oven or separate annealing furnace.

Marver. A polished metal or stone slab on which the gather of molten glass is rolled to give it a symmetrical shape before it is blown out.

Melt (noun) : The glass batch after it has been melted in pots in a furnace and is in a fluid or viscous state.

Metal: A semi-technical term used for glass in the molten state, and less frequently for glass when cold.

Muffle: A small oven used to bring enameled or gilded glass articles to the heat necessary for fritting, or melting the applied decoration, thereby permanently attaching it to the glass body.

Molded glass: Glass given a partial or final form and/or decoration by being blown in a mold.

Mold-line: Those marks left on the plastic glass from the seams or joints of the mold.

Parison (blow) : An inflated gather of glass.

Padding technique: The application of small pads or blobs of glass to a glass body which are afterwards cut in relief designs.

Part-size mold: A dip mold or piece mold used to impress a design on a gather of glass.

Pattern-molded: A term used to differentiate between glass molded for pattern or decoration only in a part-size dip or piece mold and thereafter expanded and glass blown and patterned in a full-size piece mold (contact mold) .

Pellicle: A thin film or skin of acid-resistant material—usually wax, gutta-percha or powdered asphaltum.

Pontil mark: The scar left on a glass article where it has been separated from the pontil rod (In many cases this scarred condition is ground down to a smooth finish on a wheel) .

Pontil rod (punty, pontie, ponty, pontil, puntee) : An iron rod used for holding glassware during the manufacture.

Pot: The fireclay crucible in which the founding or melting of the glass takes place.

Plated ware (cased glass) : Articles in which one or more layers of glass are plated over an inner shell of glass. The term "plated" usually refers to the skin of glass externally applied; "cased," on the other hand, meaning the glass skin applied to the inner surface of the article.

Pressed glass: Glass pressed manually or mechanically in a mold.

Prunt: A molded seal of glass pressed to leave little points or figures in relief on a glass article.

Resist: A pellicle or wax coating to protect glass from the action of the acid in the etching process.

Ring plate: As used in the manufacture of pressed glassware, a dummy plate put into position in the mold to reserve a space for the casting on, or pressing into place of another design, usually of glass of another color. The term is also applied to the ring plate placed at the mouth of a mold which governs the overflow of glass during the pressing operation.

Soda-lime glass: A common mixture for glass, the principle ingredients being soda, lime and silica.

Splosh: Colored glass crushed into a powder and sprinkled on glass articles while being worked at the furnace.

Striae: An undesirable quality in glass manifested in fine cords, wavy lines or streaks forming threadlike striations in the metal.

Struts: With specific reference to diatreta, the small glass rods which connect and support the outer network of glass to the inner cup of glass.

Threading: An applied decoration consisting of threads of glass coiled or wound about a glass article.

Vetro di Trina: Glassware exhibiting a fine network of intersecting lines of white enamel or colored glass threads, formed between two walls of glass and creating a series of diamond-shaped sections. The center of each diamond formed thereby has an air bleb of uniform size.

Index

Italic numbers refer to illustrations